MW00528217

Advance Praise for *Unwavering*

"Powerful and deeply moving, this is a war story like no other. If the first duty of every citizen is to remember, *Unwavering* will remind us of those captured or missing in Vietnam, and the remarkable women who kept faith with them for more than half a century."

–Rick Atkinson, bestselling and Pulitzer Prize-winning author of seven works of narrative military history, including *The British Are Coming, The Guns at Last Light, The Day of Battle, An Army at Dawn, The Long Gray Line, In the Company of Soldiers,* and *Crusade*

"This is a brilliantly written, beautifully emotive, and utterly accurate portrait of the families left behind during America's long war in Vietnam. It reads like a suspenseful work of fiction, and tugs at the heart—but is also full of rock-solid policy recommendations. Every word is true, and this is a book every military family should cherish."

–Admiral James Stavridis, USN (Ret), former Supreme Allied Commander at NATO and author of *To Risk It All: Nine Conflicts and the Crucible of Decision*

"A cinematic recounting of how the wives of POW/MIAs during the Vietnam War compelled U.S. policy changes, forced tradition-bound military services to adapt, and ultimately, inspired other countries to seek answers to their missing loved ones. A beautifully written and enthralling story that amply displays these ladies' courage and strength."

–Dr. George J. Veith, author of *Drawn Swords in a Distant Land: South Vietnam's Shattered Dreams*

"With a brisk economy and verve, Taylor Kiland and Judy Gray tell a little-known story of love and devotion that deserves our attention and admiration. *Unwavering: The Wives Who Fought to Ensure No Man Is Left Behind* is a tremendously moving account of the wives of American POWs and MIAs, whose advocacy for their husbands was unflagging, inspiring, and effective. Their actions bulldozed military and civilian bureaucracies into making their loved ones' treatment and return home with honor a national priority. For the courage and faithfulness they exhibited toward that end, they, like their husbands, deserve to be remembered as American heroes."

–Mark Salter, former chief of staff and coauthor for Sen. John McCain

"Taylor Kiland and Judy Gray have chronicled—as no one else has—the dramatic, heart-rending saga of a small band of unlikely heroines who came to reshape US foreign policy. While very diverse in backgrounds and personalities, they united around the common cause and soon learned how to call public attention to the plight of their men, and to bring pressure to bear on the government to take action. I witnessed firsthand their impact when I served as Director of the Defense Intelligence Agency in the early 1990s. This is a compelling, enlightening, and readable narrative of how these courageous crusaders forged a new benchmark for U.S. policy on POW/MIAs."

–Lt. Gen. James Clapper, U.S. Air Force (Ret.) and former Director of National Intelligence

"A heartbreaking, compelling story of a group of courageous military wives forced by circumstance to simultaneously confront a staid military culture and an indifferent political bureaucracy to create transparency and find the truth about their missing and captured husbands. In doing so, they created the art of the possible where military leaders and politicians had failed. More importantly, they established a new standard of care and responsibility for our military forces that operate in harm's way. As a nation we should all be grateful."

–Thad Allen, Admiral, U.S. Coast Guard (Ret.) Commandant, US Coast Guard (2006-2010) James Tyler Distinguished Leadership Chair, James Loy Institute for Leadership, USCG Academy (2014-2021)

"Those of us who served in the military know well the story of the unbelievable survival of our Vietnam POWs, but what many of us do *not* know is the role their wives played in making their safe return the cause that rallied our nation like none other during the Vietnam War. Authors Kiland and Gray, both veterans themselves, have dug deep to showcase how these women fought for their husbands and ended up changing America's foreign policy. Hats off to this group of unsung heroines of the Vietnam War."

–Christopher Michel, Founder Military.com

UNWAVERING

TAYLOR BALDWIN KILAND
& JUDY SILVERSTEIN GRAY

A KNOX PRESS BOOK
An Imprint of Permuted Press
ISBN: 978-1-63758-737-9
ISBN (eBook): 978-1-63758-738-6

Unwavering:
The Wives Who Fought to Ensure No Man is Left Behind

Cover art by Cody Corcoran

All people, locations, events, and situations are portrayed with fidelity to the research conducted by the authors.

Permuted Press, LLC
New York • Nashville
permutedpress.com

Published in the United States of America
1 2 3 4 5 6 7 8 9 10

From Taylor: To my budding little author, Kiland Hatcher.

From Judy: To a pioneering spirit who endlessly inspires, Nada Reichmann Gray.

TABLE OF CONTENTS

PART II - IN THE THICK OF THE FIGHT (1970–1973)

PART III - THE LONG AND WINDING ROAD (1973–PRESENT)

INTRODUCTION

This is a story about a small group of women, in the 1960s, who did what few women in that era could. They bucked tradition and, in fighting for the men they loved, forever changed U.S. foreign policy. It is a story about a tribe of ladies who became accidental activists during one of the most tumultuous times in our nation's history. Amidst the din and confusion of the Vietnam War, the antiwar movement, civil rights marches, and the Watergate scandal, this band of wives galvanized a president and a nation around the plight of their husbands, some 1,500 men held as prisoners of war or missing in action in Southeast Asia.

This is more than a wives' tale. Unintentionally, this small cadre of women made the POWs and MIAs so valuable that getting them home became the only victory left for our nation. Bringing home a small group of men who represented a fraction of the 58,000 war casualties became the focus of the peace negotiations.

Every war produces prisoners. But only since the Vietnam War have prisoners become political hostages, so valuable that preventing them in future wars has become a strategic imperative—not for humanitarian reasons, but to avoid having to make compromises to get them home. The United States will still tolerate casualties but will not tolerate missing men or POWs. Our military's increased use of unmanned technology helps avoid this threat. We now expend unlimited resources, deploying special forces to rescue *just one* POW, whether that man is in Bosnia, Iraq, Somalia, or Afghanistan.

It is no accident that America ended its longest war, in Afghanistan, without a single POW or missing man. The United States says that we hold sacred the mantra "leave no man behind," but that has not always been true. Every other war in our nation's history produced thousands of unrecovered missing men: 81,600 in World War II and 6,497 in the Korean War.

Only since the Vietnam War have we upheld this promise. Only since the Vietnam War have we spent hundreds of millions of dollars every year combing the globe for missing men from all our wars. Only since the Vietnam War have we hoisted the black and white POW/MIA flag above the White House, the Capitol, and each post office in the United States to remind us of our sacred promise to find every missing man—dead or alive. You cannot drive five miles in this country without seeing one. With its stark white silhouette, the flag signals that wars are not over until all troops have returned home.

Credit for our dedication to leaving no man behind belongs to the small group of women who in October 1969 took diplomatic matters into their own hands. Turn the page and travel back in time with us to take an intimate look at the upended lives of a handful of women as they coped with the capture or disappearance of their husbands. We immerse you in the action and the history of this tumultuous era, as these women moved from the sidelines to the frontlines of advocacy.

Bravely marching up to enemy headquarters on the outskirts of Paris, they insisted on a seat at the diplomatic table. In doing so, they set in motion a wholesale shift in military policy. These are their stories.

PART I

To the Frontlines (1964–1970)

CHAPTER ONE

TEA IN PARIS (OCTOBER 1969)

The Parisian suburb seems unusually quiet. It has been raining for days, scattering and matting clumps of leaves on the sidewalks. A noticeable chill hangs in the air. The sound of heels clicking on the sidewalk pierces the silence as five American women stride in a single file toward a dark stone building surrounded by an imposing wall. Sybil Stockdale has organized the group in formation to keep them focused, on track, and on time. She sighs at her reflection in the puddles. The rain has flattened her new haircut and she is not certain she likes the effect. At forty-four, she feels careworn compared to the younger women, but she picks up the pace, taking the lead. The overcast skies do little to warm their welcome as they reach the iron gate of the modest building.

Smoothing her skirt, Candy Parish fishes her lipstick from her purse and refreshes the color on her lips without a mirror. Taking a deep breath, she musters the last bits of energy she has stored for this meeting. A former airline hostess with a striking resemblance to British fashion model Twiggy, Candy is known for her bubbly personality. But the stress of the past year has dampened her spirits. The mother of an exuberant toddler, she spends her days chasing Hunter around an empty house. Her emotions seesaw between delight in raising her little boy and anxiety over her missing husband. Waiting for any news about his fate has been a torment.

Perhaps it is her burning desire to introduce her son to his father that has brought her to Paris. Maybe it is the urging of naval intelligence officials who have coached her to recall names and faces so she can identify specific people. Or it could be the lure of a confrontation with the North Vietnamese enemy who might be holding her husband captive. Perhaps it is all three. Whatever it is, Candy knows she must take matters into her own hands.

Sybil and Candy are not alone. Three other women and one man accompany them, several meeting for the first time at John F. Kennedy International Airport. The group is advocating for men from each of the armed services, Americans held as prisoners of war, or missing in action in South Vietnam, North Vietnam, or Laos. Sybil Stockdale is *de facto* den mother. Doe-eyed but stoic Mary Ann "Pat" Mearns, a nurse and former airline hostess, is the mother of two young girls. She, too, is seeking answers about her husband, an Air Force aviator missing since 1966. An introvert, she follows Sybil's lead and gets in line. Slender and perfectly manicured Andrea Rander is the only wife of an enlisted man. She is also the only Black woman. Her husband is a POW, captured in South Vietnam during the Tet Offensive in 1968. Statuesque Ruth Ann Perisho, the wife of a naval aviator missing since 1967, rounds out the pack. The lone man, Tom Swain, is the father-in-law of a missing Marine and chief of staff to the governor of Minnesota. He acts as chaperone. This is the 1960s. A group of women traveling for business without male accompaniment is uncommon.

Sybil has had a hand in recruiting the women to represent a cross section of missing and captive men. They have been holed up for six days at the Intercontinental Hotel in Paris, waiting for the meeting. The plush hotel is far beyond the budgets of these military wives. The bill for their travel and accommodations is being underwritten by defense contractor Fairchild Hiller Aircraft and *Reader's Digest* magazine. American and international media have been alerted to the risky summit the women are trying to arrange, attending press conferences at the airports in New York and Paris.

The women have gone to great lengths to arrange for childcare, as family and friends step in to assist. Sybil frets that nosy reporters might frighten the four boys she has left behind in California. And, as American antiwar protesters grow increasingly aggressive, she yearns to shield her sons from incessant news reports about the growing divide between antiwar activists and those supporting U.S. troops and President Richard Nixon. She knows it seems paranoid, but she worries Communists might kidnap her sons while she is overseas.

All the women are concerned that the meeting with the North Vietnamese might never happen. Nerves are fraying. Candy's suitcase is lost, and she does not have enough cash for new clothes in a place like Paris. Women did not have credit cards in 1969. She keeps recycling the puffy-sleeved outfit she wore on the plane and she borrows Ruth Ann's hair rollers.

Other than letting the women embark on one two-hour shopping excursion, Sybil has sequestered the group in the hotel. She has forbidden them from talking to anyone—especially to the media. They feel like prisoners in one of the most beautiful cities in the world. Tempers flare and bickering ensues.

To combat fears and boost morale, Sybil sets rules and a daily schedule. Each morning, she musters the group in her room. Armed with a yellow legal pad, and whipping out the pencil stashed behind her ear, she drills the wives. She has them rehearse the statements they are going to make—*if* they secure a meeting. Then she fires questions as they sit side-by-side on a settee, Sybil coaching their delivery until their answers are just right. If reporters show up, *only* she and Tom will talk. That week, Sybil "was both den mother and dictator," Andrea remembers. "I looked up to her." By day four, the women know how to make their case.

(L to R) Andrea Rander, Pat Mearns, Sybil Stockdale, Candy Parish, Tom Swain, and Ruth Ann Perisho, at a stop near the Luxor Obelisk and the Louvre, Paris, October 1969. Reporters followed them whenever they left their hotel. (*Photo courtesy of Pat Mearns.*)

Dressed conservatively, Sybil resists the ubiquitous and trendy miniskirts. Her jowls belie her age and weariness, but she has a hearty laugh that lights up her face. That is, when she allows herself to laugh. Serving as the anchor for this group, she is determined and decisive, but can seem unapproachable.

Her husband's long absence—longer than any of the other women's husbands—weighs her down. She is also weighed down by a secret she keeps. Sybil knows that her husband and other POWs in Hanoi are being tortured. She cannot share what she knows or how. The others attribute the anguish etched on her face to age and weariness. This is a serious mission. Candy overhears Sybil telling Pat Mearns that she would *manage* the upstarts on the trip. Put off by the comment, Candy may not grasp the burden Sybil carries.

Sybil wants the group to place the North Vietnamese on the defensive. There isn't much the women can control on this trip, but they should master their emotions. Be calm and cool, she tells herself—and the others.

Before breakfast, Sybil dials the North Vietnamese delegation on the black rotary phone in her hotel room. In a rehearsed and professional voice, she firmly requests a meeting. A representative from the delegation answers icily and curtly: *The ladies will have to wait*. Each afternoon, Sybil sits by the phone, in anticipation of a return call. She has been advised not to contact the U.S. embassy in Paris unless there is an emergency.

Officially, there is no government sponsorship of this trip. They are on their own. But Sybil, Candy, and Ruth Ann received *unofficial* guidance from their contacts in the military intelligence community. They were shown photos of North Vietnamese officials and taught to remember what they might see, hear, and observe, especially, any notable physical reactions.

As the sun sets each afternoon, the group grows more anxious. Five long days tick by, each blending into the next. They are in Paris, the city of lights and love, but surrounded by overcast skies, and only a few miles from the enemy. How patient should they be? They are not experienced in international diplomacy and have limited financial resources. October 4, the sixth day, dawns gray and drizzly. It is a Saturday and hopes for a weekend meeting are dim.

Sybil sips her coffee, thinking about how to keep the group engaged. Nearly jumping out of her chair, she grabs the armrest when the phone rings. Her heart skips a beat when she hears the cold voice that she has been talking to every morning. "Please come to Choisy-le-Roi, this afternoon at 4:00 p.m., for tea." Click.

The building that beckons in Choisy-le-Roi serves as the Parisian offices of the delegation from the Democratic Republic of Vietnam (North Vietnam). For more than a year, protracted negotiations called the Paris Peace Talks have been taking place there between the Communist regime of North Vietnam, the Republic of Vietnam (South Vietnam), and the United States. Little progress has been made. Back home, nightly news broadcasts highlight how long it takes to agree upon laborious details like the size and shape of the negotiating table. Meetings are held weekly, something Sybil is grateful the POWs do not know. "It wasn't a very convincing demonstration that either side was anxious for progress," she noted. Increasingly, she is cynical about the war and her country's leadership.

As she performs her last rehearsal alone, in front of the hotel mirror, Sybil's anxiety is overwhelming. She is exhausted, even though she has been taking a sleeping pill each night. She has been dry heaving. But she does not want anyone to know. Candy recognizes her emotional distress. "She was on her way to a nervous breakdown.... Something was off. It just wasn't right."

Sybil plows on. This is their one shot to request an *in person*, honest, and full accounting of the men the North Vietnamese are holding captive and those that are missing. She reviews the script and the plan with the group one last time. They grab their notes, powder their noses, and head out for the forty-minute taxi ride. North Vietnamese officials meet them at the gate, escorting them into a dimly lit room. Spacious, it is sparsely decorated. Oriental rugs cover a worn wooden floor, low-slung furniture is arranged around two Formica-topped tables, a picture of oxen hangs on a wall, and a model of an oxcart sits on the table. Coarse linen curtains make the room seem even darker and the mood heavier. But they do not muffle the dissonant sound of someone playing billiards nearby.

Four slender and diminutive North Vietnamese officials in drab suits with Mandarin collars stand silently, watching the group intently. When the men sit down, their too-short pants reveal skinny socks and pale, scrawny legs. Sybil is in a deep easy chair with heavily upholstered cushions facing Xuan Oanh, the senior representative of the delegation. Later, she describes him as "enigmatic looking." The other three men never introduce themselves. Sybil makes meticulous mental notes of what they look like, assigning them mnemonic nicknames: "Brown Suit," "Mr. X," and "Glasses."

The deep seats make it awkward for the women to sit politely in skirts. Andrea's knees rise close to her face. Convinced the seating is intended to unnerve them, Candy almost giggles out loud, while she struggles for modesty. An image of Ho Chi Minh, the recently deceased North Vietnamese prime minister and president, looms over the group. It may be a photograph, but he is an ominous presence.

The gloom casts a sense of doom over the group. Andrea's eyes dart around, as she squints at the doors. What is behind them? Naïvely, she believes her husband might be at this house ready to return with her to the United States. Tea, stale crackers, and Vietnamese candies are served. It is a strange tea party. The group sips from cups, trying to balance their saucers and steady their shaking hands from clanking the porcelain cups. The North Vietnamese stare blankly at the women.

Sybil gives the signal to Candy. She clears her throat, sits forward, and recites her statement, pleading for information about her husband, Navy Lt. Charles "Chuck" Parish, missing for more than a year. Why can't they tell her if he is alive or dead?

"Well," responds Oanh, "it is difficult to know whether men are missing in Vietnam or not because of various reasons, either because other countries are involved, or because some planes are shot down over water, some are lost at night, some are on fire." He asks her to write down the specifics of Chuck's shoot down and loss date. Then: "He told me I reminded him of his younger sister." He says her husband has just been killed by an American bomb. Oanh pauses, letting his statement sink in. Candy is not naïve. She knows what he is trying to do. Somehow, she finds him personable. Even though she knew he was a politician, skilled in poker-face diplomacy, "he seemed warmer than the others, at least to me."

Ruth Ann speaks next, then Andrea, who is terrified. Unlike the other missing and captive men, Donald works in military intelligence and has briefed her to *never* discuss his work. "But I had to say who I was...and that I knew by then that he had been captured in the south."

Andrea wonders if their hosts suspect the women are dupes of their government. And what do they think of *her*? "They see this brown face in there. Look what's going on in the United States, you know? People are being killed, and the civil rights are going on." They must wonder, she thinks, how did *she* get involved?

Next up is Pat. Carefully, she recounts what she knows of the incident where her husband, Air Force Maj. Arthur Mearns, was shot out of the sky on November 11, 1966. She beseeches her hosts: "What do I tell my children?" They have been without a father *for almost three years*. Silence. "They just sat there. Their faces were placid."

Tom speaks about his missing son-in-law. Finally, it is Sybil's turn. Although she has practiced her statement many times, she is too nervous to recite it from memory. But she cannot see. Darkness is descending, and the room is awash in shadows. Sybil asks to borrow reading spectacles from "Glasses." He acquiesces, slowly handing them to her. For a few seconds, all pretenses fall away, giving her a fleeting sense of control. Sybil relishes the moment.

She relays her husband's shootdown and capture. "I know Jim was injured, but I have no evidence his injuries have been given proper treatment." Sybil wants a report for each captive's circumstances and an accounting for the missing, as required by the 1954 Geneva Convention.

An awkward silence fills the room. Suddenly, stone-faced Oanh stands up, pulling a folded *New York Times* article with a photo of Sybil from his pocket. "We know all about you, Mrs. Stockdale." Sybil blinks, staring back at him. The ticking of a clock in the background mimics her pounding heart.

He leers, "Does it not seem strange to you that for so many months the government was not concerned and talking about the prisoners and missing? And then the government started talking about them and women started coming to Paris. Your government is using wives and families to draw attention away from the crimes and aggressions they are committing."

Sybil can almost feel the blood congealing in her veins. Oanh continues: "We know you are the founder of this movement in your country and we want to tell you we think you should direct your questions to your own government." This is what the U.S. government had been warning the wives about for years. Talking in public might hurt their husbands and hamper the U.S. government's ability to negotiate their release. *Keep quiet*! they have been told repeatedly during the past four years.

Clenching her jaw, Sybil composes a careful response, citing the list of government offices she and the rest of the wives have visited on Capitol Hill and elsewhere.

She does not reveal that she has been unable to get an audience with the new president, Richard Nixon. Dull stares from the North Vietnamese: it does not seem to matter what she says. Her spirits sink.

Out of his pocket, Oanh fishes a letter from a group of North Vietnamese women to American wives of POWs and MIAs. He apologizes for the poor translation and reads aloud: "You don't really know what trouble is compared to our trouble. We want to live in peace with you. American prisoners get food which some of us have to go without so the Americans can be well fed." Sybil knows otherwise.

Candy watches the tennis match of words between Sybil and Oanh intently, trying to memorize the faces of the four North Vietnamese men. "Mr. X's" beady eyes reveal his disdain. He sneers when Sybil speaks. Candy absorbs details about the room and the conversation so she can debrief Pentagon intelligence officers when she returns home.

The women hand over a thick stack of letters—some 700 of them—from 500 families of missing and captive men, requesting delivery. Oanh reluctantly takes the bundle, making no guarantees. Furthermore, he questions why the women claim they are receiving so little news from their men. "I believe that letters from your husbands are being confiscated by the Pentagon or the State Department."

Dismissively, Oanh says it is not necessary for more relatives to visit the delegation. And inquiries about men captured in South Vietnam should be addressed to Madame Binh, the Communist leader representing the National Liberation Front at the Paris Peace Talks. They will be answered by mail. But when and where? He refuses to say.

The women are ushered into another room to watch two propaganda films. The first documents the impact of U.S. napalm attacks in Vietnam. While it is designed to repulse, the graphic videos do not shock them. For Candy, "The napalm was horrific, but it was war." They have seen worse images on the evening news, which has fueled the growing antiwar movement in the United States. Just six months ago, students took over the administration building at Harvard University to protest the war. One month earlier, thousands of young people descended onto a farm in upstate New York for a rock music festival featuring performances from popular musicians including Jimi Hendrix, Creedence Clearwater Revival, Arlo Guthrie, and Joan Baez, some performing explicitly antiwar protest songs. The three-day festival, dubbed Woodstock, is a symbol of the counterculture movement wending its way through society. Resentment toward the war and those fighting it has been growing exponentially. An element of American society has come to believe the North Vietnamese are innocent victims, that most soldiers are "baby killers," guilty of atrocities, fighting an unjust war. The propaganda film supports those assertions, but the women are undaunted. They have faced resentment from fellow Americans everywhere they go.

The next film documents "humane" treatment of American POWs in North Vietnam. The women wince at the sight of gaunt men, straining to see if they recognize any faces. Then, the overhead lights are turned on and the North Vietnamese search for reactions from the Americans. Along with Tom, the five women put on their best poker faces.

After several cups of tea, several of the ladies desperately need the restroom. Their hosts escort them down the hall. Once alone, the women let out a collective sigh, exchanging furtive glances. They dare not speak candidly, for fear the bathroom is bugged. Sybil is the last to leave and has a few moments to herself. She stares at herself in the mirror. The fluorescent lights accentuate the look of exhaustion. Refreshing her lipstick, she blots her lips neatly on one of the guest towels, leaving a kiss for the North Vietnamese.

After the screening, the ladies are brought back to the "tearoom" for more refreshments and more lectures on how tough life is in Vietnam. As Andrea sneaks a piece of stale candy into her purse "to prove I was there," she and the rest of the group are given a primer on the dessert they are being served. It is candy made of rice flour, honey, and sesame seeds, prepared *by* Vietnamese women *for* women. Vietnamese men only eat hard candy. Would they like the recipe?

After two and a half hours, the Americans emerge from the peculiar encounter into the black of night. A small group of reporters emerges from the darkness. The women are not surprised to see them, but they are weary and wary.

"What will you do now that you've had your visit here?" one reporter asks Sybil as he thrusts a microphone toward her face. "Go back to the hotel and get some rest," Sybil replies. "We're *so* tired."

A male reporter sneers: "Ohhhh, yes." Some members of the international press corps seem unsympathetic to the plight of the POW and MIA families. Their taunting tone is disheartening. Tom Swain deftly briefs the reporters: the North Vietnamese have reassured them they will investigate and notify families about the status of their missing and captured relatives. After the questions stop, the women and Tom are alone on the deserted street. The silence is disquieting.

The women try to buoy each other's spirits. "We felt very dejected afterwards," Pat admits. "The one thing we accomplished is we were *there* and we made a statement by our presence." While they agree the meeting *was* risky, they believe it was worth it. Pat is convinced that "Glasses" knows her husband. She detected a glimmer of recognition when "Arthur Mearns" was mentioned. That lifts her mood a bit. Ruth Ann points out that it was an opportunity to get to know the North Vietnamese. Ironically, the wives have been unable to schedule an audience with their own president, Richard Nixon.

With only a verbal promise from the North Vietnamese and no real expectation it will be fulfilled, letdown settles in. Perhaps it is the gloomy weather, or the pressure has taken its toll. The growing din of antiwar sentiment—from the media, from other average Americans—is drowning out the women's voices. Why will the Nixon administration, the State Department, and the most powerful military in the world not do more to secure better treatment for the men and get them released? Why are they, private citizens with no political experience, forced to be the face of international diplomacy? And why won't President Nixon meet with them?

Shortly after Sybil returns home, a new group of American antiwar activists called the New Mobilization Committee informs her that the North Vietnamese government plans to release any comprehensive list of POWs to *them*, not the U.S. government nor the wives. The North Vietnamese will manage the POW/MIA issue to their advantage. The wives who went to Paris will be forced to work with the antiwar movement for any tidbit of information. The irony is not lost on Sybil.

The State Department suggests she respond to the North Vietnamese. Since the U.S. government is not planning to protest this arrangement, Sybil complies. "To force the prisoners' families to apply to such a political organization is an unnecessary exploitation of their helplessness. It only diminishes the humanitarianism of the gesture your country is making in releasing the list of the prisoners. The world will see no logic, only vindictiveness, in such an arrangement." Her telegram is delivered to Xuan Oanh. She receives no reply.

CHAPTER TWO

RISKY BUSINESS

HOW MANY ARE THERE? (JANUARY 1969)

On the eve of his inauguration, telegrams are pouring in for President-elect Richard Nixon. More than *two thousand* yellow cables with brown borders stream into the White House and State Department. Top aides take notice and so does the president. The message? "Please remember those who have offered so much for our country, the men who are prisoners of war in Vietnam. Don't forget them now. Please insist on their immediate release through negotiations in Paris."

The telegram campaign was an idea hatched by Sybil Stockdale and thirteen other Navy wives sitting around her dining room table in her cottage on A Avenue in Coronado, California.

Nixon, president-elect for more than two months, had promised a new peace proposition for Southeast Asia. Sybil's husband Jim had been a POW for more than three years. The husbands of the other thirteen women were also missing or captured in Southeast Asia. The group had been meeting informally for more than two years but they had not yet attracted the attention of the White House. President Lyndon B. Johnson and his administration relegated the POW issue to the sidelines. The ladies hoped President Nixon would place a higher priority on their captive and missing men. Sybil knew the timing was right to make some noise. The women understood the urgency of getting the attention of their new president.

With their children at school, the ladies had no distractions as Sybil explained the plan to place the POW issue squarely in the new president's lap—and on his policy agenda.

To her consternation and mounting frustration, her meetings with State Department staffers and those at the Pentagon had produced nothing. Sybil longed to bypass the bureaucracy and go directly to the Oval Office. Easier said than done. The "sit-ins" of the civil rights movement were grabbing headlines and generating discussions of policy change. That was exactly what *she* wanted to do. The Quakers had staged an antiwar protest in front of the Pentagon in 1965 and the anti-segregation sit-ins staged by Black people at lunch counters in the 1960s were also grabbing headlines. Something like *that* would certainly get the attention of the president!

But the POW and MIA wives had children and jobs. Sybil had four boys to raise, and so did the others, some of whom were schoolteachers, secretaries, social workers, or stewardesses. How could this sorority demonstrate critical mass without protesting in front of the White House?

The "Telegraph-In" campaign contacted thousands of military families, requesting them to send telegrams *en masse* to the White House on Inauguration Day. Sybil's group sent a form letter to all the POW and MIA wives they knew, asking them to contact other POW and MIA wives around the country. Forbidden by the Pentagon from having a list of other families with missing men, they had created their own through phone calls and letters.

The "Telegraph-In" was activism with a twist, in keeping with the social constraints placed on military wives and the public's expectation of how they should behave. It elevated the urgency of the POW/MIA issue *respectfully*. Nevertheless, it was a protest.

Though expensive, the effort would be worth the price. Sybil could almost see the satchels of beige and brown telegrams arriving at the White House and was convinced it would make an impact. However, they *were* breaking Navy protocol. Communicating directly with their commander-in-chief violated the service's sacrosanct "chain of command." But after years of clamoring for a new POW/MIA policy without results, Sybil was learning that circumventing the Navy's bureaucracy paid off.

Prior to meeting her husband, Sybil had no experience with the Navy, except for a brief tour of a ship that pulled into New Haven Harbor on Memorial Day weekend in 1935. She knew little about life as a naval officer's wife. But a popular handbook of the day, *The Navy Wife*, told her everything she needed to know: Her role was to support and love her man. In detail, the book advised young wives how to be good homemakers and how to set their husbands up for successful careers in the Navy. It was also a primer, a navigation chart for civilians on the tradition-bound service.

The book painted a picture of an exciting and glamorous life for young women lucky enough to marry a naval officer: social activities, world travel, and exposure to national and international military leaders, diplomats, and politicians. The tome also counseled patience: Navy wives must get used to *waiting*. "What is more, they must learn to wait patiently.... In such situations it's bad enough to feel tense and jittery, but it is worse to show it." Wives had to love the Navy—and its hardships—as much as their husbands did.

Until Vietnam, this expectation permeated military culture. "A Navy wife should be proud of the Navy and her connection with it, and never by word or deed should she cast any discredit on it. Times will be hard, and separations may be long, but she should present to the world a cheerful agreeableness rather than a resigned stoicism. The Navy doesn't particularly care for a wife who is *too obviously* carrying her load," it said. Those words would prove true.

Sybil had read *The Navy Wife* and found it thrilled her each time. Her new life would be a far cry from her childhood on a dairy farm in West Haven, Connecticut. Her father took great pride in the family business, started in 1884 by her grandfather, but she had not enjoyed farm chores. While cleaning out chicken coops, she fantasized that she was a princess whose handsome prince had been chosen.

Summers, she dressed up with friends and held mock weddings. Sybil danced all the time, pirouetting, prancing, and practicing on the front porch. Her parents indulged her passion with ballet and tap-dancing lessons. Dancing, like farm work, imbued in their daughter stamina, a sense of discipline, and a work ethic. She dreamed of becoming a Rockette and worried her legs were not long enough. But dancing at Radio City Music Hall was a step too far. Sybil's mother, a stoic New Englander, would not allow her daughter to become a show girl. She emphasized good manners, culture, and education. She and her husband were caring and stable parents, but not overly warm and demonstrative. As a result, Sybil would never be described as carefree, or giddy, or glamorous. She could be jovial but was reserved and occasionally, aloof.

Working hard in high school for entry into Mt. Holyoke College, Sybil earned the pride of her mother who had wanted to attend a "Seven Sisters" college, the female equivalent of the once all-male Ivy League schools. Before Sybil began her freshman year in 1942, Mary Emma Woolley was appointed eleventh president of the college. Ten years earlier, Woolley had served as the only female delegate to the Conference on Reduction and Limitation of Armaments in Geneva, Switzerland. Her pioneering style and her advocacy for both women's education and international affairs made a powerful impression on young women of that era.

When Sybil met Jim on a blind date in the spring of 1946, she was a high school teacher, and he was about to graduate from the Naval Academy in Annapolis. Instantly, she knew he was the man she wanted to marry, and they tied the knot one year later. By the time Jim deployed to Vietnam, they had been married for almost two decades. Jim had a football player's build and piercing blue eyes. A thinker and brooding intellectual with a penchant for philosophy, Jim's somber personality was leavened with a wry sense of humor that made Sybil laugh. His down-to-earth Midwestern upbringing was a good match for Sybil's practical New England one. Their marriage was a partnership, a union of intellect and temperament. Their mutual respect was evident to all. Sybil loved being the wife of a naval officer on the fast track to making admiral.

The Navy Wife was not serving her now. There was no chapter about lobbying the commander-in-chief. She was taking a risk with the "Telegraph-In." What would Navy leadership say when they learned of her activism?

President Nixon responds to each missive: "I assure you that the subject of their release and welfare will have an urgent priority in our talks in Paris." *Urgent* is a word the wives have not heard from their leaders before. Privately, President Nixon finds the telegram campaign mystifying. Sensing trouble from an unknown constituency, he wonders *how many* POW and MIA wives are out there? What kind of influence do they wield? It is a refrain he will repeat often.

GATHERING FORCES (OCTOBER 1966)

The "Telegraph-In" campaign was three years in the making. The women had first met at Sybil's when she needed to connect, to vent with other women whose husbands were missing. The women had heard about their common plight through the aviation community grapevine, in the checkout line at the commissary, at school drop-offs, and on the tennis court. Sybil was not sure how many wives of missing or captive men would show up. Some were too scared to talk on the phone, much less assemble in person. "I could understand their fear. For all they knew, I was a reporter."

As air strikes against North Vietnam increased in frequency and intensity, the number of POWs and MIAs grew. Likewise, the number of POW and MIA *families* was growing. But they are isolated from one another, told by the U.S. government not to talk about their predicament to anyone, for fear the knowledge could be manipulated by the North Vietnamese. They were prisoners without walls, fed empty assurances from Pentagon officials that their captive husbands were being well-treated and that their government was working hard for their release.

In the summer of 1966, Sybil had met with the Chief of Naval Personnel Vice Adm. Benedict Semmes. She asked him to write to POW and MIA wives assuring them that they were not forgotten. "What would I say?" he shrugged. Persisting, she proposed that *she* write a letter to the wives and asked him to distribute it *for* her. She offered postage. He remained noncommittal.

Sybil was exasperated with the Navy's leadership: the issue of the missing and imprisoned men was being neglected. She could not understand why the U.S. government had not voiced public concern about the evidence of North Vietnamese violations of the Geneva Convention. She needed to vent to others in the same predicament.

Carefully, she dialed the phone numbers of POW and MIA wives she knew, and some she did not, asking them to call others. Come for lunch. No agenda, just a friendly get-together.

Conversation is tentative at first, until Navy wife small talk breaks the ice: who just got promoted, who is transferring, which squadrons are about to deploy, and which are about to return. Then Sybil takes charge. Wife of the senior-ranking military officer of the group, she is the top-ranking woman, the *de facto* leader. Acknowledging the elephant in the room, Sybil wants to know: What have they been told about the status of their husbands?

One by one, the women describe tone-deaf casualty officers and condescending Pentagon officials. A flood of pent-up emotions pours out: grief, anxiety, and frustration. The women share tidbits of both official news and rumors. Most cling to morsels of information. Many have endured months of silence from officials in Washington. A realization ripples through the room: They are each receiving the same brush-off. Little is being done to help their men.

Lunch lasts all afternoon. They decide to meet monthly and determine the military does not need to know about this new tribe of fourteen. The women reluctantly leave Sybil's house to pick up children and make dinner, knowing they have not solved their problems. But the emotional relief is palpable. They *do not* have to suffer in isolation.

Today, they have found a release valve in their camaraderie. And they will no longer keep quiet—at least among themselves. *Keeping quiet* has been unbearable. As unbearable as the muzzle they received the year before.

KEEP QUIET—THAT'S AN ORDER! (MAY 1965)

The Navy commander who shows up at Sybil's front door is a baby-faced redhead with a moustache. His uniform does not fit well over his pudgy frame. An hour late, he saunters into Sybil's living room, removes his military cover, or hat, working the room like a politician running for office. A public information officer, he seems to relish his role of Navy spokesman for the aviation community.

As the wife of the air group commander aboard the aircraft carrier USS *Oriskany*, Sybil is responsible for mentoring the wives of the men who work for her husband. She takes her role seriously, and even more so when the men are deployed. They have been gone for several weeks, but the ladies and their children are facing months of separation. Sybil has invited this naval officer because she has heard he has useful things to say about what to do if anything happens to naval aviators deployed to Southeast Asia.

"What I am about to discuss with you today should not be discussed with others," the commander intones. In unison, the ladies lean forward.

Be prepared, he tells the women, for the possibility that your men could become captives of enemy forces in Vietnam. Ticking off the rules of engagement, he says, "In the event your husband is captured, every effort will be made to notify the next of kin personally." *Next of kin,* the official term for wives, parents, and children. "They should be warned not to release any information about the prisoner and not to be interviewed by the press concerning his background."

Married to a senior officer on his fifth deployment to the Western Pacific, Sybil has never heard a talk like this. She looks around at the spellbound audience. Plates of food are balanced on laps, but no one seems to have eaten a bite. Sybil thinks to herself, "How dreadful it would be if any of them had to face such a possibility."

He continues, "The standard answer to all news agencies should be 'Mrs. ______________________________ has no comment for the press at this time.'" Next of kin should *not* talk to the media, he insists. What's more, a wife should *not* acknowledge to *anyone* but family that her husband is a prisoner. "Prisoners at present are being well-treated and authorities have every reason to believe that this condition will continue." He warns that this is only true if the next of kin abide by these rules. "Any information other than name, rank, serial number, and age can be skillfully used in psychological warfare to coerce the prisoner to aid the Communist propaganda program."

Next of kin must let professionals do their work. "Families are strongly urged not to intercede on behalf of the prisoner without State Department approval. Independent intercession on the part of the individual could seriously damage negotiation being conducted on behalf of the prisoner by the State Department."

The commander waits for what he has shared to sink in. Sybil doubts he has ever had this much attention from a roomful of women. She cringes when he adds, "If this happens to you, you cry on my shoulder and tell me your troubles." He seems to have styled himself as a veritable comforter-in-chief.

The women should not expect the worst if their husbands are taken prisoner. Navy Lt. (junior grade) Everett Alvarez and Navy Lt. Robert Shumaker, two American aviators, have been shot down and captured. The commander believes that the men are being well-treated. He passes around photos released by the North Vietnamese of Lieutenants Alvarez and Shumaker and a letter Lieutenant Alvarez wrote to his wife.

Sybil tries cutting him off, but he waxes on about how much Mrs. Alvarez and Mrs. Shumaker rely on him. Later, in one of his lengthy letters, Jim cautions Sybil: "Captain Connelly has had some unpleasant experience with [this commander]—has twice told me to tell you to give him a wide berth." If only she had been given that piece of advice earlier.

After two hours, the commander leaves, and the party breaks up. A few wives linger, peppering Sybil with questions they did not feel comfortable asking the chubby commander. One, barely out of her teens, shakily asks, "You know, Mrs. Stockdale, we haven't been married very long and I don't know much about these things. Do you think there's anything to be afraid of?" Sybil quashes the girl's fear: "Oh heavens, no. My husband's been flying for years, and I've never heard anything like this before. Don't give it another thought. I'm sure they'll all come home safely."

THE DOORBELL RINGS (SEPTEMBER 1965)

Nobody rings doorbells in Coronado, California. Friends and neighbors walk in, with a little "Hello-o-o!" as they help themselves to a seat on the couch or a drink from the fridge. A doorbell ringing at 9:30 at night is unusual.

Sybil does not hear it. She has dozed off upstairs with her sons Sidney, a sixth grader, Stanford, a kindergartener, and Taylor, a preschooler. The younger boys frequently want Mom to lull them to sleep. Their 1920s-era Craftsman cottage makes scary noises at night.

The family is settling back home after another blissful summer spent on the Connecticut coast with her parents and getting ready for school. The oldest, fourteen-year-old Jimmy, is busy with pre-season football practice. Tall and stocky for his age, he sports wavy brown hair and has a strong resemblance to his mother.

Like the Stockdales, most residents in Coronado go to sleep early because most of the men wake up early. This is a decidedly Navy town, full of aviators who fly jets and helicopters at Naval Air Station North Island, and Navy SEALs who train in and out of the water at the Naval Amphibious Base. Coronado feels like a small southern town—but in southern California. The village has one stoplight, one high school, one library, one all-night diner, and lots of gossip. It also boasts a historic hotel, the Hotel Del Coronado, with its iconic red turrets. The Del is a popular playground for the rich and famous who travel from all over the world to see the Victorian resort perched on the edge of the Pacific Ocean and to experience the island's near-perfect, year-round climate. It is seventy degrees and sunny nearly every day.

Called an emerald isle, Coronado is a paradise for military families, a cocoon in which to wait for the many dads who deploy to war zones for months on end. No one locks their doors and kids bike everywhere. They spend weekends surfing, playing beach volleyball, and burning beach bonfires.

The head of the Stockdale household is gone again for nine months, deployed to the Pacific. He had been home only four months before leaving again. However, this second cruise is important, a capstone in Commander Stockdale's career. He is the "CAG," or carrier air group commander, the most senior officer of the squadrons on the aircraft carrier USS *Oriskany*. He oversees all aviators, air crews, and aircraft aboard the ship. A coveted assignment, it is required for those who wish to achieve the rank of admiral. Knowing how important this assignment is and that it might be his last deployment for a long time, Sybil and the boys endure. Only Sybil and Jimmy, her confidante of sorts, know how dangerous the assignment is.

Tonight, Sybil's blissful nap with her three younger sons is interrupted by the sound of voices downstairs—and not just her night owl teenager. Who could be visiting at this hour? Jimmy should be in bed! Heading down the stairs, she is startled to see her good friend Doyen Salsig.

Like Sybil, Doyen is married to a naval aviator, one who is privy to confidential and urgent message traffic to and from crews patrolling the Pacific. The Salsigs have already heard the news.

Doyen hugs Sybil tightly and softly says, "There's been a message. Jim is missing."

Sybil is shaken. "Missing? How can he be missing?" she wonders out loud.

Doyen leads Sybil downstairs, where Jimmy is talking to a Navy lieutenant. Standing still, noticeably anxious, the chaplain holds his cover in his hand. He doesn't look much older than Jimmy.

Trembling, he informs Sybil that her husband's plane has been shot out of the sky, on his last day on the firing line. After this mission, USS *Oriskany*, her crew, and Jim's air group were scheduled for much-needed liberty in Hong Kong.

Jim's mission was to bomb, once again, the Thanh Hoa bridge, a rail and highway structure spanning the Song Ma River. That bridge just would not be destroyed. Each time it was bombed, the enemy patched it up. Jim was frustrated that the targets handpicked by the White House seemed intended to irritate the North Vietnamese—not decimate them. "Here we were, wasting good lives on targets that often weren't worth it while we flew right by prohibited targets that were crucial to North Vietnam's war machine." That morning, rain squalls had rendered the target invisible, so Jim had flown his A-4 Skyhawk fighter-bomber farther up the coast to destroy idled trains in a rail yard.

Under the clouds he was easy to spot. Boom! Boom! Boom! The sound of anti-aircraft guns pierced the air. He was hit, and badly. Well-ingrained training took over and he pulled the ejection handle.

The chaplain says that witnesses saw a good "chute," but that Jim's beeper did not activate, and there was no sign of him after his parachute hit the ground. His whereabouts are unknown. Commander Stockdale is officially "missing."

Sybil cannot stop shaking. Doyen brings her a glass of sherry. She offers to stay the night, but Sybil sends her home. She wants to talk with Jimmy.

Lying on his bed in his basement lair, he gazes at the ceiling. The Beatles song "Help, I Need Somebody" croons from his bedside radio. Jimmy hesitates, "Do, do you think Dad is alive or dead?" Sybil stares into the darkness: "I honestly don't know." He turns over and she instinctively rubs his back. Neither one cries. Yet.

Word spreads the next day, and a parade of friends and neighbors invades the Stockdale home. The phone rings off the hook. Jimmy's football practice beckons. He hops off his bike and walks to the field where his coach embraces him in a long hug—embarrassingly long for a teenager. But it gives the boy time to furtively wipe his tears. He puts his helmet on and heads down the field to run drills.

CHAPTER THREE

PREMONITIONS, PROOF, AND POLICY CHANGES

PROOF OF LIFE (APRIL 1967)

Barely able to contain themselves, Alice Stratton and her friend Pat Foy enter the corner market in Palo Alto. Alice is on a mission. Instantly, they spot the magazine rack, zeroing in on the familiar black and white cover of *Life* with its signature red logo. The headline on the April 7 issue blares, "North Vietnam Under Siege." Snatching a copy, the two impatiently flip through the magazine. It falls open to a large photograph of Alice's husband, Navy Lt. Cdr. Richard "Dick" Stratton, in Hanoi.

"Oh my!" Alice says, in her taciturn way. This is the first visual proof she has that Dick is alive. Struggling to calm her racing pulse, she tries processing the idea that this image of her husband is in a magazine in grocery stores, drugstores, and bookstores all over the country. Her emotions have been seesawing for hours and she is exhausted. She cannot stop looking at the photograph. It is horrifying—an image that will continue to haunt her. Pat fishes thirty-five cents from her purse to pay for the magazine. The two dash back to the car, heading back to the Foy home, Alice clutching the magazine to her chest.

A study in contrasts, Pat is blonde, short, exuberant, and athletic, exuding an air of confidence. The two have been friends since Alice moved west in 1958 and began working in San Mateo County. Alice is measured, tall, lanky, and bookish, with a wry sense of humor. Their bond is unshakable. She has been through the wringer lately, and Pat is worried. She watches her friend out of the corner of her eye, as Alice pores over the magazine with Pat's husband, Tom. All three sit in stunned silence.

In the dark and grainy full-page photograph, Dick is wearing vertically striped prison pajamas, white socks, and slippers. Alice would know that profile anywhere: Dick's call sign is "The Beak." Yet something is off kilter. His hands are cupped at his sides, and he is bowing deeply. Tilting her head and the magazine, Alice tries to understand the grainy photo, but she is stymied. Dick appears more subservient than his spirit suggests. But after three months of agonizing uncertainty, she is thrilled to see proof that her husband is alive. The trio reads and re-reads the description of the press conference where the photo was taken. The title, "U.S. Prisoners and an Eerie Puppet Show," is frightening. Journalist Lee Lockwood minces no words in his description of a North Vietnamese officer barking orders to Dick as bright lights bathe the room.

"Like a puppet, the prisoner bowed deeply from the waist toward the audience without changing expression." Once to the east, once to the west, once to the north, and once to the south. The command is issued again. Dick repeats the somber and mechanical, yet seemingly choreographed, movements. And again. "Then, with a final sharp command from his captors, Dick stands upright, does an about face, and shuffles through a curtain and out of sight." Alice and the Foys are perplexed: Is he drugged? Brainwashed?

Several days prior, Alice was startled by a radio broadcast purported to be a taped statement given by her husband. The announcer said that Dick confessed to war crimes. Alice wasted no time calling Cdr. Bob Boroughs, her Navy contact, who was unaware of the tape.

Later that day, he phoned her back, confirming the voice *was* Dick's. He also told her that a *Life* reporter had just returned from Hanoi, and that he had seen Dick, *alive*. She did not pay attention when he told her to brace herself for the photos that would be published in the magazine.

Conditions are worse for POWs than suspected.

Even-keeled Alice has been distracted since her husband deployed to Vietnam, even more so since he went missing three months ago. Nearly everything in her world feels discombobulated, and her sense of humor is missing in action. Yet she has managed to maintain her calm demeanor. It is a deep-seated survival technique she has relied upon since childhood, when her father's depression caused him to withdraw for several years. It has been helpful since her husband's plane was shot down. Not much was known about Lieutenant Commander Stratton after he was forced to eject from his A-4E Skyhawk attack aircraft somewhere over Thanh Hoa Province in North Vietnam.

The past three months have tested Alice in ways she could never have imagined. She has tried to be patient about the lack of information from the Navy, fighting off the gnawing feelings of hopelessness.

Dick and Alice had made plans for such a predicament. Together, they decided that if something happened to him, Alice would move closer to the Foys in Palo Alto, where they would be her safety net. Their kids were the same ages, the school system was solid, and nearby Navy bases offered medical care and a commissary. The two families could attend church services at Our Lady of the Rosary together, and the Foys would include Alice and the boys in social outings. Palo Alto was familiar territory for the Strattons, who had lived there while Dick was earning his master's degree at Stanford University. The Foys offered rock-solid support and friendship. Alice and Pat had met at work in 1958 and knew each other well. Living near one another in Palo Alto again would allow them to settle back into their familiar friendship.

Alice Marie Robertson and Richard Allen Stratton on their wedding day, April 4, 1959, at Naval Air Station, Alameda, California. (*Photo courtesy of the Stratton family.*)

Alice has grown tired of the sadness enveloping her life. Living among other naval aviator families near Naval Air Station Lemoore, she is constantly reminded of Dick's absence. She needs a fresh start. Her children do, too.

On this first weekend in April, with signs of spring everywhere, Alice and her three young sons have had a good visit with the exuberant Foy brood. For two days, the Strattons enjoy a sense of normalcy. Alice sets aside her worries, basking in the joy of adult conversation and the comfort of friendship. She savors the pleasure of her boys giggling while playing with their friends.

Then a ping-pong table falls on her middle son Michael. A trip to the emergency room sets Alice on edge. Her three-year-old has a femur fracture requiring traction. It means the Strattons must remain in Palo Alto for two more weeks, throwing a monkey wrench into their schedule. Once again, the Foys step in and step up, offering the Strattons an extended stay and their unwavering support.

The next day, Alice remembers it is her wedding anniversary. She tries remaining stoic but can't. Biting her lower lip, the tears flow. "I exposed, once again, the Foys to my discomfort, my painful hurting, and they gave me the soothing balm of their support and friendship…."

Widespread media coverage of Stratton's robotic behavior at the press conference sparks national and international revulsion at Hanoi's propaganda ploy. Journalists and government officials suspect that Stratton's bizarre appearance is the result of prolonged torture. *Time* magazine refers to the spectacle as "Pavlovian" and "Orwellian."

State Department officials are uncertain how or if to respond: they fear public criticism might worsen treatment of POWs, but worldwide outrage forces their hand. The "Stratton Incident" cannot be ignored. President Johnson's POW point man, Ambassador Averell Harriman, writes a letter of protest to the Democratic Republic of Vietnam issuing a statement to *Life* magazine for its April 7 issue. His rebuke is restrained but pointed, "…it would appear that the North Vietnamese authorities are using mental or physical pressure on American prisoners of war…. Without such independent verification, North Vietnam's professions of 'humane treatment' cannot be accepted."

While bureaucrats and politicians deliberate the Stratton Incident, Alice is glued to the grainy photograph of her husband. Longingly, she gazes at Dick's profile. Has it only been *three* months?

Sitting near the family Christmas tree, in their Palo Alto, California home, Alice Stratton reads a letter from her captive husband to her three sons, circa December 1971. (*Photo courtesy of the Stratton family. Originally taken by the* Palo Alto Times.)

THE BLACK SEDAN (JANUARY 1967)

At first, Alice does not see it: the black vehicle parked by the curb.

She is unwinding from her day. A social worker, she patiently coaxes and guides challenged young clients. At a time when few women of her generation worked, Alice continues her career after marrying and while raising her three boys.

Helping others imbues her with a sense of purpose. Her family says it is in her DNA to help others. Perhaps she learned early in life to be nurturing and resourceful, watching her mother who worked as a nurse. Presciently, Dick had always considered her income good insurance, in case they lost his.

The Stratton family in front of their Hanford, California home, summer 1966, prior to Dick's Western Pacific deployment. From L to R: Michael, 3, Charlie, 10 months, and Patrick, 4 ½. (*Photo courtesy of the Stratton family.*)

Alice relishes time to herself during her commute and the anticipation of arriving home to the babysitter and her boys who are usually playing in the yard with other neighborhood children. She enjoys their enthusiasm and energy. Charlie, the baby, is one year old; Mike, three; and Patrick, four and a half.

Catching up with neighbors completes her day. Alice is an empathetic listener and her front yard is a welcome gathering spot. Dick has been deployed to Vietnam for three months, and Alice and the boys have established a solid and satisfying routine, which sometimes includes macaroni and cheese dinners and watching *Hogan's Heroes* and *Mission Impossible.*

Steering her station wagon into the driveway, she is thinking about dinner. She sets the hand brake and switches off the ignition. Exiting the car, two men in Navy uniforms jump out of the black sedan, walking briskly toward her.

Like a raven, the dreaded black sedan is the harbinger of grim news for military families. Wives and kids stop in their tracks and hold their breath when it circles their neighborhood, praying it does not land in front of their home. On this day, it is here for Alice.

Fear shoots through her body. Is it a mistake? She feels a pressure in her chest. Respectfully removing their uniform covers, the two naval officers solemnly tell her that Dick's aircraft has been shot down. He is missing in action. Overcome by the news, Alice covers her mouth, darting inside the house. The men follow. Patrick watches the scene unfold: "My mom got a horrific look on her face. It was as if everything suddenly stopped."

Sinking into an easy chair, Alice is only able to muster enough energy for one question: "*Is he dead*?" She can only digest bits and pieces of their response. Everything moves in slow motion. A good parachute had been spotted. Dick had sent an emergency radio signal. He has not been seen or heard from since. Presumably, he has been captured. But the men sitting in her living room do not seem certain about much.

Alice wants desperately to turn back the clock by one day. *Tick, tock*. She tries to listen as the officials, in hushed tones, offer their sympathies and a promise of more intelligence when they receive it. *If* they receive it. But she hears only the *tick, tock* of the living room clock.

Friends whisk her children into the kitchen. There must have been a half a dozen women scurrying around her, working in unison, cooking, feeding and bathing her children, washing dishes, answering the phone. Alice cannot budge. She needs a good cry, but thinks she has to hold it together. She shakes her head. *No, I'm not hungry. Yes, the kids will need to get to bed*. It is going to be a long and cool January night at her home in the San Joaquin Valley. Friends sit with her. Her hands are stiff from gripping the armchair. She is holding on for dear life. *Tick, tock*. The clock reminds her that time is suddenly irrelevant. At some point, she calls the Foys. They promise to drive down the next day.

A doctor arrives. "Here, take this. It will help you sleep." But it does not. She cries most of the night, memories of Dick flashing through her mind. Alice remembers his scent, his great big bear hugs, his work ethic, and his earnest opinions. Dick has an intensity about him, but when he laughs, his entire face lights up and his dark eyes dance. Now, her Quincy, Massachusetts, man with his thick and unmistakable Boston accent is missing.

The couple met on a blind date in December 1958 at a Christmas party thrown by Alice and her roommates at their San Francisco flat. The duo instantly discovered shared interests. Both were intellects and conversation came easily. She showed him framed photographs of her family in Michigan, and digging into his bulky leather wallet, Dick shared photos of his family taken during a visit to Mt. Vernon, George Washington's home. Not recognizing the landmark, Alice mistakenly assumed he hailed from a wealthy family with an impressively large home. That first impression turned into an often-told story that always made them laugh.

Dick had completed six years in the seminary, planning to become a priest before rethinking that decision and joining the Navy. Yet he and Alice shared a deeply rooted faith. Both were private and thoughtful, and Alice enjoyed Dick's philosophical musings. A self-described noisy, independent Irishman, Dick was a gentleman, but louder and more direct than Alice, which she found amusing. When he said he was a pilot, Alice assumed he worked for the airlines. He was neither wealthy nor an airline pilot, but she did not mind one bit.

Unlike Dick's childhood in New England, Alice was raised in Michigan. Her mother was a farm girl and Alice inherited her rugged determination, steadfast work ethic, and devout Catholicism. Her mother's nursing career modeled empathetic listening skills and a lifelong concern for others. Alice's early childhood was a happy one, ice skating with siblings on Lake Michigan and putting on plays on the stage in their Grosse Pointe basement.

Her father was a quiet and hardworking chemical engineer until debilitating depression following an allergic reaction to penicillin had made getting out of bed a struggle. His illness had required patience at a time when mental health was poorly understood and rarely discussed. Eventually, he received shock treatments that cured his depression. Like her mother, he too, found religion, converting to Catholicism. The family's deep faith provided solace and strength during those challenging times. Growing up in a close-knit family that survived adversity may have strengthened Alice's compassion and self-reliance. Those lessons would now serve her well.

During her college years, Alice spent summers working at a University of Michigan Fresh Air camp and later in the school system, while earning her master's degree in social work. For one year after graduation, she worked at a psychiatric hospital for children before moving to San Francisco with two friends, who were also coworkers.

Alice was reserved and thoughtful, but Dick appreciated her ribald sense of humor. Four months after they met, they married at a 1943 vintage white stucco chapel at Naval Air Station Alameda, where he was stationed. Their traditional ceremony was celebrated with a small group of fifty family members, friends—including Pat Foy—and Navy colleagues, followed by a reception at the Officer's Club. Dick's squadron allowed him time off from standing watch, giving the newlyweds three full days to celebrate their honeymoon at the Highlands Inn in Carmel overlooking the Pacific Ocean.

Like a movie reel, images from those happy days play continually in Alice's mind.

The morning after receiving the news of Dick's disappearance, she wakes up feeling exhausted and alone. She will need patience and resilience to survive. Is she a widow? Beseeching, she prays. Why, God? Why me?

Charlie Stratton's drawing for a second-grade school assignment. He was asked to draw his "wish." (*Photo courtesy of the Stratton family.*)

MOMENTUM (MAY 1969)

Early on a Monday morning, Sybil Stockdale is getting her kids ready for school when the phone rings. A Pentagon secretary asks her to hold the line. Impatiently, she checks her watch. Dick Capen and Frank Sieverts are on the other end, and they sound elated.

Capen, a former naval officer and publisher for Copley Press in San Diego, is a thirty-five-year-old political appointee recruited by President Nixon's new secretary of defense to work on the POW issue. Sieverts is Capen's counterpart at the State Department.

"We wanted you to know that here in Washington, in just a few minutes, the secretary of defense is going to do the thing you've been wanting him to do for so long. He's going to publicly denounce the North Vietnamese for their treatment of our American prisoners and for their violation of the Geneva Convention. We know you've been working long and hard for this day, and we wanted you to be the first to know."

Three years earlier, Sybil first raised her voice in protest to the government. It was a lonely task: government leadership has been almost mute on the topic. Few others had spoken publicly about the issue—much less protested vehemently.

Until now, the vexing POW and MIA issue has been the sole purview of the State Department. Back in 1966, President Johnson chose Ambassador Harriman as his point man. Harriman was old school. A seasoned diplomat and politician, he had been tapped repeatedly since World War II to manage thorny foreign policy issues. Surely, he could find a diplomatic solution to the growing number of POWs. Although in his seventies, his energy was legendary, even if he was hard of hearing.

Harriman prefers working behind the scenes, in a "diplomat-to-diplomat" style, using familiar "quiet diplomacy" to negotiate with the North Vietnamese for better treatment and an early release for American captives. Sybil met him in 1966 and 1967, pleading with him to do more, to publicly rebuke the North Vietnamese for mistreatment of the POWs. "When I sharpened the tone of my questions with Ambassador Harriman, he didn't appear to pay any attention. It was almost as if he were giving a monologue." Patronizingly, Harriman assures her that the State Department's efforts on behalf of her husband are extensive, but classified. The women and their families need to trust him and to keep quiet, he said. But Harriman's callous rebuffs leave Sybil feeling helpless and irritable.

A new administration has brought a new secretary of defense: Melvin Laird. He is determined to change the status quo.

Laird did not seek this challenge. Content serving as a congressman from Wisconsin for nine terms, he turned down President Nixon's offer at first, calling the position "the political kiss of death." But when Washington Sen. Henry "Scoop" Jackson rejected the offer, Laird reluctantly reconsidered. Feeling a sense of duty, he pledged to serve four years and not one day longer. That is, after

Laird extracted a promise from President Nixon not to interfere with his appointments.

As a member of Congress, Laird met with several POW and MIA wives. He heard their anguish firsthand. With more than 1,000 men missing or captive in Southeast Asia, Laird has become disillusioned with the State Department's strategy to solve the vexing POW issue. He is convinced that the Defense Department must take on a stronger advocacy role for the POWs—and a more public one. *He believes the POWs have become the unmentionables.*

Quiet diplomacy has been an abject failure. Laird scratches his head at Harriman's reticence to challenge the enemy's specious claims of humane prisoner treatment. Harriman's strategy has not allowed a steady flow of mail, has not enabled neutral inspectors into Hanoi's prison camps, and has not accounted for the missing. The North Vietnamese are winning the war of propaganda and feel no pressure to abide by the Geneva Convention. The wives in Sybil's troupe know it. Their long-simmering wrath and impatience bursts forth at family briefings that Capen and Sieverts hold around the country in the spring of 1969.

They protest the government's inaction, loudly. At a meeting in San Diego, one wife smashes a painting to symbolize what she thinks of the Air Force's commitment to take care of its people.

Sybil is dismayed. "Our government still had no reason to believe that keeping quiet was not the best way to proceed and still hoped our men were being treated humanely. I marveled at the detached, casual attitude...."

Why *not* call out the North Vietnamese on their violations of the Geneva Convention? They could then be held responsible in the court of public opinion. Laird advises the State Department that quiet diplomacy from the Pentagon will be discarded for a new strategy called "Go Public." And, in shaking up the status quo, he hopes to turn the POW and MIA wives into allies.

Rumors of Laird's impending policy change fire up Ambassador Harriman. Making a rare trip across the Potomac to the Pentagon, he spends nearly an hour trying to persuade Laird to stay the course and *keep quiet*. Laird is aware that President Nixon and his national security advisor, Henry Kissinger, also want him to back down. All three are afraid that adding POWs in the mix at the negotiating table will make diplomatic efforts more difficult. Kissinger later says: "I probably thought that to make too big a public issue [of the POWs] weakened us; it didn't strengthen us." But Laird is unwavering. The policy *must* change. Exposing mistreatment and torture will produce a different outcome at the Paris peace negotiations. In the process, it might shame Hanoi into better treatment of the men.

Laird asks Capen to review intelligence about treatment of American prisoners and build his case for a change in policy. Capen consults sources at the Defense Intelligence Agency (DIA), the Office of Naval Intelligence (ONI), the National Security Agency (NSA), and the Central Intelligence Agency (CIA).

The findings Capen presents to Laird and the secretary's executive team are grim. Evidence of torture, starvation, lack of medical treatment, solitary confinement, and beatings were buried in documents tucked away in file cabinets. Harriman's diktat to remain quiet and fear of upsetting the stagnant peace negotiations in Paris prevented the three-letter intelligence agencies from disclosure.

Laird is horrified: "By God, we're going to go public." Scheduling a press conference for May 19, 1969, he and Capen and their staff scramble to develop a comprehensive publicity campaign that will engage the press corps, American Red Cross, United Nations, foreign leaders, the American people, *and* POW and MIA families. This is a chance to wrest control of an issue that so far, has been managed by the enemy.

Over the objections of Harriman and Kissinger, and with no endorsement from President Nixon, Laird strides into the Pentagon briefing room.

"Good morning, ladies and gentlemen." Reporters, expecting a low-level official, are surprised. Small chat ceases as all eyes turn to the new secretary of defense.

Laird gets right to the point: "The North Vietnamese have claimed that they are treating our men humanely. I am distressed by the fact that there is clear evidence that this is not the case." The announcement is a departure from the previous five years. This is not the usual bland assurance the media is used to hearing.

Laird states that some American POWs have been held longer in this conflict than any during World War II or the Korean War.

Andrea Rander and Pat Mearns with the Secretary of Defense Melvin Laird at a press appearance. He inscribed the photo: "To my friend Pat Mearns with my pledge of support and understanding – Mel Laird." (*Photo courtesy of Department of Defense.*)

Behind the secretary of defense there are posters with statistics about prisoners and missing men. Laird outlines the list of Geneva Convention rules that the North Vietnamese have violated: refusal to deliver mail to prisoners, denial of independent inspections of the prison camps, the use of the prisoners in propaganda films, and failure to provide a comprehensive list of those being held. That must change, he insists. The press corps takes notice.

Capen is up next, providing excruciating detail about the torture American POWs have endured. Reporters hang on his every word. Capen passes out dozens of still photos obtained in North Vietnam of haggard, malnourished American prisoners, some with untreated wounds.

Laird's press conference infuses Sybil with hope. The lobbying of the last few months has paid off. "One military official in the Defense Department told me that they knew they'd better join us, or we were going to mop up the floor with them."

The event receives only modest media coverage, but the Go Public message is heard in Paris and in Hanoi. North Vietnamese chief negotiator, Xuan Thuy, announces that his government will *never* reveal a list of prisoners "as long as the United States does not cease its war of aggression and withdraw its troops from Vietnam." Hanoi has a new problem. Their aggressive propaganda campaign will now be matched by the U.S. government.

COLD HARD TRUTH (SUMMER 1969)

Navy Lt. Robert Frishman minces no words. On stage at Bethesda Naval Hospital in front of a large audience of reporters, he displays an injured elbow hanging at his side. He is one of three POWs granted an early release by Hanoi, on August 5, 1969. The North Vietnamese are hoping to generate good will. The gesture backfires.

Frishman is indignant and emphatic. "All I'm interested in is for Hanoi to live up to their claims of humane and lenient treatment of prisoners of war. I don't think solitary confinement, forced statements, living in a cage for three years, being put in straps, not being allowed to sleep or eat, removal of fingernails, being hung from a ceiling, having an infected arm which was almost lost, not receiving medical care, being dragged along the ground with a broken leg, or not allowing an exchange of mail to prisoners of war are humane."

Frishman talks about Navy Lt. John McCain, a POW since October 1967, who has been in solitary confinement for a year and counting, despite multiple fractures. The reporters scribble furiously. Although he has never spoken to Dick Stratton, Frishman describes how Stratton was tortured, "...tied up in ropes to such a degree that he still has large scars on his arms from rope burns, which became infected."

On stage with him is Navy Seaman Doug Hegdahl, a young POW captured when he was blown overboard into the Gulf of Tonkin by the blast of his ship's five-inch gun. Initially, the Vietnamese were convinced Hegdahl was a spy. He threw them off track by convincing them that he was illiterate and incapable of following instructions. His strategy worked. The North Vietnamese abandoned hope of forcing a written confession from Hegdahl.

But Hegdahl was hyper-literate and had an eidetic memory. He committed the names of 260 POWs to memory in a ditty he recited like an auctioneer, information that would prove invaluable to U.S. military officials. Cellmates for several months, Hegdahl and Stratton forged a tight bond in captivity. A junior enlisted sailor, he looked up to Stratton, a seasoned naval aviator. In turn, Stratton was impressed with his uncanny memory. When Hegdahl refused Hanoi's offer of an early release—the American POW Code of Conduct forbade it—both Stratton and Stockdale order him to accept, with a strategy in mind. Stratton further instructed Hegdahl to contact Alice as soon as he was stateside. He shared quite a bit about his wife and their kids and wanted Hegdahl to deliver a personal message to them.

Hanoi announced on July 3, 1969, the release of three prisoners of war as a goodwill gesture to a group of American antiwar activists visiting Hanoi. Was it a potential response to Secretary Laird's new Go Public campaign?

Alice learns one of the three had been Dick's cellmate at the Hanoi Hilton. *Would she like to meet him?* She wastes no time getting to Bethesda Naval Hospital. On an upper floor that is off-limits to the public, she gingerly enters Doug's room. Alice is surprised by how young he seems. At twenty-two, his boyish face makes him appear even younger. Pale and rail thin after losing sixty pounds in captivity, Hegdahl does not smile much, a ploy he practiced in prison to seem aloof and unfazed by the captors. An introvert, he is also embarrassed by the media attention. But Hegdahl is eager to meet Alice and fulfill his promise to Dick.

First, he sizes her up. Hegdahl thinks she looks sad. He knows Alice is desperate for any tidbits of news about her husband. Feeling protective and trying to break the ice, he offers her something to eat, but she declines. Then, he talks about life in the Hanoi prison—haltingly at first. Tapping into her maternal instincts and expert listening skills, Alice puts *him* at ease. Inside, she is a bundle of nerves.

Encouraged, Hegdahl pours out every detail he can recall. He tells her that her husband is in fair condition physically and mentally, despite inhumane conditions. Then, he carefully relays Dick's message: He loves her, her unwavering love sustains him; he never wants to be separated from her again; after the war is over, Alice will make the decisions for the family because his family is more important than his career.

Then comes the tough part, the truth about Dick's treatment as a POW, how he was shot down and captured, the forced confessions, the prolonged interrogation and torture sessions, the starvation, and the solitary confinement. The picture he paints is horrifying. Sitting upright, Alice does not flinch. Poker-faced, she thanks Hegdahl for his candor and the information. "I remember walking out of that room and into an elevator in a total state of shock."

Now she knows. It had been easier when she did not.

Publicity in the United States has exposed the treatment of POWs in North Vietnam. Hanoi officials seem to be feeling the pressure. Six months after Secretary Laird's press conference, the North Vietnamese Communist Party Politburo issues a resolution with a new directive on the treatment of prisoners. It emphasizes the party's conviction that the war is undeclared and therefore, the men are not POWs. Hanoi is therefore not legally bound to abide by the Geneva Convention rules. Nonetheless, "we should apply the points of the Geneva Convention that are consistent with our humanitarian policies." Prisons must adequately feed, house, clothe, and medicate the prisoners; cells must be "clean and airy"; prisoners should be allowed to write one letter per month, attend regular religious services, and get exercise. The directive instructs prison leaders to ensure low-level prison employees implement these policies and "increase their spirit of responsibility." Finally, the Ministry of Foreign Affairs "will study the possibility of allowing the Red Cross Associations of some countries to visit the prisoners."

By the fall of 1969, prison conditions improve significantly.

CHAPTER FOUR

WAIST DEEP

GHOSTS IN THE GULF (AUGUST 1964)

Jimmy Stockdale is having a tough time falling asleep. It is 10:30 p.m. but he is full of energy. He is excited to have his dad home in the middle of a deployment. His grandfather is dying and Jimmy's dad, Navy Cdr. Jim Stockdale, has been granted rare leave from his Navy ship in Southeast Asia to say farewell.

From his room in the basement under the kitchen, Jimmy hears voices besides his parents' and wonders who is visiting at this late hour. Tiptoeing up the stairs, he investigates. The thirteen-year-old hopscotches over the creaky boards to avoid making noise. If he is caught, his cover story is that he needs a glass of water.

Peering through the doorway, he sees his parents in the living room with their best friends, Budd and Doyen Salsig. Budd is also a Navy fighter pilot, Doyen the daughter of a career naval officer. The two couples understand each other and are close. The Salsigs arrive with champagne after Jimmy and his three brothers have gone to bed, or so they think.

Jimmy slows his breath so he will not be discovered. He loves the sound of his dad's voice. It will be a long time before he hears it again.

Commander Stockdale relays what he saw last week in the Gulf of Tonkin on August 2 and 4, 1964. What he saw contradicts what the government has announced. He did not see an attack on August 4. Those reports may have been fabricated.

Diverted from a routine training flight on August 2, Jim and his wingman were directed to assist USS *Maddox*, a ship reportedly being harassed by North Vietnamese patrol boats. Arriving on scene, they switched to the ship's radio frequency. Stockdale tells Sybil and their friends, "It sounded like we had just tuned into World War III." An excited radio operator aboard *Maddox* breathlessly reported: "Under attack by three PT boats…Torpedoes in the water…I am engaging the enemy with my main battery…." Circling overhead, Stockdale saw three small patrol boats leaving the scene. He and three other Crusader pilots fired Zuni rockets at the boats, damaging two, rendering the third dead in the water, ablaze.

What the pilots did not know was that *Maddox* was carrying sophisticated electronics intelligence-gathering equipment along with Vietnamese-speaking personnel and specially trained photographers. The equipment was housed in a big box called a COMVAN, hunkered between the stacks on the deck of the destroyer. *Maddox* was not on a routine deployment to the western Pacific as part of a larger battle group. The ship had been sent to the Gulf of Tonkin to participate in clandestine patrols dubbed Operation DeSoto. Begun in 1962, the patrols were intended to monitor the North Vietnamese coastline and gather information on its military fleet, maritime traffic, and supply lines between the north and south. *Maddox* was eavesdropping on the North Vietnamese.

Intelligence collected by the DeSoto patrols was fed directly to the NSA. This information assisted the CIA and the Military Assistance Command, Vietnam (MACV) in their plans to direct covert South Vietnamese-led naval commando attacks, using boats procured and maintained by the U.S. Navy. The attacks, intended to signal the North Vietnamese to back off, had been growing in intensity during the previous few months. The U.S. was not participating in the raids to allow plausible deniability. But Americans were intimately involved in planning, training, and logistics. President Johnson was unhappy with the results. He preferred a more aggressive approach.

In response to President Johnson's displeasure, in June 1964, the National Security Council, Joint Chiefs of Staff, and the MACV developed a *new* plan, designed to eliminate North Vietnam's insurgency into the South. It recommended placing ground forces in Cambodia and Laos to damage the Viet Cong supply line with attacks on coastal installations and aerial bombing.

Assistant Secretary of State for Far Eastern Affairs William Bundy drafted a resolution granting the president the right to commit U.S. forces to defend any nation in Southeast Asia threatened by Communist aggression. Broad and open to interpretation, President Johnson shelved it. Without threat or provocation by the North Vietnamese, the resolution would have been difficult to justify to Congress. Two months later, an attack on U.S. ships in international waters may have given President Johnson the justification he needed.

From July 30 to 31, *Maddox* was in the Gulf of Tonkin, monitoring a raid against Hon Me Island, where South Vietnamese commandos were destroying radar. Two days later, on August 2, three North Vietnamese patrol torpedo boats attacked *Maddox*.

Very few members of the crew were aware of the capabilities of the large black box on deck. Even fewer knew the ship was on a top-secret mission. Trained to understand Vietnamese, some crew members had been monitoring radio chatter all day. They *knew* enemy boats were heading their way. *The attack was no surprise.*

Most likely the attack was retaliation for commando raids on Hon Me. But the U.S. military and the White House called the attack "unprovoked."

Two days after the first assault on *Maddox*, on August 4, Jim was relaxing in the squadron ready room, where pilots gathered aboard the aircraft carrier. He was startled to learn intelligence reports indicated that *Maddox* was anticipating *another* PT boat attack and that his Crusaders were once again being summoned to assist. Jim volunteered for the sortie, suiting up and displacing a more junior pilot.

For the next three hours, the excited radio operator reported muzzle flashes, torpedoes, enemy boats, and searchlights. Jim nicknamed him Clem McCarthy, after the famous 1930s radio sportscaster. In response to this phantom assault, destroyers *Maddox* and *Turner Joy* fire blindly in the dark. Jim zigged and zagged, firing upon the same spots as the destroyers. Blow-by-blow, the radio operator narrated a rapid turn of events, multiple radar contacts, and incoming torpedoes. Jim maneuvered at low altitude, spinning his aircraft around the two destroyers with his lights off. His flight suit drenched in sweat, Jim strained as he searched in vain for the source of aggression. He saw…nothing.

The mission was the most bewildering moment of his military career. Flying above the two destroyers, he heard a play-by-play account of a fierce sea battle through his headphones. It was raging all around him, claimed the air controller on the ship. Jim found it baffling. "I had the best seat in the house from which to detect boats—if there were any."

In a final and desperate move, Jim fired a Zuni rocket into the fray, hoping to hit a target he could see. Instead, it fell into the blackness of the ocean. Low on fuel, Jim was forced to return to *Ticonderoga*, landing his Crusader in a screeching halt on the flight deck. Jumping out of his cockpit, a coterie of squadron mates, air group personnel, and intelligence officers bombard him with questions. "Did you see any boats?" they asked. "Not a one," he replied. "No boats, no boat wakes, no ricochets off boats, no boat gunfire, no torpedo wakes—nothing but black sea and American firepower."

Turning in for the night, Jim looked forward to getting some rest. Yet a few hours later, a young officer jostled him awake, telling him to prepare to launch air strikes. The United States was going retaliate for the North Vietnamese attacks on the destroyers earlier that evening. Jim felt as if a cold bucket of ice has been thrown over his head. What was going on? "We were about to launch a war under false pretenses."

But Jim had no choice. They are military officers, obligated to follow orders. He and his wingman fell in line. Concurrently, President Johnson announces live on television that American forces were about to launch reprisal air strikes on military targets in North Vietnam, giving the enemy a heads up on the impending attack. So much for the element of surprise.

President Johnson promised quick passage of a Congressional resolution "making it clear that our government is united in its determination to take all necessary measures in support of freedom and in defense of peace in Southeast Asia."

Jim's mission that night was an attack on oil facilities in Vinh, lasting only a minute and a half. It took ninety seconds to lock America into the Vietnam War. There was no going back.

Two hours later, a twenty-six-year-old aviator flying an A-4 Skyhawk from the aircraft carrier USS *Constellation* was shot down on a bombing mission northeast of Haiphong Harbor. Navy Lt. (junior grade) Everett Alvarez became the first American prisoner of war in Hanoi and would be among the 591 held captive until their homecoming in 1973.

A week after the bombing mission that catapulted the nation into war, Jim is back in his living room in Coronado. He believes he has an obligation to share the truth in case he does not come home at the end of his deployment. Although he might be violating operational security, he has a gnawing sense of anxiety about the events in the Tonkin Gulf. Sybil and the Salsigs are dumbfounded. Jimmy, crouched at the top of the stairs in the kitchen, does not understand all the military terminology, but he understands the word "lie."

Sybil Stockdale and her four sons at their Sunset Beach, Connecticut summer cottage, circa 1964. (*Photo courtesy of Dr. James B. Stockdale II.*)

ONLY DETAINEES (SEPTEMBER 1964)

Six weeks after his capture, Lieutenant Alvarez is perched on a stool for his first formal interrogation. Three North Vietnamese officials look down at him from elevated chairs. In perfect English, one tells him: "You were captured attacking our country and we have come to find out all you know." Alvarez is filled with dread. "While he talked, I tried frantically to come up with a game plan to handle the questions. Nothing in survival training had taught me how to react to a quiz under these circumstances. There was obviously no formal state of war between our countries." Alvarez refers to himself as a prisoner of war, but his captors chuckle. He is *not* a POW, they chastise him. With a sneer, they inform him that he is a war criminal who will be tried in court for his crimes. The threat of execution looms heavily.

The Pentagon decided to list Alvarez as a "detainee," not a POW. The choice was intentional, according to U.S. policy formulated a month earlier. It was meant to downplay his capture. He could not be a POW if the war was undeclared. According to the Department of Defense, "This terminology is more appropriate to present conditions than 'captured or interned' which customarily is associated with a condition of declared war."

Although Alvarez is a member of the military, the State Department is responsible for negotiating his release. Pentagon leadership is frustrated at being sidelined in assisting servicemen. But the tug-of-war between career foreign service officers working in Foggy Bottom and career military officers housed in the five-sided building across the Potomac River reflects vastly different cultures. The Pentagon is historically more aggressive and supports taking the fight to its adversary. By contrast, the State Department, created in 1789, has a more permanent presence around the world and pursues a methodical, defensive, and reactive stance.

In truth, State is hoping to negotiate a quick release of Alvarez through diplomatic channels, the way it has resolved other Cold War incidents. Just six months prior, an Air Force RB-66 photo reconnaissance plane had strayed into air space over East Germany. Shot down by a Soviet aircraft, the Air Force crew was taken into Soviet custody. Secretary of State Dean Rusk appealed to Soviet Ambassador Anatoly Dobrynin, assuring the diplomat that the incursion was an accident and that the pilots were not engaged in intelligence-gathering. A few days later, the men are released. The State Department is convinced the same tactics will work with North Vietnam, although it will be more difficult in a country where the United States has no formal relations.

Back in February 1964, the Joint Chiefs of Staff sent a memo to Secretary of Defense Robert McNamara expressing their concern over the difficulty in recovering military captives from Communists. In their view, "stronger, nondiplomatic pressures should be considered" to secure the release of U.S. personnel in Communist custody. In addition, they recommended punitive countermeasures in response to future captures. They want to unleash U.S. military might.

As a result, the Pentagon initiates a study of all prisoner releases since the Korean War, hoping to determine what measures worked best to ensure a quick release for so-called detainees. No clear patterns emerge. If any conclusions are drawn, it seems that Communists freed their prisoners when the value of POW intelligence diminished. While the idea of applying military pressure on North Vietnam had proponents in the Pentagon, the State Department has serious reservations about its effectiveness. In a May 1964 memo from the State Department to the Pentagon, the diplomats allege that military pressure on North Vietnam would "run the risk of being confused with military pressures for other goals," and that such confusion could impact the overall U.S. policy in Vietnam. State wants to continue *quiet* diplomatic overtures to the captors and wants the Pentagon to stay out of the POW business.

Downplaying Alvarez's captivity, Secretary Rusk said, "We tried to wage this war as 'calmly' as possible, treating it as a 'police action' rather than as a full-scale war." In a full-scale war, POWs are repatriated when hostilities cease. Without a declaration of war, U.S. leaders could delude themselves that a quick release was possible. Historians later concluded, "In Washington there appeared to be an unspoken resolution not to give in to the idea that the captives faced an imprisonment stretching into the indefinite future."

THE BUNDY FACTOR (NOVEMBER 1964)

President Johnson has won his bid to serve a second term. With the election behind him, he must turn his attention to the deepening crisis in Vietnam. He announces the formation of an interagency committee headed by William Bundy, his Assistant Secretary of State for East Asian and Pacific Affairs.

The Bundy Vietnam Working Group toils around the clock for two weeks, thinking through military and diplomatic options. It never debates withdrawal from Vietnam. Instead, it considers three policy choices. Option A consists of more of the same: economic assistance, military advisors, and reprisal strikes. Option B comprises massive, intense bombing of North Vietnam, or the "fast squeeze." Option C calls for a gradual escalation of the bombing of North Vietnam, or more of a "slow squeeze," with the objective of forcing Hanoi to the negotiating table. Most of the working group is leaning toward Option C, the most flexible choice.

But Bundy is uncomfortable with this recommendation. He spends the weekend reconsidering its viability. He vacillates over the "domino theory" prevailing among foreign policy wonks in Washington, the belief that Communist infiltration into South Vietnam would result in the fall of all of Southeast Asia to the "Reds."

Over the weekend, Bundy drafts, edits, and rewrites a lengthy memo, outlining a personal and thoughtful recommendation: walk away from the Vietnam morass. Bundy—and anyone reading the memo—knows that this recommendation is acceptance of a Communist takeover of South Vietnam. Could the United States live with that? He thinks so. If one domino fell to the Communists, would they all? Would a Communist Vietnam lead to a Communist Southeast Asia? Not necessarily. But can he convince President Johnson?

Bundy and his brother, McGeorge, or "Mac," Bundy, serving as Johnson's national security advisor, were appointed by President John F. Kennedy. Raised in a well-heeled Boston family, both brothers were educated at the Groton School and Yale University. They are affluent, socially prominent, pragmatic, and well-connected. The Bundy brothers bring out the worst of Johnson's infamous insecurities. The president's humble upbringing in rural Texas (he calls himself a "hillbilly,") and his education at a state teachers' college are strikingly different from that of the erudite New England Brahmins.

Despite their limited military experience, Mac and Bill Bundy are self-assured of their war time strategic expertise. With Bill at the State Department and Mac ensconced at the White House, they are in prime positions to get eyewitness reports of the rapidly deteriorating political and military situation in South Vietnam.

On Monday morning, November 23, Bundy shows his private memo to colleagues before meeting with Secretaries McNamara and Rusk for a formal presentation and discussion. The secretaries reject the memo in its entirety. Bundy later writes that they flatly told him: "It won't wash." A few hours later, every copy of the memo is collected, so no written record of it exists.

The idea of walking away from Vietnam is set aside, and the evidence destroyed, so the Bundy working group presents Option C to President Johnson on December 1. Option C opts for gradual escalation in Southeast Asia, even though two large-scale war games conducted earlier in the year had proven this strategy was ineffective. Simulating air attacks on North Vietnam, mining its harbors, and deployment of a limited number of ground troops demonstrated a strong likelihood that none of these military tactics would force Hanoi to pull back. In North Vietnam, the population is predominantly agrarian and not highly dependent on modern infrastructure. Resilient and adaptive, the population can melt into the countryside.

President Johnson agrees to the slow squeeze. But in a telegram to U.S. Ambassador to South Vietnam Maxwell Taylor on December 30, he criticizes the bombing strategy: "Every time I get a military recommendation it seems to me that it calls for large-scale bombing. I have never felt that this war will be won from the air...We have been building our strength to fight this kind of war ever since 1961, and I myself am ready to substantially increase the number of Americans in Vietnam if it is necessary to provide this kind of fighting force against the Viet Cong."

The peace candidate is becoming the war president.

Having given his assent to Option C, President Johnson agrees to a gradual escalation of air assaults. Operation Rolling Thunder begins on March 2, 1965. In a three-and-a-half-year campaign, 643,000 tons of bombs will be dropped over North Vietnam and hundreds of American aviators will be shot down, captured, or lost.

CHAPTER FIVE

THE PROPAGANDA WARS

PROPAGANDA PARADE (JULY 6, 1966)

The sultry evening light casts an eerie sheen over the pale and gaunt American POWs. Handcuffed and blindfolded, the men walk like zombies in the twilight. They have been told they are going to meet the Vietnamese people. After being piled into trucks, they are herded into a stadium before heading out. In the glare of television cameras, they shuffle solemnly in pairs through the streets of Hanoi. In numbered prison pajamas and sandals, fifty-two of them walk a gauntlet of thousands of angry North Vietnamese. The first two Americans greeted by the frenzied mob are Air Force Capt. Alan Brudno and Navy Lt. Bill Tschudy. The crowd jeers, jabbing with sticks at the Americans clad in prison garb. Some are beaten to the ground. The North Vietnamese crowd begins hurling bottles while the guards stand by, doing nothing to ensure the safety of their prisoners. The mob presses closer until there is little room for the captives to maneuver. Then the unbridled anger of the crowd reaches a crescendo as they break noses, smash teeth, spit, and punch the Americans. The POWs endure an all-out assault on their bodies and their dignity.

Watching the scene unfold on television from the duplex she calls home on the Yokota Air Base outside Tokyo, Pat Mearns is transfixed and terrified. The grainy black and white footage shot by foreign correspondents on July 6, 1966, is gruesome. Watching the news is a nightly ritual in her household. The big Sony television with its wooden console and "rabbit ear" antenna sits in the bedroom her two young daughters share. "The girls loved watching Japanese cartoons," Pat says of Missy, 7, and Frances, 5, who at their tender ages both understand the Japanese language well enough to giggle at cartoons.

Pat winces as the wrathful horde taunts and heckles the American Navy and Air Force aviators, pelting them with stones, bricks, and trash. Many of the men are bleeding. Others are able to duck the onslaught of projectiles. Pat scours the crowd, searching for the faces of men she knows from her husband's squadron. Her eyes squint at the TV set until there is a flicker of recognition. Leaning in and squinting at the television, she recognizes Maj. Neal Jones! Then, Maj. Larry Guarino, and finally, Capt. Quincy Collins, all members of her husband's 80th Tactical Flight Squadron. One week ago, Jones's F-105 Thunderchief fighter-bomber was reportedly shot down. Though relieved to see him alive, Pat finds the spectacle shocking.

Although Hanoi is more than 2,200 miles from the Yokota Air Base, it makes Pat feel vulnerable. The POWs are fellow Americans and military aviators just like her husband, Maj. Arthur S. Mearns. She has never witnessed anything like this, and it fills her with dread. "The men were paraded like targets," she remembers. "It was unfair and completely against the Geneva Convention."

But the North Vietnamese are seeking publicity. Calling the aviators "air pirates," they want to show the world their people are being victimized by the U.S. bombing of North Vietnam. They vow to put the men on trial for war crimes against the people of North Vietnam. *War crimes*? The word reverberates like a shock wave.

Hanoi does not accept that the men are POWs, as there has been no formal declaration of war between the Democratic Republic of

Vietnam (DRV) and the United States. The previous year, the Viet Cong had executed three American captives, in reprisal for a public execution by the South Vietnamese government of a Communist terrorist. The Geneva Convention of 1949, which governs the treatment of POWs and guarantees their humanitarian treatment, was signed by the DRV. But American diplomats feel they are being disregarded.

The Vietnamese people in Hanoi are enraged by the relentless bombing campaign, known as Operation Rolling Thunder, which has been intensifying: 79,000 sorties in 1966, up from 25,000 in 1965. Casualties in North Vietnam are mounting, with estimates of up to 2,000 per month in the spring of 1966. Rage fuels the crowd's hostility toward the POWs. They want revenge. North Vietnamese leadership is capturing their wrath on video, hoping to engender international empathy and support for North Vietnam and its besieged population.

The plan backfires. Worldwide media coverage of the zombie "parade" and violent attacks on defenseless captives spark outrage. The International Committee of the Red Cross (ICRC) reminds Hanoi of their obligation to abide by the Geneva Convention. Prime Ministers Indira Gandhi of India and Harold Wilson of Great Britain appeal to Moscow to restrain North Vietnam. Pope Paul VI, the World Council of Churches, and the United Nations secretary general denounce Hanoi's plan to hold war crimes trials. Eighteen U.S. senators make a "plea for sanity" to North Vietnam, warning that violence against American POWs "would incite a public demand for retaliation swift and sure."

Secretary Rusk issues a flurry of diplomatic cables to U.S. embassies in Seoul, Tokyo, Taipei, Jakarta, Hong Kong, Vientiane, Colombo, Saigon, Kuala Lumpur, Manila, Rangoon, Singapore, and Bangkok, directing them to warn Hanoi not to follow through on their threats. Although he considered Vietnam "a losing horse" as early as 1961, Rusk has nonetheless supported the commitment of ground troops in South Vietnam, a place he views as inextricably linked to the security of Southeast Asia. In his opinion, "the die for American commitment to Southeast Asia was cast in 1955" when both the United States and South Vietnam signed the SEATO treaty, a pact committing its signatories to defending the region from communism.

Rusk argues in his cable that "substantive violations of the 1949 Geneva Convention by North Vietnam make fair trials impossible. In particular, North Vietnam has failed to comply with the most fundamental procedural safeguards established by the Convention. It has refused to identify the POWs under its control; to allow the ICRC to visit prisoners and to investigate conditions under which they are held; to allow any neutral state to act as protecting power to safeguard prisoners' interests; and it has ignored the request of the ICRC to assume humanitarian functions normally performed by a protecting power. It has also paraded prisoners through streets filled with excited mobs in violation of Article 13, which states that prisoners 'must at all times be humanely treated.'"

It is the most pointed diplomatic effort yet made on behalf of the POWs. International condemnation of Hanoi follows. The government of North Vietnam takes note.

Three weeks later, Ho Chi Minh's public posturing shifts significantly. Notably, he omits the term "war criminals" from his cables to U.S. antiwar activists. On July 22, a French war correspondent in Hanoi reports that war crimes trials have been postponed. In response to an inquiry from a CBS reporter, Ho Chi Minh states, "No trial [is] in view." While U.S. officials are relieved, they admit they "are by no means out of the woods." Hanoi still refuses to accept responsibility for the POWs as required by the Geneva Convention.

Following the march downtown, the POWs are returned to their prison camps. While they nurse their wounds, one recently captured POW, Navy Lt. Cdr. Cole Black, tries to lighten the mood: "Man, do you guys do this every night?" Without missing a beat, Air Force Capt. Chuck Boyd replies, "Nope, just on Wednesdays."

LOVE IN CODE (OCTOBER 1966)

Planting a kiss on the envelope, Sybil slips it in the mail slot and listens for the drop. "There's no taking it back now," she murmurs to her toddler son, Taylor.

It only took Sybil and Taylor ten minutes to bike to the Coronado post office, but this piece of mail has been six months in the making. Carefully chosen words should alert her husband Jim it contains a tool to send secret messages. The photo she has wrapped inside the one-page letter holds the key. Riding home with Taylor in tow, Sybil prays Jim notices the clues and that the North Vietnamese do not.

The planning began on April 15, 1966, when two letters with her husband's familiar handwriting peeked through a stack of mail. The first letter was dated December 26, 1965. Her husband sounded upbeat if a bit wistful about missing the holidays. Mostly positive about his physical state, he mentioned a "bum" knee. Candidly, he wrote about how difficult the solitude had been and that it affected his emotional state.

This first letter included odd comments: "I've hoped that the old shipmates that I liked so well stopped by to see you—Don Houck, Paul Engel and all. Incidentally, I wish you would repay Paul a couple of stamp books. Just drop by—he lives right across from Shugarts." This was strange, as their good friends the Shugarts lived more than 400 miles away at Naval Air Station Lemoore in northern California. Several other incoherent statements were scattered throughout. For days, Sybil puzzled over them. What was Jim trying to convey?

Jim's second letter also gave Sybil pause. Dated February 3, 1966, it stated: "On this chilly afternoon I am so glad to be permitted to write my monthly letter and to let you know that I am still

OK. One thinks of Vietnam as a tropical country, but in January the rains came, and there was cold and darkness, even at noon." Sybil was convinced Jim was referencing the book, *Darkness at Noon*, by Hungarian-British author Arthur Koestler. The book describes grim conditions in a Communist prison, including solitary confinement, starvation, and torture. *Torture*. The thought made Sybil recoil.

Nonetheless, she had assurance that Jim was alive. That lightened her mood. And while his letter was unusual in places, he sounded like the man she knew and loved. As instructed, Sybil dutifully called her Navy casualty officer when she received the letters. Two local intelligence officials were immediately dispatched. "We don't want to pry into your personal affairs, but we are most interested in any bits of information about Jim's circumstances—other than the purely personal."

Sybil appreciated their sensitivity. She wanted to do the right thing, but "I don't want copies of my letters circulated all over the place." The men nodded in agreement and pledged to honor her confidence. Convinced Jim would want her to cooperate, she pointed to confusing references. She was certain they hinted that treatment of POWs was not as rosy as his letters conveyed and she wondered whether he was trying to identify his location. The men nodded, poker-faced. "They both urged me not to worry too much about the parts of Jim's letters that seemed unusual. I got the impression they knew more about these strange passages than I did."

A few weeks later, a Navy intelligence officer from the Pentagon called. Cdr. Bob Boroughs invited her to Washington for a face-to-face meeting, noting that the government would pay her expenses. Excited at being consulted, Sybil agreed. Boroughs greeted her at the Pentagon's mall entrance, but he did not resemble her idea of a military intelligence operative, or "secret agent." His sandy-colored hairline was receding, his chin was non-existent, his complexion sallow and he had a noticeable slouch. He would have faded into the woodwork of any room. Perhaps being forgettable was one of his best assets.

His cluttered basement office was a hub of activity. Analyzing and developing target information for pilots was only one-half of the tasks assigned to his staff of three at the Office of Naval Intelligence (ONI). Collecting information on each of the missing and captured Navy pilots was the other half. In that role, Boroughs realized that the families might be a critical asset and a useful conduit of information.

A seasoned professional who had served in World War II and the Korean War, Boroughs had an extensive network of colleagues at the CIA, and specifically, in the agency's "toy factory," that made special weapons and intelligence gathering devices. One was David Coffey, a real life "Q," the fictional character who makes tools for James Bond. On his own time after official work hours, Coffey assisted Boroughs in his clandestine efforts. Together, they developed a special code for families writing to imprisoned loved ones. Boroughs hoped Sybil would become one of his first recruits.

Boroughs built Sybil's trust over coffee, confirming that the strange references in Jim's letters were cryptic clues. Jim may have been revealing the names of fellow prisoners, men the military might not know were alive and held captive. The news was thrilling to Sybil: "I was excited that Jim had been so clever and that I was allowed to share this secret."

Boroughs had a proposal: Would she be willing to collaborate with him on a campaign to pass secret messages to Jim? Sybil's reaction was visceral: "That sounds dangerous. What if he gets caught?" In a somber tone, Commander Boroughs answered. "He'd be on his own."

Sybil wanted to mull it over.

In the meantime, he wanted her to include a picture in each letter so it would appear habitual. If Sybil agreed to be Boroughs's co-conspirator, he wanted her to send the first encoded letter in

October. Though she harbored reservations, Sybil was certain Jim would condone the effort. His axiom was: "Always try to turn a disadvantage into an advantage."

On her visit with Commander Boroughs three months later, she committed. While the POWs were tapping a secret code on the walls between prison cells, Sybil would learn to write letters to Jim in another kind of code. The thought of playing a role in assisting Jim gave her purpose.

Boroughs introduced her to an Army photographer on loan to the ONI. "He may want you to think of a way you can signal to Jim in the text of your letter to soak a picture in water without the North Vietnamese catching on. We will have prepared the picture ahead of time so it will pull apart when soaked and he'll be able to read an enclosed message." He suggested she consider including a photo of one of the children with a message about their baptism.

Sybil had a better idea. Already thinking like a covert agent, she suggested sending a photo with a look-alike of his mother swimming in the ocean. Her mother-in-law had a strong aversion to water, which would alert Jim that something was up. The letter could include the line that all his mother needed was "a good soak." Hopefully, that would prompt Jim to extract her message and the piece of invisible carbon paper that, when pressed with a stylus, would allow him to write back in invisible ink. It seemed like something out of a 007 movie or *Get Smart,* the popular and humorous spy show. Ironic, given her husband's full name was James Bond Stockdale.

The hidden message would indicate that letters written to Jim on an odd numbered date would contain carbon paper. All letters would contain a photo, but the ones with a rose in the photo should be soaked. He could use the carbon paper multiple times, to write secret messages *on top* of a regular letter. To alert Sybil to a secret message, he should begin with the salutation *Darling* and end with *Your adoring husband.*

Back on Coronado, after Sybil prepared her first encoded letter, she hopped on her bicycle with Taylor for the short ride to the post office. Anxious and unsettled, she looked at the envelope containing the special missive one last time, when she noticed she had forgotten stamps. "God almighty, what a dumb thing to do! I hoped it wasn't prophetic." Once rectified, she mailed the letter.

Three months later, a red, white, and blue mail truck parks in front of her home early on the morning of January 11, 1967. A uniformed postman knocks and hands Sybil a special delivery letter from Jim, one of twenty-one letters carried from Hanoi by U.S. members of Women's Strike for Peace. Ripping open the envelope, Sybil is overjoyed to read the salutation: *Darling*. When she flips the page over, there is the signature she is hoping for: *Your adoring husband—Jim*.

FROM COVERT TO OVERT: THE USS *PUEBLO* INCIDENT (JANUARY 1968)

Shy, introverted, and terrified of speaking in public, Rose Bucher hides behind dark sunglasses, biting her lip as the flashbulbs of cameras snap and pop around her. Stunned by the news of her husband's capture the previous day, all she can say to the throng of reporters is that she is praying for him, and is confident the Navy is doing all it can to secure his release.

A television anchor broke the news to her. Rose and her two sons were waiting out her husband's six-month deployment in the Bahia Motor Hotel in San Diego. Overlooking the sun-drenched, placid waters of Mission Bay, she was enjoying a cup of coffee when a newscaster cut into a report about the troubled Apollo space project to announce the capture of a Navy ship and her crew by the North Koreans: "The ship has been identified as the USS *Pueblo*." Stunned, Rose freezes in her green overstuffed easy chair. Her husband, Navy Cdr. Lloyd "Pete" Bucher, is *Pueblo*'s commanding officer. He and his crew have been deployed for two months. Rose knows he participates in intelligence gathering—the ship's nickname is the "floating antenna." But seized by the North Koreans? "No, it's somebody else's ship. They have made a mistake."

Within minutes, the phone starts ringing and does not stop. Within hours, the first newspaper reporter calls for a comment and Rose is suddenly thrust into the international spotlight. The sister of a World War II POW and wife to Pete for fifteen years, Rose was no stranger to having a loved one serve in harm's way. But she never expected to be put on camera.

True to form, the Navy has discouraged her from saying much. Also, true to form, the same Navy commander who offered his shoulder to Sybil Stockdale and her troupe of Navy wives almost three years ago, the comforter-in-chief, is now offering it to Rose. He tells a local reporter: "My heart goes out to Mrs. Bucher. You just tell her if there is anything I can do for her, anything at all, you can get ahold of me at the Yacht Harbor Inn, try the cocktail lounge. I'll be there for the next two hours." When Rose seeks his help at her first press conference, she is told he has a trip to Disneyland planned that day.

The ship is boarded and seized without firing a single shot in self-defense. One crewmember dies from wounds suffered during capture, and eighty-two men are imprisoned in Pyongyang. Accused of spying and straying into territorial waters, the men have been repeatedly beaten and coerced into writing and videotaping confessions of espionage. North Korea announces the men will be tried and punished as war criminals. North Korea will not release the men until the United States issues a formal apology.

Officials in Washington are caught off-guard.

Behind the scenes, President Johnson, Secretary Rusk, and Secretary of Defense Robert McNamara consider a rescue operation, retaliatory air strikes, mining Wonsan Harbor, and even capturing a North Korean merchant vessel in retaliation. All options are rejected. Military action is considered too risky. "We knew that if we wanted our men to return home alive, we had to use diplomacy. If we resorted to military means, we could expect dead bodies," President Johnson reasoned. "And we also might start a war." The American people would never tolerate a second Asian war.

Once again, the Johnson administration decides to rely on "quiet diplomacy" to secure the men's release. As Secretary Rusk remembers, "Throughout the months of its captivity, we made no inflammatory speeches about the *Pueblo*. In diplomacy many situations are better resolved if decision makers work behind the scenes and keep their mouths shut in public." It is the same strategy they have been pursuing with the POWs in Vietnam.

With the crisis playing out in both national and international media, opening talks through the Military Armistice Commission commence on February 2 at Panmunjom, just ten days after the crew was captured. Negotiations are slow and hostile. North Korea insists on a statement from the United States admitting that the *Pueblo* had entered North Korean territorial waters and was spying.

The crew's written and videotaped "confessions" are publicized for maximum North Korean propaganda value. This terrifies Rose. A recording of her husband's alleged confession astounds her. He does not sound anything like the man she knows.

The incident dominates the daily news cycle. Americans hear a lot about the captive men of the *Pueblo*. Rose receives letters from concerned Americans, as many as 400 every day. With the sympathy of thousands behind her, she feels emboldened to take her case to the media. Though she is afraid of offending the press, the State Department, President Johnson, and the Navy, Rose recognizes that she might be able to play a role in keeping the plight of her husband and his crew in the headlines, *and* force Washington to respond. Just maybe, the squeaky gate will get greased.

She appears on national television talk shows holding a sign saying, "Remember the *Pueblo*." Distributing 60,000 bumper stickers with the same tag line, she delivers a stirring appeal to thousands of military veterans at the American Legion's national convention: "My purpose...here today is to urge your support, indeed your leadership, in reminding the leaders of this great country that they have apparently abandoned the crew of the USS *Pueblo* and have allowed our nation's honor to be questioned as never before in our nation's history.... Apparently, our nation has decided not to solve crises but to file them and hope they eventually solve themselves." She receives a standing ovation.

Her friends tell her the ordeal has changed her personality. Some Navy wives think she is too outspoken. Clearly, she is breaking Navy protocol *and* policy. Many of them refuse to sit with her at official luncheons, upset that Rose has become so overtly critical of the U.S. government. Yet, passivity had not worked. Beating her chest has. She has kept the crew of *Pueblo* in the news and in the conscience of Americans. Rose wonders how Pete will adjust to the new Rose when he comes home. *If* he comes home. "If he knew I sat back in my rocking chair and did nothing, he'd be disappointed in me." Rose Bucher is not backing down.

Jumping the chain of command, she writes and calls President Johnson. He assures her the *Pueblo* is not being forgotten. She insists on a meeting with Secretary Rusk, one of the longest-serving secretaries of state and a fervent anti-Communist who vigorously defends the nation's intervention in Vietnam. Sitting across from the World War II veteran, Rose demands to know if the CIA was behind the *Pueblo* affair. Rusk denies the allegation. Is it true her husband has killed himself? Rusk chews on the ends of his glasses, picks at his nails, and smokes a cigarette. "I believe your husband is alive," he answers. How does he know, she asks? "What proof do you have that he isn't?" Rusk replies.

It takes eleven months of meetings and talks before the United States agrees to do what the North Koreans have demanded all year: Admit wrongdoing, apologize, and give assurances it will never happen again. Even though the United States has proof that the ship was indeed in international waters, the top American negotiator signs the document *and* repudiates its content while the ink is still wet. The North Koreans surprisingly accept this duplicity.

As flashbulbs go off and the Navy band plays the *Pueblo*'s song "The Lonely Bull," a radiant, tearful Rose and her two sons rush to embrace Pete on the tarmac at Naval Air Station Miramar. He and the *Pueblo* crew are home for Christmas.

Secretary Rusk issues a statement, thanking the American people: "This has been a most frustrating episode.... [T]he crew has now been released in time to have Christmas with their loved ones."

Meanwhile, Jim Stockdale spends his fourth Christmas in captivity in Hanoi.

SIDELINES TO FRONTLINES (OCTOBER 1968)

Curled up in bed on a cool and foggy fall morning, Sybil Stockdale reads and rereads her quotes in Sunday's *San Diego Union*. She has spoken her mind in a public venue. Sybil has held her tongue for more than three years, but she will remain sidelined no longer. There is no going back. The U.S. government has made a mistake in keeping her quiet.

Unlike Rose Bucher, Sybil and her squad of POW and MIA wives have been obedient. They have followed the rules. *Until now*. Sybil has not shared doubts in public. Doubts about the State Department's claim it is doing everything in its power to secure the men's release. Doubts about an edict from Navy leadership that speaking out publicly could backfire and be used against their husbands, captives in North Vietnam.

Sybil and her tribe of thirteen women have been doing a little more than just having a monthly confab at Sybil's cottage. At Bob Boroughs's suggestion, they have incorporated themselves into a formal organization called the League of Wives of American

Prisoners of War. They elect officers and adopt bylaws. Now, no longer are they writing to the Pentagon and the State Department as individuals. Communication from them arrives on League stationery. Boroughs feels the strength of an organization behind them—regardless of the small numbers—will be more effective.

But their copious letter-writing to U.S. government leaders has only elicited individual, placating responses filled with government talking points. Their efforts to date have not resulted in any vocal repudiation of the North Vietnamese and their treatment of the captives. Quiet acquiescence from her league of wives and silence from the U.S. government have not produced a full list of men Hanoi holds captive. Silence has not released the sick and wounded. And silence has not led to regular mail: Sybil has not received a letter from Jim in seven months. Their silence has not led to third-party inspections of the North Vietnamese prison camps, where at least 200 American men are believed to be held. And it has not led the North Vietnamese to provide a full accounting of the hundreds of missing and captive men.

Especially painful is when journalists and antiwar activists return from Southeast Asia with praise for Hanoi's humanitarian treatment of American POWs in North Vietnam while their comments go unchallenged by the U.S. government.

Sybil knows Americans are being fed propaganda that POWs are being treated well. She also knows that her government knows the propaganda is false. Proof was in one of the first encoded letters from Jim, in January 1967: "Experts in Torture...Hand and Leg Irons...16 hours a day." The horror in reading that line has stayed with her. When she read it, and when she passed along the information—she felt certain her leaders would take drastic action. But they have not, not in a year.

Though many in the press seem to believe POWs are being treated well, others are starting to write about the U.S. government's casual attitude toward the growing POW problem.

Celebrated journalists Jack Anderson and Drew Pearson publish a disturbing article on August 8, 1967: "One high official complained to this column that prisoner problems have been given a low priority at the State Department.... The prisoners' families have been warned not to talk to reporters lest the slightest publicity be used against the captives to increase their torment.... The great Pentagon hush-up seems to be aimed less to protect the prisoners than to protect the authorities from criticism."

In telegrams she shoots off to Secretary of State Rusk and Chief of Naval Operations Adm. Thomas Moorer, she demands answers: "I am certain all the families of war prisoners were shocked by the Drew Pearson article referring to the great Pentagon hush-up today. Do you feel this report is basically true or false?"

The response from Admiral Moorer is immediate, but perfunctory: "In reply to your telegram of yesterday please let me assure you that every effort is being put forth by responsible officials of your government to secure the release of prisoners as well as bring the Vietnam conflict to an early successful conclusion. Let me further assure you that your government has made strenuous attempts to assure humane treatment for American prisoners of war and to obtain more information for their families. I know of no basis whatsoever for Mr. Anderson's accusation of neglect or responsibilities in these matters."

Moorer knows that is *not* true. A soft-spoken Alabaman and highly decorated combat aviator in World War II, Moorer is also frustrated by "quiet diplomacy" and the Johnson administration. In a 1976 interview, he reveals: "I'll just say one more thing about the POWs. I'm sure they felt deserted, but this was not the case so far as the senior military people were concerned. If I ever had my way about it...I would have given an ultimatum to the North Vietnamese to release the POWs or else. I would have demolished the whole outfit. But they didn't. I think we could have forced them to release the POWs."

The summer of 1968 becomes the season of Sybil's education about Communist treatment of prisoners. She has been reading everything she can get her hands on: *The Prisoners of Korea, The Road to Calumny, In Every War But One, In the Presence of Mine Enemies.* The books give her nightmares. She awakens each morning in a cold sweat, worn out.

In September of that year, another chilling report comes from an article, syndicated by the Copley News Service. It cites unnamed sources alleging that the POWs are being exploited as political pawns, in "flagrant" violation of the Geneva Convention. It sets Sybil off.

In telegrams to President Johnson's new secretary of defense, Clark Clifford, and Ambassador Harriman, she demands answers: "What steps are being taken to prevent these present and future violations of the established codes?" The response is perfunctory. "I can tell you that we have no information to substantiate the assertion in the article that our prisoners will be exploited in connection with future negotiations on a settlement in South Vietnam…I am sure you realize that the welfare and early release of our men held prisoner continues to be uppermost in my mind."

Sybil is enraged. She does not believe Harriman. Clearly, he will stick to his time-worn strategy of behind-the-scenes diplomacy.

If Sybil wants to change anything, she must do it herself. What if she took her story to the press? Would it accomplish anything? Could the North Vietnamese use it to further traumatize Jim? It is a gamble. She has overcome her inhibitions about speaking her mind to Navy and State Department leadership. Can she overcome her wariness of the media?

Quietly, Commander Boroughs approves, and Sybil pitches her story to a contact at Copley News Service. Recognizing the precedent Sybil is setting by talking about her husband's treatment, Copley sends a reporter to Sybil's cottage. Sybil cannot hide that she is jumpy. But the female journalist puts her at ease. Sybil can no longer keep her words and emotions in check, and they come pouring out. Complaining about the lack of mail from her husband—seven letters in three years—she demands: "Where is the evidence, then, that Hanoi is a responsible government in the world community?" And for the families of the missing: "Only occasionally, however, would a name or a picture be released, leaving the rest to wonder whether their missing loved ones lived or died behind the wall of silence." Defiantly, she concludes: "The North Vietnamese have shown me the only thing they respond to is world opinion. The world does not know of their negligences and it should know!"

Curled up in bed with a coffee cup, she eyes the article her efforts have generated. Anxiously, she watches the clock *and* the phone. Will there be backlash from Washington? Has she "nudged" other wives to follow her lead?

CHAPTER SIX

VEERING OFF COURSE

SILENT NIGHT, HOLY NIGHT (DECEMBER 24, 1969)

Carol McCain is driving down a lonely, dark road. The temperature outside is dropping, and a light snow is falling on the Pennsylvania countryside. The night is damp and silent. Silent night, holy night. It is Christmas Eve.

Carol has not sent Christmas cards for three years, not since her husband was captured in North Vietnam and imprisoned at the Hanoi Hilton. But in keeping with the holiday spirit, she has exchanged gifts with her best friend, Connie Bookbinder.

On the way back to her parents' home near Philadelphia where she and her three children are spending the holiday, she has a few rare minutes to herself. She has been feeling out of sorts today, uncomfortable and agitated. Normally, she can talk herself out of a funk. But not tonight. Earlier in the evening, her emotions got the best of her. Carol burst into tears in front of her bewildered youngsters. "You don't let us cry, so you're not allowed to cry, either," seven-year-old son Andy admonished her. Wiping her eyes, Carol agreed: "Okay, you're right." Alone in the dark car, her emotions surge again.

Perhaps she is distracted, or maybe she is driving too fast. It is too dark to see very far. Approaching an intersection, Carol misjudges the distance to the stop sign. She slams on the brakes, and hits black ice. The car skids sideways, careening into a telephone pole. Smash! The car is almost cut in half. The impact is so forceful Carol's body is hurled like a rag doll through the windshield and into the air until she lands on a snowbank. Crumpled on the frozen ground, Carol cannot move, pain searing through her body. Her muscles stiffen. The only warmth comes from her shallow breath.

How long can she hang on? "I might not make it," she thinks. Someone reports an abandoned car near the hanging rock on Route 322 in Gulph Mills. Hours later, police find her mangled body in the snow.

At nearby Bryn Mawr Hospital, emergency room physicians and nurses replenish the blood she has lost. They assess her vital signs. "If you can hear us, wiggle your fingers." No response. "If you can hear us, blink your eyes." The team sees little response. It will be several days before Carol can communicate.

Dr. William "Bud" Stewart is the orthopedic surgeon on call. He takes note of the serious injuries his patient has sustained. Carol has broken both her legs, an arm, her pelvis, and has ruptured her spleen. The latter is life-threatening. Dr. Stewart works feverishly through the night to stabilize her. He inserts rods in her fractured legs. The outcome is unclear and her condition uncertain. It will take time and patience.

Drifting in and out of consciousness, Carol overhears doctors discussing amputation of her left leg. She tries to scream, "No! Don't do that. I'll be fine." But the words don't come. More than twenty-four hours later, Carol regains full consciousness and the medical team levels with her. They have ruled out amputation, but she may never walk again.

Carol will spend more than six months in the hospital, before emerging on her two legs, but on crutches and four inches shorter. During the next several years, she endures twenty-three surgeries and four hours of daily physical therapy. Her persistence and grit pay dividends and she learns to walk without assistance. However, she has a pronounced limp that slows her down for the rest of her life.

Before Dr. Stewart leaves the hospital on Christmas morning, the State Department calls. "Do you know who you just operated on?" Carol McCain. Her husband is Navy Lt. Cdr. John McCain, a prisoner of war in Hanoi. Her father-in-law is commander of the U.S. Pacific Command, responsible for all U.S. forces in that region. Concerned the North Vietnamese might use this information to subject Lieutenant Commander McCain to more torture, the caller sternly warns Dr. Stewart: "Don't give any info to anyone." Carol *also* asks for confidentiality, hoping to keep the news of the accident from her husband. She believes he has already suffered more than she.

Since October 1967, Lieutenant Commander McCain has been imprisoned in Hanoi. The North Vietnamese captured him two years after Carol and John were married, one year after their daughter was born and a decade after they met—when he was a midshipman at the Naval Academy. Young men at the Academy frequently came to Philadelphia for football and basketball games, and many pursued Carol. A statuesque and lanky brunette, Carol had creamy skin and brown eyes unusually rimmed with bright blue. She was unabashedly feminine, vivacious, flirtatious, and poised. Socially fearless, she loved a good party and filled a room with her coquettish, high-pitched voice and full-throated laugh. Carol was a hot ticket.

The attraction had been instantaneous, at least for John. "When he would ask me out at the Naval Academy, I always said, 'No.' You know, when you're about nineteen years old, you think you're just the best." Plus, Carol had eyes for someone else. John's classmate Alasdair Swanson won her heart, and she dropped out of college to become his wife.

Carol's mother, Mary Madraza Shepp, of Cuban heritage, was not pleased. Carol, an only child, was a daddy's girl. "Mom was hard on me and not very nice." Was Mary jealous of Carol? "I think so." Mary was a former ballerina with New York City Ballet who had abandoned her career to marry Joseph Shepp, a tall, skinny Philadelphia insurance agent, the descendant of Welsh coal miners.

Mary was a disciplinarian, but her strict ways backfired. "I was a brat," Carol shares, "and when I was mad at my mother, I would run away to my aunt's house on the Main Line of Philadelphia. She had no children and was really nice to me." At Centenary College in New Jersey, where Carol majored in English, her mother forced her to take typing and shorthand, practical skills for a woman in the 1950s. Carol did not want to become a secretary. Instead, she became a sought-after local model.

Given its proximity to New York City and its stylish and trendy department stores, Philadelphia had a thriving modeling scene. While shopping at Bonwit Teller & Co., Carol was "discovered." Graced with height, a slim figure, and size 5 feet, Carol was ideally suited for the runway. She joined the exclusive Models' Guild that secured gigs for her on the runway for Gimbels, Wanamaker's, Saks Fifth Avenue, Lord & Taylor, and Lit Brothers. Photographs of her appeared in catalogs and advertisements for Albert Nipon, Jantzen, and Geoffrey Beene. She earned a good income and made a name for herself in the local fashion industry *and* Philadelphia society. Yet her mother was unimpressed. "She did not think modeling required much talent," Carol says with a smirk.

Mary was equally disenchanted with Carol's suitors. "My mother wanted me to marry someone local, like a shoe salesman. That's probably why I didn't." When Ensign Swanson asked for her hand in marriage, Carol agreed. "My mother claimed that I was taken in by the Navy uniforms—all those brass buttons." She was right. Carol's fiancé was training to be a naval aviator in Pensacola, Florida. Marrying a naval officer and living near the ocean was enticing and offered a getaway from her mother's watchful and disapproving eye. Carol and Al were hitched in December of 1958 in the Lansdowne Presbyterian Church she had attended as a child. Her father gave her away, while Connie Cunningham, her college roommate, was maid of honor.

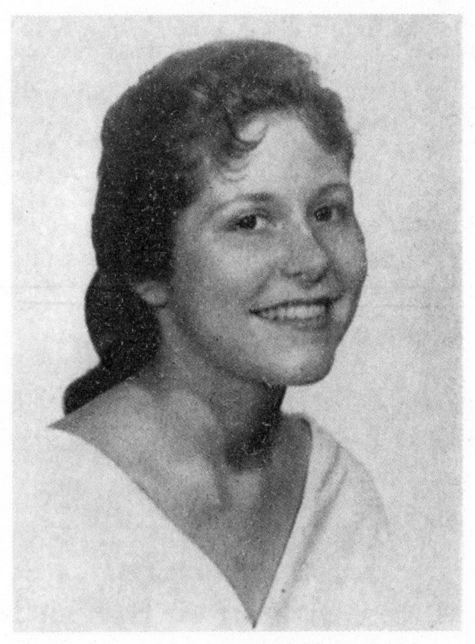

Carol Shepp McCain's 1957 college yearbook photograph in *The Hack*, Centenary College in Hackettstown, New Jersey. Her nickname was "Sheppy," and she included her chosen quote: "I warmed my hands before the fire of life." (*Photo courtesy of Centenary University.*)

Son Doug was born the following year, in 1959, and a second son, Andy, in 1962. Life in the Navy beach community of Pensacola, with its sugar white sand and aquamarine gulf waters, was idyllic. Carol and Al rented a furnished apartment for eighty dollars a month. Aviators and their wives and girlfriends hung out every weekend at watering holes or the officer's club. Live bands played Beach Boys music every weekend. John McCain routinely corralled everyone for adventures—including Carol and Al. This was where Carol got to know John. "His Academy yearbook calls him the Navy's answer to John Wayne, and I always felt that was probably a pretty decent description of him." When he imported dates for weekend revelry, some of the gals even stayed at Carol's and Al's house. She and John saw a lot of each other.

Six years later, citing infidelity or physical abuse, Carol filed for divorce from Al, moving back to Philadelphia with her sons. She resumed modeling, organizing department store trunk shows to support her young family. On a visit to Pensacola to console a friend whose husband, a member of the Navy's Blue Angels who died in an aviation accident, she reconnected with John. His reputation as a reprobate bachelor who did not take his Navy career seriously was intact. But, jumping at the second chance he saw with Carol, he took dating her *very* seriously. Carol was intrigued. At the wheel of a Corvette convertible in his Navy uniform and cowboy-style black boots, his quirky charm was irresistible. He reminded her that the ranks of available bachelors her age were dwindling. "He would tell you that the crowd had thinned out by then, so when he asked me out, I went."

Shunning his weekend routine of drinking, gambling, and carousing, John instead took a student pilot on a training flight to Philadelphia most Friday afternoons. It was an excuse to see Carol. She picked him up at the airfield and the two spent the weekend together, eating lobsters at the restaurant owned by her friend Connie Cunningham's new in-laws, the Bookbinders, going to college football or basketball games. John grew close to Carol's boys, Doug and Andy.

John thought Carol good-looking, bright, and compassionate. "We had been dating less than a year when I realized I wanted to marry Carol," he said. "The carefree life of an unattached naval aviator no longer held the allure for me that it once had. Nor had I ever been as happy in a relationship as I was now."

Carol was in no rush to remarry. And her mother was not thrilled about the idea of her marrying another naval aviator. "She was afraid I would get divorced again." But John was persistent. "He was always kind of a legend.... He's very lively. He's always got something going on. He's very smart. He has a very, very, very good sense of humor."

The two got married in Connie Bookbinder's Philadelphia living room in front of a small group of family and friends on July 3, 1965. The new Mrs. McCain and her boys joined John at his naval training base in Meridian, Mississippi, where he was serving as a flight instructor. Although the town was dry, the local sheriff offered liquor for sale. Carol stocked up at the commissary.

Both extroverts who could strike up conversations with anyone, Carol and John threw dinner parties, themed costume bashes, and black-tie soirees for the close-knit naval aviation community. "We all entertained a lot. It was fun. That part gave me a lot of practice in how to have dinner for six or dinner for twenty. It was a happy time, and it was an easy time. When everyone lives on base, it's sort of a great equalizer." A year later, John adopted Carol's young sons, Doug and Andy. The family was complete when in September, daughter Sidney was born. It was a blissful time.

Carol McCain with her three children: Andy, Doug, and Sidney McCain, circa 1970. (*Photo courtesy of the McCain family.*)

Now, the Vietnam War has broken apart her happy family and the accident has broken *her* apart. The only sound in the spartan hospital room is the beeping of the EKG machine. At her bedside, ashen-faced Connie is tearful. Carol reaches for her hand: "Don't cry."

REELING (JANUARY 1968)

Steadying her hand, Carol sips coffee and picks at a cookie as traffic whizzes by. Checking her watch, she tries to hide her apprehension, but her stomach flutters. Her husband is in a Hanoi hospital room, recovering from injuries sustained three months ago when he ejected from his A-4 Skyhawk attack aircraft and he splashed into a lake in Hanoi, parachute in tow. Here, in Paris, is where she hopes to find out how badly wounded he is.

A tall and slender man with slicked-back blonde hair approaches. Looking more like a movie star than a war correspondent, he tamps out his cigarette on the sidewalk. Then he offers his hand: "Bonjour, madame. Are you Carol?" She smiles hopefully. "*Oui*," she replies, shaking his weathered palm gingerly. "François Chalais. May I sit?" he asks. "*S'il vous plaît*." With his eyes locked on hers, he sits down, placing a metal film canister on the table.

Chalais is a well-known journalist whose career began during the German occupation of France in World War II. He was in Hanoi on assignment for a French television program to produce a segment on life in North Vietnam. While there, he interviewed the North Vietnamese prime minister and John McCain. The North Vietnamese realized they have a prize prisoner: a four-star admiral's son. They planned to exploit this. Bedridden, McCain relays his shoot down, details about his squadron, the extent of his injuries, and talks about his father.

Lieutenant Commander McCain agreed to the interview because Chalais has offered to carry a message to his family. Chalais wrote Carol, telling her that he has visited her husband in Hanoi. Is this a hoax? Then she reads: "John says he will be back. He wants you to take care of Doug and Andy and Sidney. For your birthday on February 19th, you should be sure to buy yourself a nice present." This is music to her ears. Someone has seen John. Talked to him. He is alive.

The letter pulls Carol out of the daze in which she has been wandering for months, unable to sleep, going through the motions of living. She is on a mission: she needs to see that interview.

Carol calls her Navy intelligence contact, Cdr. Bob Boroughs, or "Uncle Bob," as she and many of the POW and MIA wives have begun to call him. He provides off-the-record advice, secretly directing their actions, and tacitly approving some of their more controversial moves. Carol tells Commander Boroughs that she wants to meet with Chalais and get a copy of that film. He approves.

Parceling out her three children to neighbors, she grabs a seat on Admiral McCain's private Navy plane heading to London. From there, she makes her own way to Paris.

Chalais taps the film canister. "He had no intention of giving it to me, but I asked him for it." He hesitates. "I plan to sell this to American television. I'm sorry, but I have to make a living." She pleads with him. She *must* see it before the world does. "You have my word. I will not sell it." He slides the film closer to Carol. Furtively glancing at the other tables, she picks it up and puts it on her lap.

Carol is not finished. She has an idea, a way to infiltrate the Hanoi prison system to determine firsthand how many Americans are in captivity. Commander Boroughs had approved of the risky, clever idea before backtracking, worried how it might affect John. She makes the proposition anyway.

She wants Chalais to take her on his next trip to Hanoi, undercover as a member of his film crew. "I could pretend I'm a French photographer. Who would know?" Chalais shakes his head emphatically. "It would be a good idea but I'm probably not going to be allowed back in. I've already used up my one chance I had to do it."

Until this meeting, Carol has been grasping at straws, desperate for any information about John. He was shot down so soon after deploying: a month. The night before he left, he and Carol played double solitaire into the wee hours. They did not want the night to end because morning meant saying goodbye. His aircraft carrier, USS *Oriskany*, was on station in the Gulf of Tonkin and John was to join the ship midway through her deployment. As John checked in at the airport, Carol said: "I could just barely stand it. I was so upset. I didn't want him to go, obviously, but I know that he has to go." Sidney, a year old, sat on John's foot and wrapped her arms around his leg. "She was like a little muffin."

The disorienting news of his capture arrived four weeks later, on October 26, 1967. John's parents, Jack and Roberta McCain, were on the line from London. They wanted to be the ones to tell her.

At the time, Adm. Jack McCain commanded all naval forces in Europe. He adored Carol and was elated when she joined his family. "Carol is that greatest thing, the tallest thing that ever happened to our family." John affectionately called her "Long, tall Sally."

Roberta, the erudite and stately admiral's wife with patrician good looks, was not as thrilled. A divorced single mother, Carol was not the daughter-in-law Roberta envisioned for her son, whom she expected to become a flag officer. But she admitted that Carol possessed charm and class. Once John and Carol were married, Roberta set about grooming Carol to be an admiral's wife.

Wives of naval officers were expected to be dignified and reserved and never complain. Roberta epitomized the part with ease and grace. Perfect Navy wife, role model and coach, Roberta taught Carol to shop efficiently at the commissary and the exchange; what the insignia, ribbons, and medals on Navy uniforms symbolized; the byzantine Navy rank structure; and the elaborate protocol for entertaining. Roberta's favorite cookbook, *The Cook Is in the Parlor*, became a staple in Carol's kitchen explaining how to simmer meals while entertaining. Roberta was an asset to her husband's career. She wanted to ensure that Carol was, too.

Roberta dug deep to remain gracious while her husband fought in World War II, but her resolve crumbled in the face of every military mother's nightmare: a child missing in combat. Chief of Naval Operations Adm. Thomas Moorer bluntly assessed the crash. "We don't think there are any survivors." Roberta could not marshal the energy to be hopeful. On the phone to Carol, she admitted, shocked and raspy voiced. "I think Johnny's dead. I think we'd better just accept it." Carol shook her head. "I don't intend to. It's not possible." Jack agreed with Carol. "We have to believe he is alive."

After hanging up, Carol sat alone at her kitchen table, staring into space. He was only supposed to be away for six months.

Bewildered about what to do next, she broke into tears. Doug, the oldest child at eight, wandered in, eager for a ride to his first day of Cub Scouts. Seeing his mother upset, he rushed to her side. "What's the matter?" Carol gingerly explained that his father's plane has been shot down over North Vietnam. "We don't know very much but as soon as we do, I will tell you what I find out." Doug seemed to understand and stepped into his new role as Carol's protector. "This isn't good," he replied with a sober look that belied his age. Six-year-old Andy did *not* understand. "When will he be home?" was his first question.

The next day, the Navy chaplain paid Carol a perfunctory visit. He offered condolences and prayers and his availability: "You can call me anytime. I'll be happy to help you. I'm in my office between eight and four."

In the months since that terrible phone call, Carol has relied on sheer hope—until this letter from a stranger across the Atlantic that has brought her to the city of light. The canister in her hands contains evidence he's alive. Clasping the precious film, Carol travels to London to watch it with her in-laws.

"It was horrible because he was so obviously beat up. His father kept saying, 'I don't know. Look at his eyes. It looks like he's been drugged.'" But at least they know he is alive. "Once we knew that he was okay, we knew that it could be a long, long time. His dad kept telling me, 'Carol, this could be years.'"

The grainy black and white footage airs on CBS. John is lying in a hospital bed in a chest cast, holding a cigarette. He blinks as he looks at the camera and his lips quiver: "I would just like to tell my wife I'm gonna get well and I love her and just hope to see her soon."

OFF-KILTER (DECEMBER 26, 1969)

Pat Mearns piles into a taxi with her husband's high school friend Bob Sullivan, an attorney. They are heading to downtown San

Francisco. Traffic is heavier than she remembers from when she lived in the city in the 1950s. Back then, she was a blithe spirit who shared an apartment with other airline stewardesses.

As the taxi snakes its way closer to Union Square, she sees families cheerfully toting bags crammed with gifts. *Don't they know there is a war going on*? It is chilly and overcast on this day after Christmas, and the world is bleak and off-kilter. Suddenly, there it is again: that unsettling feeling that Pat has left something—or someone—behind.

Pat and Bob duck into a hotel off Union Square, remove their coats, and settle into wingback chairs. Then they wait. Madeline Duckles is late. With a husband missing for three years, Pat has mastered the art of waiting. But this morning, time passes at a maddeningly slow pace.

It has been more than two months since she made the trek to Paris and confronted the North Vietnamese with her nagging question: Is she a wife or a widow? They have provided no answer. Until today. Duckles bears news from North Vietnam. What she might divulge fills Pat with trepidation. "I was scared and dreaded to hear what she'd say. All morning, my hands would get very cold just thinking about our meeting."

Only four days earlier, while Pat was putting dinner on the table, her Air Force contact called. As she scooted her younger daughter into her chair, balancing the receiver of her rotary phone between her shoulder and ear, Col. Milt Kegley told her that Duckles and Cora Weiss had returned from Hanoi where they visited POWs and met with North Vietnamese officials. Where the Air Force had been unable to provide information about her husband, these women might. Bob immediately cold-called Duckles at her Berkeley, California, home, beseeching her for a meeting. If Duckles has news about the fate of Art, Pat wants to hear it firsthand.

There had been no news for three years, since Art's F-105 "Thud" jet was shot down on Veteran's Day, 1966. Singlehandedly, she packed her household and moved her children from Yokota Air Base in Japan back to California. Living next door to her parents in a Los Angeles three-plex, she had found purpose working as a school nurse in the troubled Watts neighborhood. The girl who had dreamed of travel and becoming a Trans World Airline hostess was grounded. Without a community of Air Force families nearby, loneliness crept in. Pat remained hopeful, writing faithfully to her husband. Each trip to the mailbox came with a certain weight of expectation. She never became used to the empty chair at the dinner table, nor the empty space in her bed.

Duckles seems intimidating in newspaper interviews and on the evening news. Pat wonders how she will be in person. Asking an antiwar activist for information about her husband rankles Pat to her patriotic core. Yet U.S. government officials have given her so little news over the years that she has no choice but to meet with this unofficial envoy of the North Vietnamese, handpicked to deliver news to anxious families.

Pat betrays none of her feelings. Her legs are crossed, feet tucked to the side of her chair, her reddish-brown hair pulled off her face. Secured with a barrette, it cascades below her shoulders, giving Pat the poised look of the Breck shampoo model, although she thinks of herself as just an ordinary girl from Burbank.

Without a word of apology, Duckles sweeps into the lobby, flings her coat on the couch, and begins talking. Pat and Bob have agreed that he will take the lead. Pat listens intently as Bob steers the conversation to Duckles' recent trip. A longtime peace activist, Duckles joined the Women's International League for Peace and Freedom in 1943. Decidedly antiwar, she works with Weiss, who has become the conduit of communications between POWs and their families, through their Committee of Liaison with American Servicemen Detained in Vietnam (COLIAFAM). Their small group of antiwar activists, wives, and mothers are citizen diplomats ferrying letters and packages back and forth.

Pat is suspicious of this unorthodox channel of communications. For years, the North Vietnamese have rebuffed requests by the United States government and POW/MIA families to provide lists of American detainees and have steadfastly denied correspondence. Surely the North Vietnamese are using Duckles and Weiss in their propaganda campaign that asserts they are treating American prisoners humanely? The letters must be censored.

In constant motion, barely pausing to tuck a loose wisp of hair behind her ear, Duckles turns to Bob and then Pat, as she describes her meetings in confident tones with her high-pitched, patrician inflection. Her report counters everything Pat believes. As do most POW/MIA families, she pores *over* every tidbit of news, both formal and informal, including Congressional testimony and interviews with released POWs. Yet Duckles portrays the North Vietnamese as benevolent. Pat *knows* American men are being tortured and denied medical treatment.

She surmises Duckles visited only sanitized prison cells on a cleverly designed tour to bolster support for the North Vietnamese. "The North Vietnamese women are suffering a great deal more than any American woman has ever suffered," Duckles asserts. "I have great admiration for their government and do not trust ours." Pat's tries ignoring the comments. Duckles is not young, but she sure seems gullible.

Her mind wanders to thoughts of Art as Duckles talks and talks.

Pat met Art in Phoenix, Arizona in late-1956 when her roommate asked her to take a present to him, her brother, during a layover. Upon meeting her, Art invited Pat and another airline hostess to a Flight Suit party during which all partygoers, including females, dressed in aviator uniforms. Pat thought it was great fun. She and Art had plenty to discuss. The duo felt an instant and strong connection. Pat remembers the intensity of their connection as "electrifying."

Pat Mearns's graduation photo from the Los Angeles County General Hospital School of Nursing in 1954. She later became certified as one of the first 1,500 advanced registered nurse practitioners in the state of California. (*Photo courtesy of Pat Mearns.*)

They married in the Air Force chapel at Luke Air Force Base in Phoenix, Arizona on January 16, 1958, surrounded by family. Her mother's uncle, a coal miner with calloused hands, traveled west to present her with a small gold-toned cross. "It wasn't fancy or expensive, but he came a long way to give it to me," remembers Pat. It is a talisman she treasures and still wears.

The couple delighted in military life, and an assignment to Japan, where Pat immersed herself in local traditions and cultural exchange programs. Their girls adjusted to Asian culture and loved their bedroom, with classic Japanese children's art, and bedding that gave off a rosy-pink glow, reminiscent of cherry blossoms. A natural at parenting, Art enjoyed interacting with his girls and playing board games. The couple went on dinner dates and listened to records from Art's impressive collection. Growing ever closer, they confided in one another.

Art and Pat Mearns at the Luke Air Force Base chapel, Phoenix, Arizona. (*Photo courtesy of Pat Mearns.*)

In hushed tones, they discussed Art's secret missions to Thailand, but Pat never worried. His aviation chops were impeccable. "Whenever things were in a state of change, which was most of the time, he was one of those I would move from hot spot to hot spot and he always did the job the way I wanted," wrote Col. Jack Broughton, Art's former supervisor and good friend. Pat is certain her husband, with nearly one hundred combat missions under his belt, would always return safely. She believes he is invincible.

The somewhat disheveled Duckles is an unpleasant reminder that Pat was wrong. Duckles launches into what seems like a well-rehearsed speech. What about Art? Prison officials, she tells Pat, claim he is one of five men listed as "known dead." Pat winces. Duckles appears upset for her. She repeats the assertion: *"Known dead."* The words send a jolt of fear shooting through Pat's body. They are painful to hear.

Bob questions Duckles. Where was Art last seen? Why do the North Vietnamese claim he is dead? Pat is surprised by the hesitancy in Duckles's answers and believes she is unsure of her own assertions. Ignoring the plan for her to stay silent, Pat jumps in. What *evidence* did the North Vietnamese present that Art is dead? Duckles is caught off guard. She admits there is *none*. But "the North Vietnamese wouldn't say such a thing unless it was true," she insists, as if trying to convince herself. Pat's pain turns to irritation. The activist's admiration for the enemy is incomprehensible. "That woman just does not care how MIA families feel."

A half-hearted smile spreads across Pat's face. Duckles is not as confident when facing an MIA wife as when talking to reporters. "Duckles wanted out of that meeting quickly, and so did I."

Pat has won this parry. It may be small, but it is a meaningful victory. "Here I am, sitting next to an American woman who has traveled to a known enemy country, professing her disdain for American leaders and her admiration for the North Vietnamese. Why would I believe anything she said...and with no proof?"

Frances, 6, and Missy Mearns, 8, at their home on Yokota Air Base on November 11, 1966—the day their father was reported "missing in action" following a shootdown of his aircraft near Hanoi. (*Photo courtesy of Pat Mearns.*)

Mustering the last vestiges of civility, Pat thanks the activist for her candor. The confidence she displayed when praising the North Vietnamese has all but vaporized. Seemingly chastened, Duckles asks Pat for her phone number and promises to call if anything new emerges. Silently seething, Pat gives her the information. Duckles jumps up, gathers her things, and exits the hotel, fading into a crowd of holiday shoppers. A heaviness washes over Pat. She does not like the news from Duckles, but she must keep going. One foot in front of the other.

If only those Christmas carols would stop.

YOU MUST BE LONELY (SUMMER 1969)

Pat Mearns was more confident six months earlier on Capitol Hill, lobbying for answers about her husband and drumming up legislative support for the MIAs.

Working out of a relative's office and bunking with a friend, she spent two weeks roaming the hallways of Congress alone. She scored dozens of meetings with staffers and with the occasional elected representative. Clutching an accordion file with alphabetical lists of legislators, Pat tucked a pencil behind her ear that she whipped out to jot down notes after each meeting. Learning how to chart patient vital signs and history as a nurse has paid off, she thought. "I could handle the leg work, research, and actual lobbying," recalls Pat. "But I just couldn't type quickly." Colleen Ducheck, wife of Art's Uncle Max, graciously did some of that for her. Still, she signs each of the hundreds of letters she sends to legislators.

Lobbying offered a change from the helplessness of not knowing where and how her husband was. Like many of the other wives of MIAs, Pat coordinated calls and massive letter-writing campaigns. Once avowedly apolitical, she changed. A lunch with Sybil Stockdale motivated her. Sybil encouraged her to organize, advocate, and publicize their shared plight.

This summer, she could no longer abide the MIA and POW issue being sidelined. She wanted to meet people with influence face-to-face. She wrote all 435 members of the House of Representatives and one hundred senators, signing each one. The letter implores the legislators: "A forgotten by-product of what has become a diplomatic and political stand-off war is our men held prisoners…. Tell about the refusal of the North Vietnamese and the NLF to even give a list of prisoners or to abide by any of the other articles of the Geneva Convention, such as the release of the sick and wounded, the allowing of neutral inspection of POW camps and the free flow of mail."

Once in Washington, Pat followed up those letters with phone calls and time in the halls of Congress. On her way to meet a senator's aide, she stopped by the Hall of Statues to admire the artwork and artifacts. A statue of Kentucky Sen. Henry Clay, known as the "Great Compromiser," caught her eye. Both her parents hailed from pioneer families, and she enjoyed listening to their stories. A plaque explained that Clay was one of few legislators to serve in both House and Senate. Pat took this display of talent from her ancestral state as an omen that things would go well.

She hopped on the underground subway. Pat loved that subterranean train in Congress: it reminded her of her student nurse days at the Los Angeles County General Hospital School of Nursing, where her classes were held in the basement. A short ride later, she hopped off the open-air railcar into the Dirksen Senate Office Building with its gleaming marble hallways. Glancing at her typewritten list of appointments, she reminded herself that each minute counted.

In the inner sanctum of the congressman's office, Pat waited for the legislative aide behind an imposing mahogany desk. On the credenza, the senator and his young family smiled in silver framed photos. The aide proudly told Pat that he held down the fort when his boss was home meeting with constituents. Pat ignored the ego-charged comment, diving into the topic at hand: her husband, Art, missing in Vietnam for more than two years. She recounted his story and hers, the glaring lack of government interest and information. She painted a picture of hundreds of American POWs languishing in North Vietnamese prisons. And what of the hundreds of MIAs with unknown fates? Think of them, she implored. Think of their families. *Is Pat a wife or a widow?* Only the North Vietnamese know.

Tapping his pen on the desk blotter, the aide asked, "What would you like the senator to *do?*" Pat sighed. "Well, for starters, he can make some noise at the State Department, the White House and the Pentagon. Demand that the North Vietnamese provide a full accounting of the missing. It is required by signatory countries of the Geneva Convention."

The aide took a call in the front office. Pat stood, stretched, and strolled behind the senator's desk to gaze down the National Mall. Was he even paying attention?

Yesterday, everyone on the Hill had been talking about the lunar orbit of Apollo 11. *The moon*! Today, staffers were agog over Sen. Ted Kennedy's accident on Chappaquiddick Island, Massachusetts late Friday night. The senator drove his car off a bridge into a pond and his female passenger drowned while he walked away. Details of what came to be known as "The Chappaquiddick Incident" were sketchy but engrossing.

The aide returns. Suddenly he asks, "Would you like to have dinner?" She ignores the question, thinking he is making small talk. He asks again. Pat deftly continues her conversation about MIAs. She will not be derailed. But he is tenacious. As she talks, the aide creeps around the desk toward her, edging closer. Pat backs away, continuing her monologue. A slow-motion chase around the desk ensues. It would be comical if it were not detracting from the MIA issue. Moving toward Pat, the aide asks again: "Aren't you hungry? I'm only talking about dinner."

After all, she must be lonely.

The Letter, a painting of Frances and Missy Mearns. The original hangs in the National Museum of the U.S. Air Force in Dayton, Ohio. (*Photo courtesy of Pat Mearns.*)

CHAPTER SEVEN

TAKING IT TO THE ENEMY

KUSHNER TO CAMBODIA (NOVEMBER 1969)

Nguyen Hoang Kinh, the second secretary of the Viet Cong's Provisional Revolutionary Government's (PRG) embassy in Cambodia, ushers Valerie Kushner toward a low chair. "Here. Please sit down." She sinks in. "And" he insists, "relax."

Nearly halfway around the world and 9,000 miles from home, Valerie is in Phnom Penh, the Cambodian capital. She is on a mission with a delivery for her husband, Army Maj. Harold "Hal" Kushner, a flight surgeon held captive since November 1967 by the Viet Cong somewhere in a South Vietnam jungle.

She knows Hal, or "Spanky," as she calls him, is alive. Several recently released prisoners have confirmed this. After his helicopter crashed into a mountain at night, Major Kushner was captured trying to reach friendly forces, but wound up on the wrong side of the mountain. "He never was good with directions," Valerie laughs.

Hal has been trying to administer medical aid to his fellow POWs, many of whom are in bad shape. Unable to get medical supplies and letters to Hal either through the mail or via Red Cross envoys, "I decided that the only way I could possibly get medical supplies to him was to take them myself."

It is Cambodia's dry season, and the weather is temperate, the mood tropical. Motorcycles, pedicabs, and modern cars buzz past; it feels like a French colonial town with Buddhist overtones. Monks drape Sanghati robes over one shoulder. Many bow to one another. While awaiting her appointment with Viet Cong officials, Valerie spends three afternoons sightseeing, picking up souvenirs, including a Cambodian doll in a temple dancer's costume for her daughter.

Hal and Valerie met at the University of North Carolina, where he was a teacher's assistant in her chemistry class. A sociology major, Valerie was not keen to take the class. But her father, a prominent Ph.D. chemist who held twenty-one patents—including one for the fuel system used in the Apollo space project—insisted. Although wickedly smart, she found herself failing the course. Hal ensured that did not happen.

When they began dating, Hal brought Valerie home for weekends with his family in Danville, Virginia, a two-hour drive from Chapel Hill. His father, a World War II Army combat veteran and dentist, had an iconic name: Robert Lee Kushner. Bob was a scion of the small southern town, member of the city's small Jewish community and the only dentist serving Black patients in Danville in the 1950s.

The Kushners liked Valerie, even though she was a northerner. "Oh no, a Yankee," Hal's mom protested. Feisty, outspoken, and independent, Valerie was a contrast to most of the small-town southern women Hal had dated. The daughter of European-educated Dr. Anthony Manuel Moos and his wife Dorothy, Valerie and her younger brother Buddy were raised Catholic in Westchester County, New York. She attended Briarcliff Junior College for two years before matriculating at UNC Chapel Hill.

High schooler Valerie Moos (Kushner) in Ossining, New York, circa 1958. (*Photo courtesy of Toni Kushner Nee.*)

Valerie's intellect was a good match for Hal's, and her looks were alluring, with freckled alabaster skin, auburn hair, and ruby red lips made so from a ubiquitous tube of red lipstick. She smoked Marlboros and her thick, charcoal eyebrows seemed permanently arched, as if to suggest that she had something important to say. Hal wanted the stability of marriage and proposed to Valerie as soon as he was accepted to medical school.

After completing his studies at the Medical College of Virginia, Hal was assigned to Tripler Army Hospital in Hawaii, where he was born. Valerie was compelled to learn to be a proper Army wife, though it tried her patience and ran counter to her sense of fun. Invited to tea with a general's wife, she was instructed to wear a hat and gloves, to bring a formal calling card with the corner turned down—to indicate it had been delivered in person and *not* by a servant. No junior officer had servants, but Army society in the 1960s held firm to the practice. Valerie abided, with a smirk.

When Hal deployed to Vietnam, Valerie was all too eager to escape the confines of Army life and considered moving in with her parents, who were living in Manhattan. But Hal's hometown of Danville was more affordable, and she was able to secure a local job teaching. Being near Hal's parents and a supportive, close-knit community made sense while she was a single mother to three-year-old Toni Jean, and pregnant with her second child. Valerie's brother, a Marine Corps pilot, was also deployed to Vietnam. In this war, the personal stakes are high for her.

By all accounts, she loved being a mom. A cigarette dangling from one corner of her mouth, she patiently sewed clothes for her children and some prize-winning Halloween costumes. (Barbie always had matching costumes.) An accomplished baker, she once baked for her daughter Toni Jean a cake in the shape of a Brownie uniform—with all the requisite patches. As Valerie enumerated, she had three maxims, according to Toni: (1) "There's always a sailor to carry the luggage" (you don't need to do everything yourself); (2) "Always ask for what you want. The worst they can say is no"; and (3) "I'm XX years old (27, 55, 70, etc.). I don't need this shit."

Like many of the POW wives, Valerie had become frustrated with the talking heads in Washington. A meeting with President Nixon's new Secretary of Defense Melvin Laird left her nonplussed. As she described the meeting, "It was a hand-patting session because there are absolutely no channels of communication. The Defense Department is trying to introduce the subject of prisoners in the Paris talks, but the Viet Cong won't discuss it."

Toni Jean did remember one morning—and only one, probably in the summer of 1969, when she heard her mother crying in bed. Valerie refused to get up that morning, so Toni Jean made toast for them to share. But the self-pity did not last.

Valerie understands that POWs are an inevitable casualty of war. She is not protesting the fact that her husband is a prisoner. But she wants him to have the supplies he needs. Applying the same creativity and roll-up-your-sleeves activism that she uses in her children's school in Danville, Valerie headed to Phnom Penh. As Toni Jean testifies, "She wasn't fearful of the world for herself or for us."

Valerie Kushner with daughter Toni Jean and son Mike, circa 1970. Dr. Hal Kushner did not meet his son until Mike was almost five years old. (*Photo courtesy of Toni Kushner Nee.*)

Today, she is proffering Kinh seventeen pounds of medical supplies, letters, photos of her children, and two pairs of eyeglasses for her husband.

In halting French and using some English, Valerie implores him to deliver the medical equipment to Hal. Released POWs say Hal is in fair physical health and has recovered from his injuries. But his glasses were smashed in the crash. He and the other men suffer from malnutrition, dysentery, and parasites. Few medicines are available. Used razor blades are his only surgical tools.

Hal is a humanitarian, she explains to Kinh: a medical professional who wants to help. But Kinh wants to talk about *her*. "Do you have children? Can I see the pictures?" Valerie opens the envelope with the letter and photos for her husband. She holds up a photo of six-year-old Toni Jean and nineteen-month-old Mike. Kinh looks intently into Valerie's eyes and quietly told her that, like her husband, "The war has separated me from my family, too."

Valerie is taken aback by this man's attempt to find common ground. This is not what she expects. The wives who traveled to Paris to confront the North Vietnamese delegation at the peace talks encountered much more hostile rhetoric and Valerie met Kinh with her guard up. But he is disarming.

Focus, she thinks, as she listens intently. Her eyes bore into him. How can she convince Kinh to take and deliver this precious package? She slides the bundle closer to him.

Kinh shakes his head, pushing it back to her. Valerie pleads: "But these can be used for other purposes, not just for the prisoners." He refuses, citing the logistical difficulties of getting them into South Vietnam. He does accept the glasses, a medical book, and the letter and photos for Hal. He also accepts letters from two other Army POW wives, including Andrea Rander—who had been unsuccessful in her attempt to deliver a letter to the North Vietnamese delegation in Paris just one month ago.

One hour later, Valerie emerges only partially satisfied. It was a strange conversation, but she is not going to give up. She departs

Cambodia without achieving her primary goal, although she leaves the medical supplies with the Cambodian Red Cross, in hopes that Kinh might change his mind. Upon her return home, she writes several letters to him. Has her husband received her letters? Does he know he has a son?

Almost two months later, Nguyen Hoang Kinh replies: "Dear Mrs. Kushner: I have received your letter dated February 13, 1970, in which you ask me about the sending of medical supplies to your husband. I have the pleasure to tell you that, according to the lenient and humanitarian policy of the NLF and the PRG, the POW are always very treated. But in this situation of war, the POW could receive only letters from their family. We are now in the impossibility to forward postal parcels and medical supplies to the POW, because the difficulties created by the US aggression in South Viet Nam. Finally, I hope that the dirty aggression waged by the Nixon government against the South Vietnamese people will be stopped soon and you could meet again your husband shortly."

Valerie is starting to agree with him. She will not see her husband until this war ends.

PEROT'S POCKETBOOK (DECEMBER 1969)

On any given night, the bar of the Lane Xang Hotel in Vientiane teems with foreigners. A cacophony of languages—Russian, Chinese, Vietnamese, French, and English—fills the rundown place. It has the only night life in the sleepy capital of Laos. In a scene out of Rick's Café in the movie *Casablanca,* diplomats and spies eye one another warily over cocktails.

Sipping water at a corner table, billionaire Texas businessman Ross Perot surveys the crowd and listens as his advance man, Tom Meurer, lays out logistics. It is December 24, 1969, and Perot is here from Texas. Meurer, a fresh-faced and clean-shaven young Air Force veteran, has been in Asia for weeks trying to secure an appointment for Perot with a representative from Hanoi. When Meurer reveals the details of Perot's intentions—landing a massive plane in Vientiane loaded with 60,000 pounds of canned Christmas dinners, clothing, air mattresses, medical supplies, gifts, Red Cross workers, employees, clergymen, as well as a large contingent of international press—the Hanoi diplomats acquiesce and promise to meet Perot. The international spotlight is shining on them.

While waiting for Perot to arrive in Vientiane, Meurer was cornered by American Ambassador McMurtrie Godley: "What in the hell do you think you are doing bringing a plane load of gifts and press into Laos?" A secret American war was being waged in Laos, in support of the Royal Laotian Government against the Pathet Lao, allied with the North Vietnamese. Godley and the CIA ran it. Vientiane was the nerve center. Nosy journalists were not welcome.

Meurer stared at the ambassador. It never occurred to him to ask permission from the embassy to land a Boeing 707 onto Vientiane airport's narrow runway. Thinking on his feet, Meurer pulled out his old White House identification badge and, flashing it in Godley's face, feigned incredulity. "Haven't you been notified by Kissinger's office?" It was a risky move. President Nixon's national security advisor had not directed Perot nor Meurer to undertake this plan. But Godley did not know that. The ruse worked.

Tonight, amid the haze of cigarette smoke in the bar, jet-lagged Perot and Meurer strategize how to convince the North Vietnamese to issue a visa and allow them to deliver the goods to American POWs in Hanoi.

Two days later, on December 26, Perot and Meurer are ushered through the gates of the North Vietnamese compound in Vientiane to see the North Vietnamese *charge d'affaires,* Vu Tien. The requisite portrait of Ho Chi Minh hangs on the wall. Tien sits on a bamboo couch. The Americans are directed to take a seat. Messengers come and go through a doorway with hanging beads.

For the first half hour, Perot endures the North Vietnamese propaganda presentation, just as the wives had in Paris. Tien accuses the American POWs of being war criminals and asserts that the "the American people are being lied to, and that the blood and tears of the North Vietnamese people flowed daily.... Because of all the widows and orphans in Hanoi, Perot cannot visit Hanoi."

Perot proposes ideas to generate publicity, good will, and propaganda for the U.S. government. If he cannot deliver the packages to Americans in captivity, as an alternative, could he donate the supplies, meals, and gifts to North Vietnamese orphans? Rebuild hospitals and schools Tien claims the Americans have destroyed? Tien does not accept the offers.

Back in Washington, Secretary of Defense Mel Laird and his dutiful, clever aide Dick Capen are intrigued by Perot's holiday adventure. They doubt Perot can reach Hanoi. They wonder if his exploits will complicate diplomatic efforts in Paris. But the publicity value of his stunt could be worth it. And they admire the swashbuckling entrepreneur's attempt to break through the bureaucracy.

In the seven months since Secretary Laird launched the Go Public campaign, Perot has proven to be its most valuable private sector asset. Even though an increasing number of POW and MIA wives are soliciting media coverage and Congressional support to educate the American people about the plight of their husbands, Laird and Capen have thirsted for more splash. Perot's vast wealth and audacity have proven useful. The scrappy computer software magnate stands only 5'5", a comical figure with his boyish crewcut, protruding nose, big ears, and loud Texan twang. But his fortune of more than $1 billion has been wielding a lot of influence in Washington.

President Nixon had accepted a generous offer from Perot, the founder of fast-growing company Electronic Data Systems (EDS), to assist in his 1968 bid for the White House. Perot lent EDS executives to the campaign, including Meurer, who served on the advance team. With Perot's candidate installed in the White House, he wants to rally more Americans around President Nixon and his agenda.

After the president outlined his strategy for peace, his chief of staff, H. R. Haldeman, called Perot to ask for help with an initiative encouraging Americans to speak up for the president. President Nixon was attempting to blunt the growing antiwar movement and rally the majority of Americans he believed supported him. In the same week that President Nixon gave his famous "Silent Majority" speech to the nation on live television, Perot established an organization called United We Stand (UWS). Staffed with about thirty executives from EDS, who launched a nationwide advertising campaign called "The Majority Speaks," Perot ran full-page advertisements in 117 newspapers around the country. The ads aimed to tie two messages together in the American consciousness: support the president and his plan for just and lasting peace *and* publicize the plight of the POWs. President Nixon's administration hoped that widespread support for the POWs would translate into widespread support for his peace plan. Advocating for the POWs gave Americans something to be *for,* not *against.*

One week after the Silent Majority speech, another full-page ad appeared in newspapers around the country: "The Majority Speaks: Release the Prisoners." Paid for by Perot and written by President Nixon's speechwriter William Safire, the ads asked the public to sign a petition in support of the president's plan for peace. The president was photographed reading voluminous bags of positive mail. Perot's new group bought airtime on fifty-three television stations to air a thirty-minute documentary featuring a recently released POW, the wife of a MIA, and a Medal of Honor recipient.

With Christmas approaching, Perot wanted to capitalize on the ads' momentum. At his own expense, he chartered three planes. Two would attempt to land in Hanoi and one would head to Paris. The plane to Paris would carry 152 POW and MIA wives and their young children seeking an audience with the North Vietnamese delegation there.

Perot mystifies the North Vietnamese. Suspicious of his ties to President Nixon, they call Perot's global adventure a "provocation" and they call him the "dark scheme" of the Nixon administration. Though Perot reiterates the purely humanitarian nature of the mission, Hanoi is not buying it.

On December 27th, Perot is informed that, if he can get the packages to Moscow no later than December 31st, Hanoi will accept delivery from the Soviets. In a trip report Perot's team prepares, his staff claims: "The North Vietnamese have shifted the monkey to the Russians' back." There is a caveat: the supplies must be repackaged into individual, three-kilogram boxes (or 6.6 pounds). Hurriedly, the team makes plans to fly from Vientiane to Bangkok, over Burma and India, on to Rome and Copenhagen, and then to Moscow. Before landing in Moscow, they must offload thirty tons of supplies, unpack and repack them into smaller parcels, and reload the plane.

While in Bangkok, Perot receives a call from Henry Kissinger's military aide, Army Col. Alexander Haig. The White House has had second thoughts. "Ross, you've done a great job of publicity. But you best now come home." It is not a request. It is an order.

No longer in the military, Perot defies Haig's order. The mission is not complete. When he is denied permission to fly over Burma and India, Perot has his pilot fly over the Arctic Circle instead, to Alaska. There, hundreds of volunteers are recruited by a local radio station to re-sort the packages in an Anchorage airport hangar. They finish the task in ten hours. Perot then directs the plane to fly over the North Pole, landing in Copenhagen at 8:00 p.m. local time on December 30. He meets the deadline. Moscow's answer is still no.

For the 152 POW wives and children who have flown in Perot's other chartered plane, to Paris, to meet with the North Vietnamese delegation, the answer is *also* no.

Andrea Rander is one of them. This is her second trip to Paris in two months. On the plane dubbed "The Spirit of Christmas," her daughter Lysa is given Benadryl to sleep on the overnight flight. This is also Valerie Kushner's second international trip in two months. Her daughter Toni Jean is feted with rum cake for her sixth birthday. The mothers spend a sleepless Christmas Eve aboard the jetliner. Landing Christmas morning, the group emerges groggy onto a dark, rainy, and chilly Orly airfield in Paris. They have no hotel reservations. They do, however, have a couple of buses and a few hours to fulfill their mission.

Escorted by Paris police and followed by a swarm of reporters, the buses head to the North Vietnamese Mission. Three busloads of women and children pour into the street a block away. Fifty French police cordon them off. The women are expected. But the police tell them the delegation offices are closed for Christmas. Three women will be allowed to meet with North Vietnamese representatives the next day.

The buses take the ladies and their children to Notre Dame for Christmas mass. There, Andrea purchases a memento: a gold charm for her bracelet, a replica of the cathedral replete with a tiny stained-glass window.

An excited French police inspector interrupts the service. North Vietnamese officials have changed their minds. A political counselor will meet the group's three representatives *now*. Scurrying to the buses to race to the delegation offices, some children and their mothers begin crying. They are overwhelmed by sadness, exhaustion, and frustration.

Andrea and the two other designated wives spend seventy minutes with the North Vietnamese. Emerging to brief the press and family members, they report the meeting was more of a lecture, and much like the tea party Andrea had attended in October. "You might say it was a broken record." The political counselor had instructed the women to go home and tell their children that their fathers are murderers. He accused the women of political motives, and of being deceived by the U.S. government. And he informed them that POWs would only be released as part of a broader peace settlement.

However, Christmas brings a small gift: a list of fifty-eight missing pilots, husbands of the women in Paris that day. "They said gradually *all* the wives will hear," emphasizes Andrea. *Gradually*. That could be a long time.

Andrea rubs the gold charm for good luck.

HOUSE ARREST IN MOSCOW (JANUARY 1970)

Trudging through the snow blanketing Sheremetyevo International Airport near Moscow, Pat Mearns hunches forward to block the wind. She coughs as her lungs filter the icy air. Clunky rubber boots protect her from the slush and snow, but they are not keeping her toes warm. The walk to the hotel is short, yet at eight degrees below zero, feels interminable. The weather and the weak welcome have deflated her spirits.

House arrest at Moscow's airport was unforeseen. Pat has been traveling for a week with three other MIA wives from California: Carole Hanson, Patty Hardy, and Connie Hestle. Robert K. "Bob" Dornan accompanies them. He served as a fighter pilot flying an F-100 Super Sabre, surviving two emergency ejections. Now an influential conservative radio host, he tapped into his vast network of contacts to arrange meetings and secure private funding for this trip. While pleading with world leaders to intervene with Hanoi on behalf of their husbands, the four women have become fast friends. "We just had to do something *significant*," Pat explains. She has been desperately seeking information about her husband, Art, for more than three years.

Asking foreign leaders for help is a twist on diplomatic protocol. "But, why not?" shrugs Pat. "Nothing else is working." Each woman on this trip has been living in limbo for years. "Life is empty," Patty Hardy, an emergency room nurse, told a newspaper reporter. "We're all missing so much."

In Cairo, Pat and the others were fascinated to hear that POW issues were resolved almost instantly despite infamous hostilities between Arabs and Israelis. "International Red Cross representatives told us there is no such thing as a missing man in that conflict. Within twenty-four hours, either side is notified as to the status of each captured man."

In Rome, the group landed without visas, but the U.S. embassy assisted their entry. In the Basilica, hope surged inside Pat. "I felt a really good feeling as I heard the organ music playing." Then she locked herself in the ladies' room. "I had no choice, but to crawl out from the stall….I had those big, bulky rubber boots on, and they slowed my exit quite a bit." Smoothing her dress and coat, she collected herself before the group was summoned to a meeting with the Pope. "I didn't think I'd be wearing big boots to meet the Pope," she offers, smiling.

Pope Paul VI greeted the women warmly, blessing them. He said it was notable and reasonable for the wives to request status updates on the POWs and humane treatment of the men. The Pope was struck by their narratives, their determination, and their courage. This success gave the women a false sense of confidence that the rest of the trip would be an administrative cake walk, every country and leader equally receptive. The USSR definitely was not.

All had seemed in order with their passports that morning when leaving Cairo, and they were waved onboard the plane by a Russian guard. They were hoping to garner goodwill from Russian officials who might sway fellow Communist leaders in North Vietnam to divulge which Americans were their prisoners, and which had died. Yet upon landing in Moscow, the women and Dornan appear to be missing crucial documents. Without the right visas, Moscow, a mere forty-five-minute taxi ride away, is off limits. The group is told they are forbidden to leave the premises of the airport and are escorted to an Aeroflot hotel—really more of a 1930s-era military barracks with such poor heating that their windows froze over. Here they sit, in no man's land.

Pat Mearns and Carole Hanson flanking Pope Paul VI in Rome in January 1970. The Vatican was one of thirteen cities the MIA wives visited with Bob Dornan. (*Photo courtesy of Pat Mearns.*)

Their plan to take their cause overseas was hatched only five weeks ago, in Pat's kitchen in Los Angeles. "I was always convinced there had to be some leader that would agree to talk to the North Vietnamese," she insists. "Our agony and terror are something we needed to convey—the agony of waiting with no word, not a speck of information." Hoping their pleas will persuade world leaders to pressure Hanoi to provide complete lists of the imprisoned and missing men, their itineraries are intentionally packed with meetings with anyone who might be able to help. They have watched as peace activists traveled to North Vietnam and were able to influence Hanoi. Now *they* will have an opportunity to plead *their* case, in hopes that women's organizations would respond to their appeal as wives, mothers, and sisters.

Trip planning was a welcome distraction from another Christmas without their husbands. The women were motivated, capable, and organized. But with little time and no international connections, they needed help. Carole contacted Bob Dornan who wasted no time. The nephew of Hollywood actor Jack Haley, he had a penchant for the theatrical. With a booming voice and extensive connections among politicians and celebrities, he was ready to be a front man for the wives.

Over dinner, Carole, Patty, and Pat outlined their daring plan to Bob. The women told him that some leaders could influence or embarrass North Vietnamese leadership into handing over a full list of POWs, and the names of those who were known to have died. Dornan admired their brave advocacy and supported their game plan.

They would need courage now, while stuck in limbo in a hostile Soviet Union. The USSR is a close ally of North Vietnam, and the women are anxious to meet someone at the Foreign Ministry who might wield some influence with Hanoi. But how to get a message out? Two stern-faced Russian women stuffed into layers of clothing keep watch over them. In broken English, the "guards" point the way to third-floor accommodations. The women share spartan rooms with twin beds, while Dornan has his own, smaller room. "It was not comfortable, just furnished with a bed, a lamp and a desk," he recalls. Only half joking, the group wonders in hushed tones if they are under house arrest. Pat doesn't worry about her safety. "We are Americans and everyone in the world knew we were here. What could possibly happen?" Indeed, reporters have been following their travel. An Associated Press photographer captures the group at the airport, looking careworn.

Pat and roommate Connie settle in. They are resigned to the fact that their belongings will be rifled through while they grab dinner. In Romania, Carole's hair dryer was taken apart and Pat's Bible was stolen. "They were looking through our items to see if we were spies," she says, rolling her eyes.

Setting her beloved light blue and silver portable Royal typewriter on the desk, Pat leaves the case open. Her typewriter is a treasured gift from her mother for her advocacy work. Late at night, she taps on the keys, keeping a diary, and composing letters to legislators.

As she types, the snow falls gently against the night sky. *Dr. Zhivago* comes to Pat's mind, one of the last movies she and Art watched together.

Indomitable Dornan works the phone—when he can find one, trying to obtain appointments in Moscow. He calls the Foreign Ministry, the Soviet Women's Council, the Soviet Red Cross. One by one, the groups decline. Three days later, time has run out. Disheartened, the women and Dornan trudge back to the airport for their flight to Tehran.

MIA wives Carole Hanson, Patty Hardy, Pat Mearns, and Connie Hestle on Capitol Hill in March 1970 to testify about their round-the-world trip. They requested western and Communist nations pressure the North Vietnamese to provide an accounting for the missing men. (*Photo courtesy of Pat Mearns.*)

They encounter a fellow American, Minnesota Sen. Eugene McCarthy, a well-known member of the powerful Senate Foreign Relations Committee. They ask if he has discussed the POW and MIA issue with Soviet Premier Alexei Kosygin. McCarthy is vehemently opposed to the war in Vietnam but says he has compassion for all those affected: their husbands, draft evaders, and deserters. Hearing their men lumped together with draft evaders is shocking. But they ask if the senator has obtained a list of POWs. Patting the breast pocket of his navy-blue jacket, McCarthy hints he might have one. But he does not share.

SO CLOSE, YET SO FAR AWAY (JANUARY 1970)

The smell of jet fuel trails the plane as it screams down the tarmac and lifts off from Vientiane without the women. Hanoi is so close, only an hour's flight away. Carole Hanson clutches a letter to Marine Corps Capt. Stephen Hanson. She does not know if her husband is a prisoner in Hanoi, but with no word for more than two years, anything is possible.

MIA wives Pat Mearns, Patty Hardy, Connie Hestle, and Carole Hanson on the tarmac in Vientiane, Laos, January 1970, as the weekly International Control Commission (ICC) plane departs for Hanoi without them. (*Photo courtesy of Bob Dornan.*)

This was one of the last stops on the whirlwind round-the-world trip Carole, Pat Mearns, Patty Hardy, and Connie Hestle have been navigating for three weeks. Carole was denied a visa to Vietnam, as were the other women on this trip hunting for information about their husbands. The irony stings that the plane making its weekly flight to Hanoi is chartered by the International Control Commission, the organization created to implement the 1954 Geneva Accords that govern the treatment of prisoners of war.

A last-minute woman-to-woman appeal to the air hostess also failed. "Will you take these letters on your flight and mail them from Hanoi?" Carole pleads. The hostess agrees. A few minutes later, she returns, tears in her eyes. The captain has ordered her to hand the letters back. "And there we were, four Americans and a French girl, standing on the airstrip in Vientiane crying."

It's been three years since Carole's husband went missing. He was her college sweetheart whom she married in 1962. Carole Lynne Shipley met him at a party she hosted with her San Jose State University roommates. "We served peanut butter and jelly on crackers, and beer." Their small apartment was overcrowded with boys from nearby St. Mary's College. "I saw this handsome man sitting under a desk. I went over to talk, and he offered me a beer." He had sandy blond hair, cinnamon-brown eyes, and a cleft chin. "He asked if he could call me."

A tall, lively brunette with sparkling eyes and a toothy grin, Carole was a fourth-generation Los Angeleno. Raised in Burbank, she grew up in the shadow of the Lockheed aircraft plant where her father worked and among skilled laborers from nearby movie studios.

Burbank was a mostly white, small town with a Bob's Big Boy drive-in, an ice cream parlor, and a locally owned grocery. Carole loved dolls, painting, and playing the piano. An exceptionally good swimmer, she made money in college giving lessons.

After college, Steve and Carole both moved to southern California to teach, pursuing their romance at Dodger baseball games and long beach walks during foggy "June Gloom" days common in that part of the country. Those were heady times, and they were happy. Neither had been in love before. Steve proposed on the beach at Balboa Island, and they married in 1962.

Steve planned to continue teaching, but the Vietnam War changed that. Enamored with flying as a child, he had watched planes landing at nearby Oxnard Air Force Base from a platform his father built in their backyard next to his mother's clothesline. The idea was for Steve to watch the stars, but he was hooked on planes.

As news of the war in Vietnam made headlines, Steve was inspired to join the Marine Corps, hoping to attend flight school. Once he earned his wings, he was assigned to a CH-46 Sea Knight helicopter squadron at the El Toro Marine Corps Air Station in Orange County, California.

Military life was a new adventure for the couple, as neither of their fathers had served. They bought a new house outside the base with a two-car garage, but no sprinkler system. Not able to afford one, Steve began and ended his days soaking the ground cover he had planted in the front yard. When he deployed in the fall of 1966, Carole assumed daily watering duties.

Carole was looking forward to the summer of 1967. She planned to spend her days with her nine-month-old son Todd, born ten days after Steve left for Vietnam. With great anticipation she awaited a mid-deployment rendezvous in Hawaii with her husband. The end of the school year could not come fast enough, so she was almost relieved when her principal opened her classroom door, gesturing for her to follow him. He was unusually quiet as they walked toward his office. Three sharply dressed Marines were waiting. Carole was wearing a dress she had sewn herself, a light-yellow summery sheath with pastel flowers, reminding her that June was Steve's favorite month. After receiving the news that Steve was missing, "I never wore it again. I just couldn't bring myself to wear that dress again."

He disappeared on June 3 on a risky, covert, and highly classified mission to extract American and South Vietnamese troops under intense fire. The helicopter he piloted was shot down by heavy automatic weapons fire near Khe Sanh in South Vietnam. Search and rescue operations were underway, but Steve had not been recovered.

Numb and shaking, Carole agrees to let the Marines drive her home. Word among the small military community of El Toro spread fast. As was customary, a group of wives from the squadron, including the commanding officer's wife, brought dinner and a helping of empathy. As expected, she is inconsolable.

Carole was hopeful that Steve was alive, as this was not his first shootdown. A month earlier, he had survived another, and was rescued after spending a night in a cave with a Vietnamese man and his son. Steve had written to Carole about that evening. "They had fled the north some years ago when things got bad. He said all he wants for South Vietnam is for it to have even a small portion of the freedom that we have in the United States.... As I write this letter, I wonder where that man and his little boy will be in five or ten years. I do not want to hand them over on a silver platter to the North Vietnamese. They deserve a lot more than that. A chance at freedom doesn't seem like too much for any human being to ask for. Despite this war's frustration, I'm glad I had a part in helping these people. Someday, their sons will have the same opportunities our children have."

That first night after Steve's disappearance, Carole lay awake, listening to her baby breathe as his chest rose and fell. Stepping outside before dawn, she turned on the hose. Out of nowhere, a bird landed on her shoulder. It was a white dove. She coaxed the bird onto her palm and into a cat carrier, the only "cage" she had. Each day, while her cat Stuart napped, she took the carrier outside, opening the door to encourage the dove to freedom. Yet it would not leave. Her father built a wicker cage that she hung in her kitchen. The dove laid only one egg but thrived until 1999.

Four months after Steve's disappearance, his squadron returned from deployment. One of his friends asked to visit her at home. Her inquiries to the Marine Corps about Steve's shootdown had gone unanswered, so she was eager for first-person details—if they existed.

"When he arrived, I spread a large map down on our kitchen floor. It was a map of Southeast Asia. He didn't say a word. He just pointed." His finger landed on Laos. Steve was shot down in the country where Carole is now standing on the airport tarmac, disconsolate and helpless, smelling of jet fuel.

CHAPTER EIGHT

COUNTERCULTURE

NO MAN, NO MORTGAGE (MARCH 1970)

Candy Parish desperately wants to move forward with her life but is stymied at every turn. It's as if she is trapped in an episode of the television show *The Twilight Zone*. One minute she understands her reality, and the next it seems surreal. With a father and brother in the military, Candy understands more than the average civilian how the military works. But *this* conversation, with *this* man, is infuriating.

Candy is eager to buy her first home. She and toddler Hunter have been living with her parents. She has been saving and has enough for a down payment.

Puffing on a smoldering cigar, the brown-suited, heavy-set Veterans Administrator reminds Candy of Chicago's Mayor Richard Daley. "You are in a 'gray area,'" Donald E. Johnson says, with studied insouciance. Candy has difficulty understanding what he means.

He takes a long puff. She waits as he admires his cigar. Then, she asks for clarification.

He leans back in his chair and shakes his head. "You are not entitled to your widow benefits because you cannot prove to me that your husband is dead. And because you cannot prove to me that he is alive, you cannot use your power-of-attorney." Now it is clear. Johnson will not give her a VA loan.

Fuming, Candy stares at him in disbelief. She is not, however, intimidated. "You just watch me," she exclaims, storming out the door. She's going straight to Congress.

This is completely wrong, thinks Candy. And when she sees a wrong, she rights it. Thanks to years of advocating for her missing husband, Candy has a national platform. It is 1970. She has met officials from the Pentagon, State Department, and White House. She has been all over the national news and she has stared down the North Vietnamese delegation in Paris. When she calls Capitol Hill, they answer.

Her husband went missing in North Vietnam three long years ago during a mission near the city of Vinh on July 25, 1968. His F-4 Phantom fighter jet was engulfed in flames, most likely from anti-aircraft fire or a bomb that detonated at close range. The crippled plane descended in an uncontrollable spin, plowed into the ground, and broke apart on impact.

An eyewitness in another plane saw no signs of survivors. Lt. Charles "Chuck" Parish and his radar intercept officer (RIO), Navy Lt. Robert "Bob" Fant, were listed as MIA. Fant had ejected at 1,000 feet and was captured as soon as he hit the ground, held as a POW in the Hanoi Hilton for more than five years. Released on March 14, 1973, Fant said in his debrief that he did not believe his pilot had survived. He surmised that Chuck's equipment malfunctioned, and he was unable to eject, most likely dying on impact.

When Chuck's plane went down, Candy was alone with her three-week-old son. The phone rang. "Hello?" Her dad's good friend, Navy Capt. Bill Gortney, on duty at the Pentagon, was on the line. Her parents were shopping for a bicycle for her younger brother. "Can you have your dad call me when he gets home?" It wasn't unusual for senior naval officers to call the house. Her father, Capt.

Don Engen, was also a senior naval officer assigned to the Pentagon. It was not unusual for his work to follow him home.

Captain Gortney called again, and other colleagues, too. The calls did not sound alarm bells for Candy. She reasoned that the operational tempo was high for the U.S. Navy, especially for those serving in hazardous wartime naval aviation, like her father.

The phone continued to ring, but Candy's son kept her busy. Meanwhile, family friends drove to the mall to intercept Captain and Mrs. Engen, to ensure that he was the one to break the tragic news to Candy.

When her parents pulled in at 4:00 p.m., Candy greeted them in the driveway with the baby in her arms. "It's a good thing you're home—the whole world has been calling you," said Candy, as she smiled her father.

Captain Engen ducked inside. "After I placed Hunter in his crib, Daddy came into the living room and said there was bad news." Gingerly, he shared the eyewitness report: Chuck's plane had crashed. *Impact* is the word that hit her. Hard. Later she received the official telegram and the perfunctory visit from the chaplain and casualty officer. Captain Engen called Chuck's father, retired Navy Rear Admiral "Hop" Parish, and his wife.

Candy could not believe her tall and strapping husband, so full of life, could be gone. "People like that just don't disappear." He had to be on the ground evading the enemy. Soon the Navy would pick up a radio signal and "winch him up to a helicopter." She was certain of it.

It was probably destiny that Candy would marry a Navy pilot. Her father was one, and she liked the itinerant lifestyle. The only job she had ever wanted, since she was twelve, was to be an airline stewardess. She tried applying when she turned eighteen. "I marched myself in. As far as I was concerned, I met the requirements." Arm around Candy's shoulders, the hiring manager marched her back out the door. The minimum age was twenty.

She tried again at nineteen, with the same result. On her third try, with two years of college under her belt, United Airlines accepted her application. Candy turned twenty during training and started working at her dream job.

An independent soul, she is always up for adventure. When United's mechanics went on strike, the airline furloughed stewardesses, and they had some time on their hands. Candy invited them to her father's upcoming change-of-command ceremony in July of 1966. There would be parties with lots of bachelors. Captain Engen's friend set Candy up with one of his most eligible pilots. Chuck was a naval aviator and a spelunker—Candy had met her match.

"He took me into the bar, and as we entered, sitting at the first bar stool was Chuck, and he greeted me with his broad and gleaming grin, 'Oh, hi.'" It was love at first sight. "He was fun, a lot of fun, and easygoing."

Home from her second date with Chuck, Candy, unprompted, exclaimed to her roommate, "Oh my gosh, Kitty, I'm going to marry this guy!" Four months later, on November 12, 1966, she did. "We were young and happy."

OUT IN FRONT (MARCH 1964)

Andrea Haywood is looking forward to seeing her beau, Donald Rander. Into the silky lining of her trusty, hard-sided American Tourister valise she tucks her hosiery, a shower cap, and perfume. As she folded her blouses and skirts, she felt like a schoolgirl. While she is filled with anticipation for her upcoming rendezvous, she is less enthusiastic about taking the train to Georgia. It revives unpleasant childhood memories. "Once we got to Union Station in Washington, D.C., we had to switch cars," recalls Andrea, describing the humility of being forced to move to a segregated car for Black people.

The indignity of sitting in that back car grated on Andrea's nerves, yet the idea of seeing Donald and his mesmerizing hazel eyes lifted her spirits. There was something about him. She liked that they had both grown up in a vibrant, multicultural Bronx neighborhood. Andrea had attended public school, Donald the Catholic school, so the only place she saw him was at the roller rink. Each time, she dug into her skates, pushing forward with all her might to try and catch him. They made small talk, but never really got to know one another.

That is, until fifteen years later.

Heading into divorce court in 1963, Andrea faced the reality of raising her three-year-old daughter Lysa by herself. Her first husband had grown restless, spending more time at civil rights marches than with his family. A resigned Andrea sat quietly in the judge's chambers. Slender, tidy, and fashionable, she was unfailingly polite and ladylike—the definition of feminine poise. Perfectly coiffed, her nails always matched her lipstick, and the deep cherry red she often wore was a radiant contrast to her freckled, toffee-colored skin. On this day, she just wanted to get through the legal proceedings.

She caught a glimpse of those unmistakable hazel eyes. Could it be Donald Rander? He, too, was ending a marriage that day, but leaving on *his* terms. He did not want to be married anymore, no longer wishing to raise his young son and daughter. He planned to make child support payments because it was an Army requirement. But he was washing his hands of all three of them. He was so *definitive,* Andrea thought. She and Don made light of their situations. When he requested her phone number, she gave him a coy smile, jotting the seven digits on a piece of paper. Andrea's mother was unimpressed with the coincidental meeting. She did not remember Donald but wanted her daughter to finish her degree in social work before dating again.

Her parents were pillars of their community in the same neighborhood of Harlem where Gen. Colin Powell was raised. Alton Haywood was a North Carolina transplant who migrated north after college and worked in New York's Garment District. He was in the prestigious Prince Hall Masonic Order, the oldest and largest African American fraternal organization founded in 1784 by fifteen freed Black slaves. Richard Pryor, "Sugar" Ray Robinson, Supreme Court Justice Thurgood Marshall, Nelson Mandela, and Nat King Cole were all members. Alton's name was engraved on the exterior wall of the iconic temple.

Agnes was a third-generation New Yorker raised by a mother whose complexion was fair enough to "pass" as a white woman and get a better-paying job in Chicago, leaving Agnes to be raised by her maternal grandmother. A homemaker when Andrea and her brother and sister were young, Agnes later started a home-based secretarial business. She founded the Northeast Chapter of the National Council of Negro Women, or NCNW, a civic organization promoting education, health, and entrepreneurship for women of African descent. In 1985, a Bronx park and playground were named for her.

Andrea's parents taught her she could be anything she wanted. She attended Hunter College to earn a master's in social work. Agnes and Alton wanted her to live in her own apartment and finish her degree, so they financed her education. But they did not expect her to start dating so soon after her divorce.

Donald was persistent and romantic. Dating provided a nice respite from schoolwork and caring for little Lysa. Drafted into the Army in 1961 as a military policeman, Donald was shipped off to France for a year. He wanted Andrea and her daughter to join him. "I said no." When Donald returned, he proposed marriage again. "And there was mystery to this man of mine," reminisces Andrea.

She succumbed to the temptation of a romantic getaway in Georgia. After Andrea alights from the train on a sunny day at Fort Benning, Donald heads off to work. Andrea is invited to spend the afternoon with Hilda Brooks, the wife of a Black Army officer friend of Donald. "Boy was she an adventurous woman," notes a smiling Andrea.

Hilda suggests they go downtown "to test the waters" at a local lunch counter. Always game for adventure, Andrea is only marginally aware that her new friend is planning to stir up a little trouble. When they walk into F. W. Woolworth's on South High Street in downtown Columbus, she thinks they might do a little shopping. But Hilda has another idea. A stone's throw from the gates of Fort Benning, the store is a treasure trove, carrying fabric and lampshades, framed velvet paintings, colored chalk and jump ropes, pet hamsters and goldfish. Everything catches Andrea's eye. She loves to shop. But when Hilda steers her firmly by the elbow toward the lunch counter, she is confused. "Go on, take a seat," her large-boned and slightly loud new friend says, nodding in the direction of the stools with their leatherette seats. Andrea obliges. "You didn't question her directions, and I really didn't know what was happening." As she begins catching on, she recalls the sit-ins making headlines from Greensboro, North Carolina to Jackson, Mississippi. It gives her pause. "I really did not know what to think. But I followed my friend, thinking *she* knew what to do." Slightly older than Andrea, Hilda seems savvy and confident. For several minutes, the two women sit in silence. The waitress busies herself sorting dishes and scouring the counter with remarkable attentiveness. She does not acknowledge the two Black women.

Hilda is not going to put up with being ignored. She clears her throat. Raising an eyebrow, the white waitress glances in their direction. "We'd each like a Coke, please," booms Hilda, her voice infused with conviction. Impressed and embarrassed at the same time, Andrea simultaneously wants to stand her ground *and* disappear through a trap door. She does not enjoy confrontation. "From the corner of my eye, I could see a small crowd gathering—maybe a handful of people watching, and I could almost feel their gaze boring through my back."

Having been a particularly obedient child, Andrea is uncomfortable taking a public stand. She cannot bear the thought of intentionally upsetting anyone. The waitress ignores them. For *fifteen minutes.* Then, reluctantly, she plops down two Cokes and walks away. Hilda takes long, deliberate sips, while Andrea drains her glass quickly. "Don thought we were nervy to do what we did. Even then, you had to be cautious and careful, and especially in the south. He thought we were naïve about trying things out." Paying their bill, Hilda appears triumphant. But Andrea? "I was glad to get out of there."

At the end of the summer, Donald transitions from military policeman to Army Intelligence. While awaiting his transfer to Ft. Meade, Maryland, Don professes that he wants Andrea and Lysa to join him. For the third time, he proposes marriage. Finally, Andrea accepts. "I thought to myself, 'Well, maybe, I should. He looks like he cares about me. He says he loves me.' So, I did it."

The couple marries on October 3, 1964, at Andrea's Presbyterian church in the Bronx. Her daughter, her father, and two aunts attend. Her mother and siblings do not. Afterward, Don and Andrea pack their household goods and move to a historically Black, middle-class neighborhood in Baltimore County, Maryland.

Donald and Andrea rent a tidy brick row house, enrolling Lysa in one of the earliest Head Start preschool programs. Two years later, daughter Page is born. Although civil rights protests in downtown Baltimore are becoming more frequent, their village of Turner Station seems far removed from the growing unrest. Occasionally, when things turn volatile, police tell the Randers and other Turner Station families to stay inside. Sometimes, Andrea feels the pull of civil rights protests. But she listens to authority, both civil and military, and stays put.

Some things in life are mysteries to Andrea. For one, her Donald is something of an enigma. His mercurial moods vacillate from sweet and thoughtful to distant and annoyed. No one in Andrea's family has served in the armed forces and she and her two young daughters must endure his long hours conducting field training exercises, isolated from other Army families. While she believes she would have felt more connected had they lived on base, "I was happy because here was a new life. I did not have any fear."

Until February 1968.

Absorbed by documents at her desk, Andrea is working on a suicide hot line in the psychiatry department of a hospital. Unexpectedly, she is summoned to the boss's office: "We have to talk to you." Her heart sinks as she walks in and sees green. Army green. A chaplain and senior officer from Don's command relay the frightening news: Her husband was stationed in a house in the thick of the intense and bloody Tet Offensive at the Battle of Hue when Communist forces launched a series of long and bloody attacks. His unit, housed in the middle of Hue, held off the attacking forces for two days, and was eventually overrun during the overwhelming insurgency.

Don is no ordinary foot soldier. He has access to military intelligence and Andrea knows it. Now, he is missing.

DRIFTING AWAY (JUNE 1967)

Emilee McCarthy's fiancé, Air Force Capt. Jon Reynolds, is also missing. His shootdown and disappearance over the skies of North Vietnam three weeks before their December 1965 wedding ended her fairy tale.

Emilee is conflicted. The five-pronged diamond engagement ring she wears reminds her of Jon each time she sees it sparkling in the light. But things have changed in the two and a half years he's been a prisoner. And she has changed. Emilee wiggles it off her left ring finger.

"Dear Mr. and Mrs. Reynolds," she writes. This is hard. Jon's parents have been good to her. She chooses her words carefully, explaining that she has decided to marry an artist she has met at graduate school.

This is not the marriage Emilee expected. But it seems to make sense. Her life is centered in the art world and so is her new man's, a Navy Vietnam veteran, now an art professor. At the University of Georgia, they are part of a close-knit group of graduate students creating art. They travel in a pack and have transformed a vacant building in downtown Athens into a co-op art studio. It has running water and electricity, but few other amenities. Emilee and her classmates clean and furnish it and create art in this studio instead of going to a classroom.

Professors come to critique and grade their work. Emilee tacks her artwork up on newspapers glued to the wall. "It was sort of edgy, because it wasn't the typical art education background that I had come from. We had silk screening, we painted, we had easels, and most materials you ever needed came from a hardware store."

Emilee is exhilarated. She relishes being in the vanguard of a movement, learning current art trends and new ways to express herself with paint, and how to teach art and engage students. "So, you can look at a piece of work and you don't have to talk about what's there, but you could talk about the line. Is the line round? Is it curvilinear or is it hard-edge straight? You could talk about the colors. Is it soft, hard? What colors are there? Are they advancing, retreating? And texture. Is it smooth or rough? You can take any piece of work and talk about those elements."

Abstract expressionists dominate their debates. Even in the 1960s, they needed to be defended, notes Emilee. "Were they legitimate? Was Jackson Pollack legitimate because he wasn't painting with a brush? Was David Smith, who was doing sculpture, legitimate because he sent it to the foundry? He wasn't doing it himself."

For the first time, she is comfortable immersing herself in these topics. "That's what you talk about when you eat. That's what you see when you close your eyes." This vivid life is freeing, if not consuming—maybe even excessive, she admits. Older than many of the students on campus, Emilee straddles two generations: one abiding by the prim and proper social code of the 1950s, the other pushing and stretching the limits imposed by society. It is 1968, after all. Martin Luther King, Jr., whom she heard preach in Atlanta when she taught art at an all-Black high school, has just been murdered. Several hundred co-eds have been demonstrating for equal rights for female students. There is a nightly curfew and a no-alcohol policy on campus even though Emilee and her friends are old enough to legally drink.

As Emilee drifts away from the life she planned to build with Jon ("I lost my way," she says now), her mother calls her out: "What are you doing? You are still wearing that ring." Her father is disappointed. He loves the idea of her marrying a pilot, though he has yet to meet Jon.

The only child of an accounting executive with Pan American Airlines, Emilee's mother was raised in New York City where formal dinners were served and family dressed for dinner. Emilee's mother Nan loosened up after her husband Wilfred moved the family to Florida for his career and the opportunity to travel. Emilee went on her first trip to Europe at nine. When Pan Am offered Wilfred a job in Trinidad, they jumped at the chance to live in the tropics. "At the time, Trinidad was still a United Kingdom colony, so I learned to count in shillings." Like many "expats," the McCarthys had housing, a maid, and a social club membership paid for. Emilee attended the local British school.

Wilfred and Nan were loving parents, but they held their emotions in check. It was a trait Emilee inherited, one that would serve her well throughout adulthood. First-time parents in their thirties, Wilfred and Nan treated Emilee as their little princess, coiffed her like a doll in dresses with embroidery, lace, big bows, and hats and gloves for church. As a young woman, she could have passed for a Kennedy cousin, with her friendly and toothy grin, thick dark hair worn in a fashionable bob, and sharp features. Petite and fashionable, she had a bounce in her step and a bohemian spirit.

Emilee McCarthy in her high school cheerleading uniform, Miami, Florida, 1960. (*Photo courtesy of the Reynolds family.*)

Emilee was teaching art at a junior high school when Jon approached her at Tampa's MacDill Air Force Base Officers Club in in his flight suit asking politely to buy her a drink. "I noticed you and your friend in the parking lot when you two drove up in that cute car," he said with a laugh. He was right. Judy's teal Volkswagen Bug did make heads turn.

Tall and trim with an easygoing smile, Jon was disarming. He exuded calm—and charm. Emilee's roommate Judy Whitley, the daughter of an Air Force colonel, knew the ropes at the "O Club":

"All the fighter pilots will tell you they are single, even when they are not. So, be on your guard." Emilee and Jon chatted all night before he asked for her phone number and drove her home in his new, sparkling white Jaguar. She gave him a tour of her apartment. "I'm only in town for a few weeks while I attend a training program here at MacDill," he told her. "Can I see you again this weekend?"

Eight months later, Jon proposed, before deploying to Vietnam and before he had an engagement ring. He planned to take his time and search for the right stone and setting in Hong Kong. Emilee quit her job to move in with Jon's parents near Philadelphia. It was not an ideal arrangement, but it *was* practical, allowing Emilee to save money and plan the wedding, slated for mid-November. With an innate sense of aesthetics, she tended to every detail, spending her free time thumbing through fashion magazines and window shopping for inspiration.

Their wedding date loomed and then passed. Jon's return was delayed when his squadron was sent from Japan to Thailand, the staging point for Operation Rolling Thunder missions. Emilee didn't worry. Jon had survived two risky deployments—one during the Cuban Missile Crisis and one to South Vietnam when the government of Ngo Dinh Diem was overthrown. He seemed like Superman to her. She was blissfully unaware of the danger of the missions he was flying and the high pilot loss rate.

A new date was selected, and notifications printed and inserted with the invitations. The change was attributed to "unavoidable circumstances." Her parents flew in to help and to get to know Emilee's future in-laws. They had yet to meet Jon. Thanksgiving came and went in a blur.

"I'll get it!" Emilee called out when she heard a knock at the door. All four parents and Emilee were skipping church and enjoying a lazy morning. They were not expecting company until the afternoon. In Air Force winter dress blues, two men stood on the front porch. They spoke slowly and solemnly: "We have a message for Mr. Reynolds."

Emilee did not understand the significance of their visit. With little exposure to military life, she did not know what the knock on the door portended. Innocently, she asked, "Can I deliver it to him?" "No," they insisted. "We need to talk to him ourselves." Still clueless, Emilee relayed the message. Mr. Reynolds invited the men in where they delivered the grim news: Jon's plane, a supersonic F-105D "Thunderchief" fighter-bomber, had been shot down over North Vietnam. Witnesses saw him bail out of his plane with a good "chute," and heard his beeper for several hours. His whereabouts were unknown.

The supersonic F-105 Thunderchief was the primary long-range strike fighter jet employed for the early missions of Operation Rolling Thunder. The plane delivered significant bomb payloads against targets in North Vietnam and Laos. Eventually, 334 F-105s were lost in combat, 40 percent of the Air Force's inventory. And the American aerial assault on Hanoi was having insignificant effect on North Vietnam's focus or its ability to get men and supplies headed southward. As Secretary Robert McNamara said in his memoir, "That fall the Communists matched our military escalation, recruiting more troops in the South, strengthening air defenses in the North, and boosting infiltration of men and supplies down the Ho Chi Minh Trail. Quite simply, they were adapting to the larger U.S. presence." He was about to recommend a bombing "pause," as an enticement to Hanoi to join negotiations. This would not happen soon enough for Jon Reynolds.

Emilee awakened after a fitful sleep. She was strangely calm and dry-eyed. "I felt like he could defend himself. Maybe I was naïve, but I envisioned him fighting off the Vietnamese."

The McCarthys, the Reynolds, and Emilee sat down to breakfast on Monday morning, silently drinking coffee. As the news got around, the phone started ringing and neighbors dropped by to console the group. It felt as if they were planning a funeral. Perhaps they were.

Emilee had no status in the military. A fiancée received no benefits and had none of the legal protections afforded to wives. She would not be included on the list of people to receive official military notifications about Jon. On December 18, the day she was supposed to say "I do" to her "hero," Jon's father woke her up. Solemnly, he handed her the diamond engagement ring that Jon had designed with the inscription "12-18-65." It was a bittersweet and awkward moment. Wordlessly, Emilee slipped it on her finger and did not take it off—not even when she slept.

Three years later, Emilee places Jon's engagement ring along with the letter to Mr. and Mrs. Reynolds in the envelope, and seals it shut, closing one chapter of her life and starting the next.

FIRST WIVES CLUB (FALL 1968)

Within this manicured, traditional brick colonial in a quiet Virginia Beach neighborhood—far enough from military housing at Naval Air Station Oceana so as not to attract attention, two dozen women plan to let their hair down. They cannot do it anywhere else. They will vent, if only to each other. And they will drink a cocktail, or more, without worrying what the squadron commanding officer's wife thinks.

In their stratified society, the women wear the ranks of their husbands. The standards of decorum in the U.S. Navy, and rules that govern their husbands, also govern them. But these women have something else in common: their husbands are missing in action or held captive in Southeast Asia. They are in a state of limbo. They feel like outcasts from the tightknit tribe of military wives who do not want to socialize with them because they are a reminder of what might happen to *their* husbands, still fighting the war. They. Are. Bad. Luck.

Candy Parish and her friend Reiden Rupinski watch the other women mix and mingle as they perch primly on the couch. Candy is keenly conscious of her youth. Nervously smoothing their miniskirts, Candy and Reiden do not know what to do with their hands.

None of the other women introduces herself to Candy or Reiden. No one joins them on the couch. The others are a decade older, at least. The dark circles under their eyes and the wrinkles forming around them make them seem even older. As they pour another gin and tonic and suck on their Virginia Slims, the wan expressions on their faces say it all. These are wives under pressure.

Many of them are suffering through their *third* year as POW and MIA wives, single mothers. With no end to the war in sight, they carry their burdens alone. "You weren't supposed to tell people that your husband was missing. I mean, think about that," Candy says later. They are kept at an arm's length by other naval aviator wives, unseen in the larger military community of Virginia Beach, and invisible to civilian housewives. The government hopes to keep them that way.

Candy and Reiden are both in their early twenties with babies at home, and only several *months* into the dizzying experience of being a MIA wife. These older women seem jaded, worn, bitter. And a bit drunk. Candy is worried: "I thought to myself, 'Is this what I'm going to become?'"

The two friends feel as if they have not paid their dues. Candy and Reiden stick together, sitting close to one other. It is a dinner party, and protocol dictates they stay through dessert. Two hours pass. Candy checks her watch. "I just couldn't wait to leave."

ROTTEN APPLES (SPRING 1970)

Carole Hanson has perfected her presentation. She rolls her projector in and out of venues all over southern California: Rotary Club chapters, Chambers of Commerce, garden clubs, Kiwanis,

Soroptimists, American Legion, VFW. Audiences lend a sympathetic ear, and afterward, raise their hands to offer help. It is heartening. She and dozens of other POW and MIA wives in southern California have been pounding the pavement and talking to any civic group that will host them. Their goal is to bolster public support for better treatment of the POWs and to obtain a full accounting for those missing. Carole wants information about her husband Steve. She has received none since 1967.

The women have garnered significant local, national, and international publicity, but it is not enough. Looking fellow Americans in the eye seems to be the most effective strategy to gain support and help. Several times a week, Carole packs up her gear, including bumper stickers and handouts, and sets up for another talk. She has a brisk schedule.

Today, she is speaking to college students at Santa Monica Community College. She has brought along her three-year-old son Todd. A college administrator greets her off-stage at the small outdoor amphitheater. Around fifty students are attending and eat lunch during her talk.

Seating Todd on the other side of the stage, Carole puts her finger over her lips, signaling to him to keep quiet. Todd has been her constant companion, even accompanying her to the Pentagon for meetings.

Carole Hanson was selected as "Military Wife of the Year" at Marine Corps Base El Toro, California in 1970 and described as the woman "who best typifies the spirit of the all-American military wife." This photo, of Carole and 3 ½-year-old Todd, appeared in a local community newspaper. (*Photo courtesy of Carole Hanson Hickerson.*)

The administrator introduces Carole as the wife of a Marine Corps helicopter pilot missing in Southeast Asia. Before she can utter a word, the students launch their lunch. Apple cores, eggs, soda cans, and brown lunch bags fly her way. She ducks left and right to avoid the projectiles. Todd wails as the crowd spits out: "Your husband got what he deserved!"

Part II

In the Thick of the Fight (1970–1973)

CHAPTER NINE

IN THE SPOTLIGHT

PRIME TIME (DECEMBER 12, 1969)

Trying to calm her nerves and still her pounding heart, Sybil Stockdale stands tall, smiling wanly at a sea of cameras. President Nixon flashes his high-wattage grin, indicating there is no place he would rather be than next to Sybil and POW wives Louise Mulligan and Andrea Rander, and MIA wives Pat Mearns and Carole Hanson.

Eleven months prior, Sybil and 2,000 other wives barraged the newly inaugurated president and commander-in-chief with their Telegraph-In campaign, requesting a meeting. Despite the telegrams, President Nixon deftly avoided contact for eleven months. Until today. Two months earlier, on a trip to pressure the North Vietnamese diplomatic delegation in Paris, it took less than a week to secure a meeting with the enemy.

Now, a month after President Nixon's notorious Silent Majority speech, however, he finally finds it politically expedient to meet with the wives. He seems eager to ride the coattails of support they have garnered in the press and with other Americans. The POW/MIA issue might rally "hawks" *and* "doves" behind his war strategy. "I felt he knew what was going on with us and was waiting to see whether the public might be interested in the issue...we needed traction," Pat says. Indeed, who would be *against* an effort to improve treatment for the POWs? The president is keenly aware that the captive men might just be the issue that rallies Americans behind his Vietnam policy. They could provide a way to pull himself out of the quagmire of war into which President Johnson had sunk so deeply.

President Nixon and his staff debated for several months how and when to engage directly with the women. It was thorny. Secretary Laird's staff traveled around the nation meeting with some 1,400 wives, parents and other relatives of the POWs and MIAs. Their reception was mixed. Emotions were high, patience worn thin. The Pentagon's representatives were on the receiving end of blunt and hostile rhetoric about the government's handling of the POW and MIA issue. Nevertheless, given increased media attention on the wives and their visit to Paris, Secretary Laird recommended a one-on-one meeting at the White House with a cross-section of wives. "It would indicate concern at the highest levels of government for the welfare of these Americans."

Others, including armed forces aide to the president Air Force Col. James Hughes, worry about bringing distraught women to the White House: "I would not disagree with this provided they are carefully screened for emotional stability and judgment."

Henry Kissinger and Colonel Haig opposed a meeting, fearing it would signal Hanoi that the wives were their marionettes. Throughout the fall, President Nixon asked his staff to reconsider, weekly. Eventually, Secretary Laird's recommendation prevailed. A meeting was scheduled for December 12, almost eleven months after Sybil and her compadres, scattered all over the United States, first issued a request to their commander-in-chief.

White House staff had reservations. Unrehearsed, what would the women say to the press corps? Deputy Assistant to the President Alexander Butterfield wrote, "I have serious doubts about the wisdom of Sybil Stockdale speaking out while here in the White House. She has expressed in the past her great disappointment over what she terms a lack of concern on the part of the President, and in a recent telephone call to me she sounded almost bitter."

Carol McCain could not believe the invitation for coffee with First Lady Pat Nixon was real. "And then I got a phone call that said, 'Will you come?' By golly, it *was* the White House." After their ID cards were checked and rechecked, twenty-six family members from around the country were ushered into a library in the White House family residence where a fire blazed. "Mrs. Nixon greeted every one of us personally," Pat remembers. Andrea thought the First Lady was warm and welcoming, putting her instantly at ease. Then, President Nixon revealed to the women his strategy for ending the war: he wanted to separate the prisoner issue from others at the Paris peace talks. Sybil is perplexed. "That didn't make any sense to me. How could you separate one from the other when one was an integral part of the other? How could I ever explain his idea of separating them to the press?"

Afterward, five of the women are ushered into the Roosevelt Room. They represent POW and MIA wives from all the military services, and all five have been active in lobbying and publicity. President Nixon stands in the middle, flanked by Carole, Louise, Sybil, Andrea, and Pat, creating a symbol of solidarity.

Calling Hanoi's treatment of the prisoners "one of the most unconscionable in history," President Nixon turns the stage over to the ladies, "five of the most courageous wives I've ever met in my life."

All five had spoken to the media before, but never to the White House press corps. "There we were," Carole remembers, "standing there with all these flashbulbs flashing."

Sybil, the designated spokesperson, claims she is satisfied with her government's efforts on behalf of their husbands. She does not support a premature troop withdrawal. "It would be very damaging to us on the prisoner issue." Beaming, President Nixon seems to like what he hears.

Pat feels those missing in action have been left out. She chimes in, urging reporters to remember *those* men: "We send packages and we don't know whether they are alive or dead. We send mail to men who we do not know whether they are alive or dead." An awkward silence descends on the drab press room. Sybil fills it with as cheerful a "Merry Christmas!" as she can muster before she is whisked off stage. Footage on the evening news includes her hollow holiday greeting. "I just wished they had mentioned the MIAs on the broadcast I saw," laments a wistful Pat.

President Nixon's aide, H. R. Haldeman, notes that the wives impress the president. In his diary, Haldeman writes that the president "now has great interest, amazing what a little personal exposure will do. He now wants all sorts of action." In a handwritten note to Kissinger about the focus of peace talks in Paris, President Nixon is emphatic: "I have changed my mind. – From now on until further direction from me – [American diplomat Philip] Habib is to talk only about prisoners."

Sybil is encouraged by the meeting, the spotlight on the issue of missing and captive men, and President Nixon's concern. She fires off a letter to her commander-in-chief that night, requesting that he form a federal task force. "It should be composed of able and imaginative people both in and out of government. It would be an action point for focusing efforts on behalf of our prisoners. Many of us are concerned that the gradual escalation of the war in Vietnam may leave the future of our prisoners in limbo simply because there may be no specific end to the war through armistice or treaty."

Colonel Hughes "mansplains" a response: "I am sure you know of the existence of the Prisoner of War Policy Committee which is a top-level group formed in 1967 to deal with all matters with the cognizance of the Department of Defense concerning missing and captured military personnel.... Therefore, we already have a 'task force' capability which should produce results if this type of approach is to be successful."

Sybil retorts in writing the next day: "I am going to be extremely frank in the contents of this letter and I shall always deeply resent constantly being forced into the position of assuming the role of a highly incensed, screeching female. In my opinion and that of many others, the Prisoner of War policy committee is a 'joke.'" She knows the committee has done nothing but hold meetings.

She reminds Colonel Hughes how long the wives have been waiting. "Many of us have been courageous, loyal, and INCREDIBLY PATIENT.... Time is running out for our patience."

She warns that many of the wives will not continue to march in unison with this president unless they start to see ACTION.

"I'm from New England and was brought up with the adage, 'Don't tell me, Show me.' I have heard every reassurance and allusion to collution [sic] or secrecy with expected developments in the next few months, known to woman. I have seen nothing."

A CALL TO ACTION (MAY 1, 1970)

From her onstage perch, Sybil gazes in delighted amazement as the crowd shuffles into DAR Constitution Hall, the neoclassical building across the street from the White House. Every seat will be filled; 3,700 people have traveled across the country to hear *her* speak tonight at an event designed to rally Congress behind the plight of the prisoners of war and those missing in Southeast Asia, some of whom are in their fifth year of captivity.

Sybil proudly walks to the podium as POW and MIA family members rise from their seats, bursting into resounding applause. She savors the moment.

It has been more than three years since the first thirteen wives of POWs and MIAs gathered at her home to privately share their frustration, vulnerability, helplessness, and despair. It has been more than a year since she gave her first nerve-wracking media interview to the *San Diego Union.* It has been seven months since she and five other POW and MIA family members went, alone, to confront the North Vietnamese in Paris. And it has been five months since she stood before the entire White House press corps with her president.

Now, she is the coordinator of the newly formed National League of Families of American Prisoners and Missing in Action in Southeast Asia. Sybil now leads a national organization with chapters in each state and is speaking before a live crowd of thousands of people. She has come a long way, baby.

While their husbands, brothers, sons, and fathers wage their battle against a foreign enemy, family members have been pursuing a lonely fight against their own government: against ignorance, apathy, and bureaucracy. But tonight, their efforts are recognized by legislators on Capitol Hill, bureaucrats and public servants from Foggy Bottom, Pentagon brass and officials, and the White House—many of whom have sent representatives. Candy Parish is on the stage with Sybil, having worked behind the scenes for two and a half months planning the logistics. Carole Hanson is there, too. The event is a triumph for the wives in their battle to place the fate of their men squarely in front of policy makers and politicos.

President Nixon has a message in the program, with a clear priority: "This Administration has no more urgent goal than to secure information about and eventual freedom for these Americans who have done so much for this country."

Also onstage with Sybil is U.S. Sen. Robert Dole from Kansas, the champion of tonight's event. A World War II veteran who sustained life-threatening injuries while serving with the 10th Mountain Division in Italy, he has made a commitment to help their cause, recruiting a bipartisan committee of colleagues to plan the event—those who support and those who oppose the war. The list includes senators Barry Goldwater, Edmund Muskie, and John Stennis, as well as several congressmen, including Olin Teague. Astronaut James Lovell delivers the keynote speech, joined onstage by movie actor Bob Cummings, Washington, D.C.'s mayor Walter Washington, and former Navy man and relentless POW advocate, Ross Perot, who is co-chairing the event with Sybil.

Sybil's week has been busy. She has testified before the House of Representatives, attended meetings with the secretary of defense and undersecretary of state, the attorney general, and several White House officials—all while overseeing tonight's event. One thing is certain: Americans are now acutely aware of the POW/MIA issue, and Sybil believes it is a unifying cause. Institutions in Washington, D.C. are finally willing to publicly castigate the North Vietnamese for their violations of the Geneva Convention concerning treatment of POWs. Since Secretary Laird announced his Go Public campaign almost one year ago, legislators on Capitol Hill have responded, holding five hearings in the House of Representatives and Senate. Six months ago, in October of 1969, more than 275 House members signed resolutions protesting the treatment of the POWs.

Earlier today, a joint resolution was passed as an "appeal for international justice for all the American prisoners of war and servicemen missing in action in Southeast Asia." Included in the resolution was the line: "That every possible effort be made to secure their advance release from captivity." Sybil knows the wives are the reason the issue has finally received the attention it deserves.

Press coverage of her big night is overshadowed by the president announcing that he has sent ground troops into Cambodia, despite promises that he would not. In an address to the American people, he proclaimed that he was going to the "heart of the trouble": enemy sanctuaries in Cambodia. "That means cleaning out major North Vietnamese and Vietcong occupied territories—these sanctuaries which serve as bases for attacks on both Cambodia and American and South Vietnamese forces in South Vietnam." Public outrage over the perceived duplicity explodes, especially on college campuses. America is at war with herself. National Guardsmen have been summoned to quell unrest on campuses. It will prove deadly in Ohio in a few days.

The Hon. Melvin Laird, secretary of defense, greeting Candy and Hunter Parish at the International Day of Justice at DAR Constitution Hall, May 1, 1970. (*Photo courtesy of Candy Parish Ellis.*)

For now, in this hall, POWs and MIAs are the focus. Vice President Spiro Agnew takes the stage and he, too, makes clear that release of POWs "is fundamental to our negotiating stance in Paris." The evening reaches a crescendo when POW wife Louise Mulligan asks the crowd a pointed question regarding the more than 1,500 missing and imprisoned men: "*Have we become so callous that these men are going to be written off?*" Directing her gaze—and her words—to the assembled leaders, she admonishes, "*…do not turn your back on the hundreds of mothers who want their sons returned.*"

Her plea resonates throughout the hall.

"*Do not ignore the children who cry out for the love and guidance of their fathers and the hundreds of wives who have grieved for years, some for husbands who will never return!*" Some in the audience furtively wipe away a tear. Louise is not finished. She ends with an urgent and rousing call to action: "*Hear our call of distress.... May Day, May Day!!! Please help!*"

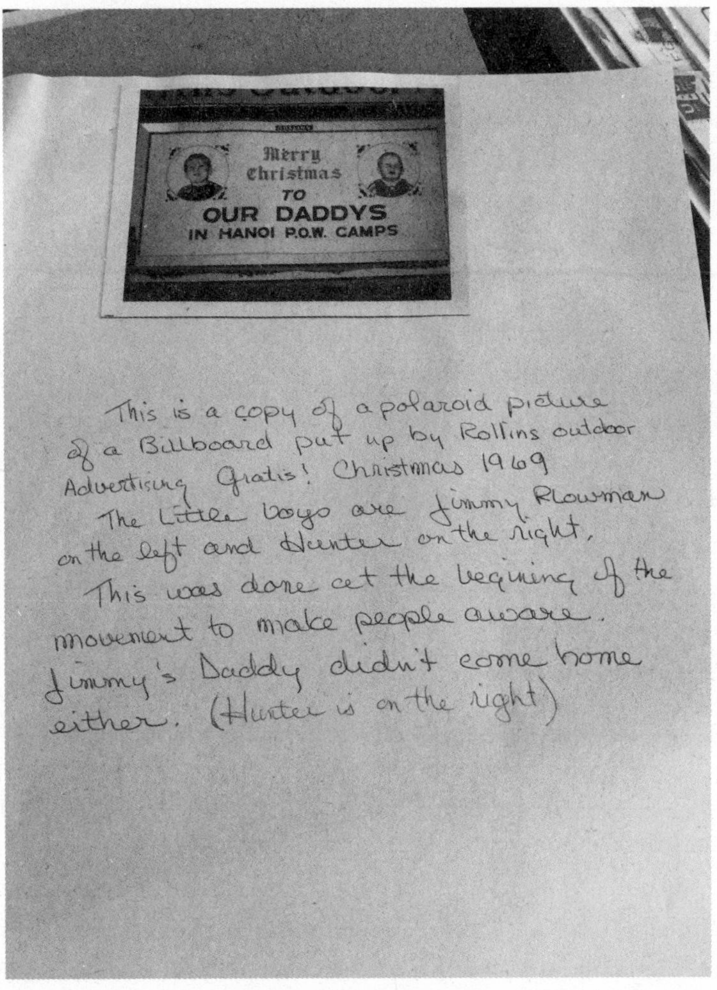

This is a copy of a polaroid picture
of a Billboard put up by Rollins outdoor
Advertising Gratis! Christmas 1969
The Little boys are Jimmy Plowman
on the left and Hunter on the right.
This was done at the begining of the
movement to make people aware.
Jimmy's Daddy didn't come home
either. (Hunter is on the right)

MIA toddlers Jimmy Plowman (L) and Hunter Parish (R) on a national billboard advertising campaign, Christmas 1969, underwritten by Rollins Outdoor Advertising. (*Photo courtesy of Candy Parish Ellis.*)

CROSSED WIRES (NOVEMBER 1970)

The American captives in a small prison compound twenty-three miles west of Hanoi have also been sending May Day! signals. U.S. officials perk up at the discovery of covert missives from the men.

On detail in the prison yard digging ditches and a well, the men arrange rocks into formations. Cleverly, they can only be read from above. The POWs work casually, so as not to arouse suspicion. Allowed to lay their laundry out to dry on the rock mounds, they write a message with the clothes—a missive to the sky.

SR-71 Blackbirds on regular reconnaissance flights capture images of the symbols in May. A seasoned intelligence technician with experience working in Laos, Air Force Tech Sgt. Norv Clinebell is the first to notice. He works for a small and obscure Air Force unit, the 1127th Field Activities Group at Fort Belvoir, Virginia, located about seventeen miles south of the Pentagon. The unit processes intelligence from American POWs, and designs programs to help downed airmen evade and escape capture. For months, Clinebell scrutinizes aerial photographs of the walled compound near Son Tay. By comparing newer photographs to earlier ones, he notices that the compound has recently been enlarged, with a new wall and a new guard tower.

Even more intriguing is the word "S-A-R" spelled out with prison uniforms drying in the sun. It could stand for "Search and Rescue." And the "K" outlined on the ground? Could it be a distress signal from an imprisoned air crew? An encoded letter from a POW has indicated that at least fifty-five men were at the camp, and some were in rough physical shape. The letter begged for an evacuation.

Clinebell and a colleague, Claude Watkins, a retired Air Force master sergeant and a former World War II POW, are struck by the detailed communications. And they are haunted by the desperate plea for assistance. Could a rescue operation be attempted? Could it be executed in time?

Planning begins for one of the most daring covert operations of the Vietnam War. Personally approved by President Nixon, the attempted rescue became known as the Son Tay Raid. Everyone up and down the chain of command supports the idea. Adm. Tom Moorer, chairman of the Joint Chiefs of Staff, wants "some focal point, something dramatic" in the war: "If we could get 50 or 60 of those boys back in the United States and let them tell in their own words what had happened to them, it would throw a new light on the character of the North Vietnamese." *He desperately needs to prove to the wives and families of the POWs that he is doing more than shaking his fist at the North Vietnamese.*

Since the peace talks in Paris are stalled, a small group of covert operators will attempt what diplomats in Paris have thus far been unable to achieve: a release of the POWs.

The team rehearses under live fire at night 170 times with an inflatable mock-up of the Son Tay prison compound at Eglin Air Force Base in western Florida. Army Col. Arthur "Bull" Simons is in charge, the same man who will, in 1979, lead a successful rescue operation into Iran to retrieve two of Ross Perot's employees. After six months of planning, the Simons team is ready. The operation to rescue prisoners deep in enemy territory is given the green light on November 20, 1970.

Since President Nixon halted all bombing strikes over North Vietnam in October of 1968, the skies above North Vietnam have been relatively quiet. That is about to change.

On this cloudless night, Navy planes launch flares over Haiphong Harbor to divert attention from the small strike force heading for this prison compound outside the village of Son Tay.

To avoid detection by enemy radar, the aircraft is flying very low. One of the four HH-3E helicopters, called "Banana 1," dives to avoid trees on its descent toward the target: a courtyard in the middle of a small prison compound. It is just after 2:00 a.m. Hanoi time.

At the controls of Banana One, the helicopter pilot performs a "controlled crash" inside the compound. The helicopter is a Sikorsky CH-3, converted for search and rescue missions, armor plated to protect against enemy fire at close range. Forced to make a steep descent to avoid the trees, the helicopter slices and sheers everything in its path. Before the bird touches ground, the assault team inside, led by Air Force Master Sgt. Richard J. "Dick" Meadows, begins firing. The violence of the crash landing propels the door gunner from the aircraft.

Clutching his bullhorn, Meadows announces: "We're Americans. Keep your heads down. We're Americans. This is a rescue. We're here to get you out. Keep your heads down. Get on the floor. We'll be in your cells in a minute."

There is only silence.

The assault team races across the prison yard and breaches one cellblock after another. They are all empty.

Where did the fifty-five prisoners go? How long ago was the prison camp evacuated? A coded message in a letter from one of the Son Tay prisoners states: "We move early July."

The only problem is that this letter has been languishing on Watkins's desk at Ft. Belvoir, one of a backlog waiting to be analyzed by the 1127th. Watkins reads it hours too late. He recounts: "I remember trying to inform DIA later that morning, only to discover the raid had just taken place."

In fact, officials also have significant photographic evidence that the Son Tay prison was emptied weeks or months before the raid. Overhead imagery taken on October 3 indicates little activity. No people milling around, weeds growing. Despite this, the commander of the operation, Army Brig. Gen. Donald Blackburn, briefs Henry Kissinger on October 8, more than a month before the planned raid, and tells him that the mission had a "95 to 97 percent assurance of success." Kissinger asks many questions: What would be the cover story if the raid failed? How would this raid affect the prisoners in other prisons? What if this mission results in more men being captured?

He does not ask if prisoners are still there.

Intelligence collected the day before the planned November 21 raid from a "sometimes-reliable agent" in North Vietnam reinforces the imagery analysis. Americans are nowhere to be seen in the camp's outdoor areas. However, there has been increased activity.

Could Americans be *inside*? Secretary Laird and President Nixon weigh the latest intelligence and, together, decide to take the risk. They approve the mission last minute.

On Capitol Hill four days later, Laird takes a political beating for the failed raid. Among the senators seeking answers is Sen. William Fulbright. At the Committee on Foreign Relations that he chairs, Senator Fulbright commends the bravery of the force that staged the rescue attempt. However, "I do not like to say it was all a bad idea simply because it failed, but it did fail. There was something wrong with the intelligence."

Laird begs to differ. "There were prisoners there, Mr. Chairman, and we knew that full well. What we have done here has shown all of those prisoners in North Vietnam that America does care. There was a chance—"

Fulbright interrupts with rancor in his tone. "Was there any doubt that America cares about them? I did not know there was any doubt."

Laird: "Yes, there was a doubt. I am sure you have had an opportunity, as I have, to talk to the wives."

Fulbright: "I have, yes."

Laird: "And mothers. I have talked to almost every wife. I talked to these nine prisoners [early returnees]. I spent time with some of them who have returned, and there is a question in their minds as to whether America is showing—"

Fulbright: "There is no justification for it. Mr. Secretary, my time is up."

President Nixon agrees with Laird. The risk was worth it. Before Colonel Simons and his band took off for Hanoi, Laird and President Nixon believed the rescue attempt would demonstrate "our love, caring, and affection for those POWs." Even if it failed to rescue one of them. Even if it resulted in casualties or more POWs.

POW brother Bob Brudno picks up the phone at home the night after the story of the raid breaks. Tech Sergeant Clinebell has a detail that Bob will not read in the news. The men know each other well. Bob's brother, POW Alan Brudno, is noted at the 1127th intelligence unit at Ft. Belvoir as one of the more effective at communicating secret information that only family members or the U.S. military can decipher. Although the Brudno family has received just a dozen letters from Alan, each one is chock full of "doubletalk" references that reveal camp locations, prison conditions, treatment of POWs, and names of missing men. Alan, in a Christmas 1966 letter to his wife, first alerts the U.S. government that the North Vietnamese are torturing the men.

Tonight, Clinebell is in tears. "Alan was there, Bob," he says, choking on his words.

CHAPTER TEN

ENDURING ICONS

TURNING POINT (SPRING 1971)

Ever so carefully, Stanley and Virginia Bates crack open the door to their daughter's bedroom, grimacing as it creaks. Peeking inside, they smile as they spy twenty-one-year-old Carol sprawled across her bed, fully clothed and sound asleep. A plump, baby-faced ingenue with blunt-cut blond bangs and piercing eyes, she is covered with checks and bank deposit slips.

Carol was up late the previous night, as she has done many nights over the past year. She is throwing all her energy into rallying Americans around the nation's POWs, some of whom are entering their sixth year of captivity in Southeast Asia. Politics is a passion inherited from her mother, Virginia Bates, who is proud of her daughter's dedication, but unhappy that Carol has dropped out of college.

With her friend, Kay Hunter, Carol is the brains behind a wildly successful nationwide campaign to raise awareness about the missing and captive men. The pair is selling aluminum and copper cuffs engraved with the name of an individual POW or MIA. Millions of people around the country sport the bracelets as a visible sign of their concern for and support of the men. Sales are exceeding expectations. Money is rolling in faster than it can be processed.

Carol is astonished as 30,000 envelopes and packages filled with order forms, cash, checks, and letters of support pile up in their office daily. The two gals can barely keep up.

Carol Bates, the brainchild behind the wildly successful POW and MIA bracelet campaign, working the phones in the VIVA office, circa 1972. (*Photo courtesy of Carol Bates Brown.*)

After mail starts to disappear from the post office and neighbors find pilfered bags burning on their front lawns, the duo hires a Brinks driver to deliver mail bags to the bank. They also hire a fulfillment company to ship the coveted bracelets. As sales keep garnering publicity and orders, the bank account grows fatter.

The campaign and its success lead to questions from POW and MIA wives. "We were very skeptical about this idea of there being bracelets," Sybil Stockdale admits later. "I remember we [initially] voted that we were not going to support the thing...and we told them that if they wanted to use anyone's name, they would have to get permission [from the family]." Pat Mearns was also wary. Where was the money going? she wondered. And how about their own organization, the National League of Families? "VIVA was making so much money and the National League had so little," Carole Hanson recalls.

Alice Stratton, looking over a stack of POW/MIA bracelets. (*Photo courtesy of the Stratton family. Image originally published in the* Palo Alto Times, *circa 1971.*)

VIVA, or Victory in Vietnam Association (later called Voices in Vital America), is the organization sponsoring Carol and Kay's activities. Carol, a Republican since the age of six, is attracted to the campus group formed in 1967 in Los Angeles. Its members are more wary of the spread of Communism than most of their contemporaries. VIVA activists supported ending the war in Vietnam by winning it.

Concerned about surging violence and unrest on college campuses, Carol and Kay want to do something positive for U.S. soldiers fighting in Vietnam and tap into local Republicans. California is a Republican state with Ronald Reagan as governor. Sam Yorty is mayor of Los Angeles, the largest city in the state, where the circle of Republican influencers is small but powerful. Many of old Hollywood's royalty are part of the GOP, including John Wayne, Charlton Heston, and Jack Benny. Carol and Kay get to know these celebrities and other notables, including local personality and fervent anti-Communist television talk show host Bob Dornan.

The girls attend tapings of his new television show and tag along to political fundraisers and rallies.

A fighter pilot who survived two ejections, Dornan feels a connection to the POWs and those missing in Vietnam. His fate could have been the same. After reading about Carole Hanson and her missing husband, and realizing that she was a southern Californian, Dornan invited her on his show. The Marines sent a chaperone to monitor what she said.

At the time, Carole was on a lonely quest to publicize inhumane treatment of American captives. She was giving away bumper stickers with the slogan, "Don't let them be forgotten—POWs and MIAs!" She wrote an open letter to 250 newspaper editors across the country. Carole was gaining traction with local media, but it was not enough. Her frustration deepened. Where was any public condemnation of the North Vietnamese, she wondered. Of the hundreds of elected officials she wrote, only twenty responded. She was convinced the North Vietnamese were susceptible to world opinion. Carole believed that, if she could spark outrage at the treatment of America's military men, she could change the tide of public opinion. Dornan's show gave her access to his Los Angeles viewers, but she needed to increase the size and scope of her national audience. Dornan vowed to help.

In late 1969, he introduced students Carol Bates and Kay Hunter to wives Carole Hanson, Pat Mearns, and Patty Hardy. They brainstormed how sympathetic college students could help the women's cause. Would petitions help? Letters to Hanoi's leaders? Knocking on the doors of Capitol Hill? Speeches on campuses? Media interviews?

Carole and Pat were nonplussed. They had been doing all that for more than a year, without garnering much attention.

The two students were moved by the wives, as was VIVA's adult advisor and board chair, wealthy Los Angeles socialite Gloria Coppin. She had been searching for a meaningful issue for VIVA, an opportunity to do more than bake cookies for soldiers.

VIVA was making headlines, standing up to so-called "peaceniks" demonstrating on campuses in southern California. But VIVA activists were outnumbered by the antiwar movement sweeping through college campuses. Enter Gloria with her Rolodex, checkbook, and free time. She was a game changer for VIVA. In many ways, she fit right in with the college co-eds. Photogenic and hard-working, she toiled around the clock, sometimes staying awake for days. She opens the doors to her spacious Brentwood mansion for Carol and Kay to use as office space, funding and mentoring them.

The idea for a bracelet campaign sparked in Gloria's kitchen. Bob wears a bracelet, a simple band of aluminum airplane scrap given to him in 1966 by a Montagnard tribesman in the Vietnam central highlands. The Montagnards were an Indigenous minority who fought alongside American Special Forces, raising the ire of the Communist People's Army. Around a campfire in the Kontum region, an elderly village chieftain placed the bracelet on Dornan's wrist and told him, "Please, sir, do not stop wearing this bracelet, and thinking of my suffering people, the Montagnard, who are being murdered and killed by the Communists. Do not take it off, till my people are free." Dornan vowed he would not.

It's a vow he still honors. He told Gloria: "When I work so hard and go without sleep, and think I can't go that extra mile, I jump in the shower and I'll often hit my arm against the shower, and I'll feel that bracelet and it will remind me that someone is suffering more than I and it'll keep me going." Impressed, Gloria shared the anecdote with Carol and Kay. They were immediately inspired. Why not go to Vietnam and find more bracelets? They could invite citizens to wear them, *to remember the POWs*.

But who will fund the coeds' trip? "My parents were absolutely horrified," Carol recalls.

Carol and Kay strategized. What if they made their own bracelets, *like* Bob's? Gloria remembers their pitch: "These two girls called me with the obvious answer, which I hadn't thought of at the time. Why can't we do this same type of thing for the prisoners of war?" Gloria embraced the idea wholeheartedly.

They wanted Bob's help. They write their idea for a nationwide campaign to support the POWs. At the taping of his Saturday night television show they shouted it from the audience. Bob was excited: "What did you just say? That's a fantastic idea."

Along with Bob, and Gloria, the girls called a metal shop in Santa Monica that engraved horse harnesses. Dornan suggested flattening the aluminum for easier engraving. On the phone with manufacturer Jack Zeider, they decided to include the missing or captive man's name, rank, and loss date. Zeider agreed to make prototypes in both nickel-plated aluminum and copper, a popular remedy for arthritis.

One question loomed: What should they charge? Carol suggested $2.50, about the cost of a student movie ticket. They searched for startup funding. Ross Perot rebuffed them, as did Howard Hughes. Eventually, Gloria's husband, the owner of an aircraft parts manufacturer, donated enough metal for the first 1,200 bracelets. At a

Salute to the Armed Forces dinner dance in Los Angeles on May 7, 1970, where Governor Ronald Reagan was the keynote speaker, Bob Hope and actress Martha Raye were announced as co-chairs of the bracelet campaign. Perot's wife received the first one.

Sales explode. Demand increased from 500 a week to 1,000 and, shortly thereafter, to an astounding 40,000 per week. Zeider hired 120 college kids and some Vietnam veterans to work around the clock creating bracelets, charging VIVA fifty cents for each one. With a 500 percent mark-up, cash started rolling in to VIVA's headquarters.

Nearly five million are sold. John Wayne wears a bracelet. Sonny and Cher wear bracelets. Princess Grace of Monaco and her daughters wear them. Johnny Cash, Fred Astaire, Billy Graham, Gov. George Wallace, and President Nixon wear them too, vowing to keep the bands on their wrists until all the men return home.

The plight of men like Steve Hanson and Art Mearns is now *personal* for millions of Americans. The campaign rallies the nation behind the men like no other tactic.

Cora Weiss is alarmed by the campaign's popularity. In a speech to the like-minded Quaker military watchdog organization National Action/Research on the Military Industrial Complex, or NARMIC, Weiss does not hold back. Her venom toward the POWs and their families is palpable. "The bracelet campaign is an insidious campaign and I think should be attacked head on," claims Weiss. "I think it's insidious for two reasons: one is that everybody who buys it pays $2.50 to $3.00 and it's a tax-exempt organization that collects the money and normally it's very hard to get an exemption and they not only don't pay taxes on all the income they get, but what do they do with the money?" She doesn't stop there.

"In the beginning they used to claim that they gave [the money] to the families. But what are they doing handing out money to families of career men who are earning tax free enormous amounts of money each year, and have practically all their special needs taken care of at no expense?"

Weiss explains that families receive a bonus from the government every year that their POW is a prisoner. That, she says, comes on top of "not bad" pay.

She is adamant that the campaign is unsubstantial: "The second thing they're doing is maintaining the myth that if you wear a bracelet you're doing somebody good. Helping to bring the guy home, helping to make him or his family feel better. All of that's a lot of nonsense."

YOU ARE NOT FORGOTTEN (1972)

The board of directors of the National League has a lot to cover. Bob Brudno and Carole Hanson glance at the agenda. Bob has taken the train from Philadelphia, and Carole has flown in from Los Angeles for a quick turnaround.

Arms folded, they review an image laid out on the table of a silhouetted POW. The prisoner's head is bowed, as if dejected. A guard tower rises behind him. Above his head is the acronym "POW*MIA." Below is a strand of barbed wire with the phrase, "You are not forgotten." The flag is the brainchild of MIA wife Mary Helen Hoff, who recognizes the need for a symbol for the POW and MIA issue. Appealing to their patriotism, she contacts the largest manufacturer of flags in the world, Annin Flagmakers. They had just designed flags for the newest country members of the United Nations. Sympathetic to the cause, Annin agrees to design a flag for the National League.

The flag's commercial graphic artist Newt Heisley, explains, "I used to fly within range of the Japanese, and I wondered how I would hold up if I ever got captured. When I did the design, I thought how easy it would be to forget these guys." Heisley is a World War II veteran, and a pilot who flew missions in the Pacific.

Hired by Annin, he has poured his heart into the design, using his twenty-four-year-old son as the model.

Heisley pitches his design to the board. Sketched in black and white, Heisley intends to add color—to make it less somber, yet still able to inspire empathy. Bob and Carole review the design, assuming it will be one more useful tool in the National League's larger campaign, along with bumper stickers, the VIVA-produced bracelets, billboards, commemorative stamps, and Christmas cards.

The board of directors approves. "We were playing on victimhood, trying to win hearts and minds," Bob admits.

A banner emblazoned with the design is first presented to Secretary Laird. As Annin begins manufacturing the flag, the image becomes ubiquitous. It is *the* symbol for the League—and for the nation—of American commitment to bring home POWs and resolve the fate of all the wartime missing. Other than Old Glory, it is the only flag that flies over every federal building and post office, as well as the White House and the Capitol. The image is on everything: T-shirts, belt buckles, coffee mugs, hats, ornaments, bumper stickers, blankets—even face masks.

Unlike the bracelet campaign that reaps a fortune for VIVA, the POW-MIA flag generates no income for the National League of Families. Bob remembers, "I recall no discussion about getting it trademarked since all we wanted was to see the war end." And Carole admits, "We didn't even think about trademarking it. We were novices."

Once the war was over, it was assumed the POWs would come home and the missing would be accounted for, making the flag obsolete. Today, you cannot drive five miles in the United States without seeing one.

Each day, the ubiquitous POW and MIA flag flies above every federal building in the United States, including the White House, the Capitol, and each U.S. post office. It is an enduring symbol and a reminder to "leave no man behind." (*Photo courtesy of Leah Spiro.*)

CHAPTER ELEVEN

BREAKING DOWN

LAMBS TO LIONS (JANUARY 15, 1970)

Her shoulders are tensed. Sybil Stockdale lowers them, but then her jaw clenches. On this wintry day, in front of a fireplace on an overstuffed antique sofa in the exquisitely plush seventh floor suite of the State Department, she is about to meet with President Nixon's Secretary of State, William Rogers. It is not the first time and she finds him likable. But she needs him to be more decisive.

In a tone and decibel that veers from her customary demeanor, she loudly and firmly makes her case for having the U.S. pressure Russia to cut off supplies to North Vietnam. It will force Hanoi's hand at the peace negotiations in Paris, she insists. "I think you're going easy on Russia, so they'll go ahead with the SALT talks. At the same time, you tell us you're doing everything you can to help our men. It. Doesn't. Add. Up." She is a foreign policy neophyte and knows it. Perhaps she has overstepped. Then again, *she* has met with the North Vietnamese. Secretary Rogers has not.

He thunders at her, gesticulating, *his* tone a departure from his customary polished approach. "You have got to believe we are doing everything we can to bring the war to an end and to get our prisoners home!" After years of excuses from one government official after another, Sybil doesn't.

Emotions get the best of her. Do Rogers and other Nixon administration officials realize how long she has battled her own government? He has only been a cabinet member for one year. "I just can't believe a country as big as ours can't win this war if they want to!" Sybil roars back.

Half a year earlier, on June 5, 1969, Rogers had endorsed Secretary Laird's Go Public campaign launch. Filled with reproach for the North Vietnamese treatment of POWs, he reaffirmed that the United States was ready for meaningful discussion, saying, "Any sign of good faith by the other side in this matter would provide encouragement for our negotiations in Paris."

Rogers appears confident in public, yet others come to recognize his lack of experience. He later acknowledges, "When I started here, my own lack of foreign policy training was certainly a disadvantage." Despite his close relationship with the president, he was never seen as an influential secretary of State.

In truth, President Nixon had chosen him expressly for his *lack* of foreign policy experience. Rogers was intentionally excluded from foreign policy decision-making, as President Nixon intended to hoard that role. Kissinger admitted, "Nixon considered Rogers's unfamiliarity with the subject an asset because it guaranteed that policy direction would remain in the White House." Kissinger was President Nixon's unofficial Secretary of State, until he was given the title in September 1973.

Sybil wonders if her exhortations are wasted on Secretary Rogers. She also recognizes a puppet when she sees one. In the elevator, she reflects on her meeting. "I felt pleased to have been sharply frank with him, even though I liked him quite well. I thought to myself, 'President Nixon put him in charge of this place only to keep these State Department types from botching up the peace efforts the president and Dr. Kissinger are working on.'"

LIONS TO LAMBS (FALL 1970)

"Oh, come on, Stockdale. Now you're an attractive gal and I'm not so bad. Let's lie down on the couch over there and give it a go." No one has ever called Sybil Stockdale by her last name. "Mrs. Stockdale," yes. But "Stockdale"? It sounds coarse. Sitting upright in the big black leather chair, she blinks. She is speechless.

Dr. Robert Moran on K Street came highly recommended by her OB-GYN. She cannot bring herself to say the word *psychiatrist*. It offends her New England sensibilities. She can almost hear her mother: "God helps those who help themselves." "If at first you don't succeed, try, try again." Only weaklings seek psychiatric help, thinks Sybil.

But she is exhausted and unable to pull herself out of bed. The cacophony of traffic in front of her new home in the northwest suburb of Washington, D.C., makes her pine for the sunshine and quiet of Coronado—which she left two months ago. Most days she stares at the ceiling in her bedroom, ruing her decision to move across the country.

She thought it would be convenient to be near Capitol Hill, Foggy Bottom, and the Pentagon for the increasing number of meetings she is attending. It would be easier to do the job of chairman of the board of the newly incorporated National League of POW/MIA Families. It would be helpful to be near Bethesda, for her young son Stanford to be treated for hypertension and problems with reading.

The traffic, the crowds, and the rent in Washington have placed her in a constant state of anxiety and dread. She has no energy and cannot make the simplest decision. Sometimes, she cannot decide what to wear. Only when her boys get home from school does she drag herself upright and wander naked from bedroom to bathroom, where she throws on a dress and a scarf to greet them. Friend and fellow POW wife Karen Butler urges her to seek help.

Sybil relinquishes her position as the National League chairman on the fifth anniversary of Jim's shootdown. "I just can't do it anymore." A newspaper photographer captures a candid image of her on her front porch, haggard, head covered in a wig.

News of Jim's condition has deepened her despair. She could only stare at the Navy captain who gave her the classified information in the State Department lobby with employees and visitors bustling in and out. A source has revealed that Jim is crippled from injuries to one or both legs. The North Vietnamese have not treated him. Worse yet, Jim has been kept in solitary confinement for a long time—for as long as four years.

How can he survive this? How can *she*?

Psychotherapy. Her OB-GYN, Dr. Cooper, tells her that a little bit of it would do her no harm.

Dr. Moran is handsome, probably a bit younger than Sybil, with a cheerful Irish face and the gift of gab. "I hardly had time to cry, he talked so much. I have since learned there are the talking kind of therapists and the listening kind and give me the talking kind every time."

Dr. Moran talks about everything, except Sybil. She hears about his wife who reads all the time, his children and his children's teachers, his friends, his love of horseback riding, and how he doesn't understand why his wife won't ride with him. It feels irrelevant. But she is amused.

Sybil has therapy appointments with Dr. Moran, first twice a week and then once a week for months. "About the time he started urging me to roll in the hay with him, I began to realize that probably everything he did and talked about was directed to the purpose of my therapy."

In response to his proposition, Sybil sputters, "No, I'm not going to do that." Dr. Moran seems to relish her consternation.

"Oh yeah? And why not?"

"Well, I don't know. I just think you're kidding anyway. I know you're not serious."

"Why shouldn't I be serious? You know we psychiatrist[s] aren't all that different from other guys. Don't you think it would be any fun?"

She truly believes he is not serious. He has a twinkle in his eye when he makes the not-so-subtle suggestion. He repeats the offer at every visit. Each time, Sybil refuses. She is beginning to enjoy the banter. "My visits to him became the high point of my life."

After six weeks of therapy, she asks when she is going to be cured.

He explains: "One thing you have to realize is that almost all people walking around out there on the streets feel like you do all the time. They never feel any better than you do at your worst. So believe me, you'll know when the time comes. Take my word for it."

Once, he puts his arm around her and kisses her on the forehead. She doesn't flinch. "That's a good sign," he notes, encouragingly. "You aren't afraid to touch people anyway." And he comments that her skin and hair are starting to look healthier.

By March, she feels a little better, even after a cancer scare and subsequent hysterectomy. Ironically, the bedrest post-surgery *is* restful. "As bad as things were for all of us, we had some nice quiet family times there together. I wouldn't ever want to go back to those days, but I can think of them with a softness now that I couldn't have done for a long time."

She postpones one appointment with Dr. Moran, and then another, realizing she *is* better. In June, she makes one last appointment to say goodbye. Sybil is, happily, moving back to Coronado. He talks her ear off again, this time about his girlfriend and their escapades. Was this therapy, too, or is Dr. Moran telling tall tales?

Years later, Sybil offhandedly asks her OB-GYN about the psychiatrist. Dr. Moran suffered a tragedy. "When he and his wife were out at the beach at their summer place, one night after dinner, out of the blue, his wife took out a gun and shot and killed herself in front of him and the kids." He never practiced again.

"Poor fellow. He was the best therapist I could ever have hoped to have."

CHAPTER TWELVE

BREAKING OUT

MOVING ON VS. MOVING IN (JANUARY 1972)

Candy and Hunter Parish (Ellis), featured on the cover of *Look* magazine, December 1970. (Look *Magazine Photograph Collection, Library of Congress, Prints & Photographs Division, LC-L901-70-5692, #1. Photo by Thomas R. Koeniges,* Look *staff photographer.*)

Candy Parish is feeling nervous, but also helpless and frustrated. Her future lies in the hands of a small panel of men—officers from the Navy, Marine Corps, Air Force, Army, and Coast Guard. They are huddled in a conference room at the Bureau of Naval Personnel discussing her husband, Chuck. Should he be declared dead? Candy is not invited to attend nor is her opinion solicited.

This status hearing is routine, as far as the men are concerned. These meetings are periodically held to review MIA cases and determine if a change in status—from MIA to POW, or MIA to KIA/BNR (Killed in Action/Body Not Recovered)—is warranted. Candy believes it is.

Candy wants them to change Chuck's status from MIA to KIA/BNR. Chuck is deceased, and he died the day his plane was shot out of the sky more than three years ago. It took a long time for her to come to this conclusion, but it is the right one.

For a long time, she prayed Chuck was alive. But, after fifteen months with no word, she was beginning to have her doubts. Her belief that he was dead began to grow a few months after she returned from that memorable trip to Paris, in the fall of 1969. Bob Boroughs had asked her: Could she come to the Pentagon again? "We have received some new photos from Hanoi of some of our captured men. I want to see if you recognize any of them."

Eager to help, Candy obliged and trekked to his basement office. Sifting through a stack of grainy 8 x 10 shots, she came across a gaunt, scared, and vulnerable-looking American man on a medical examination table. Her identification was instantaneous: "That's Bob Fant!" Candy Parish was emphatic. "Are you sure?" Boroughs asked her. Staring from a black and white photo was her husband's radar intercept officer, or RIO. He was the back seater in Chuck's F-4.

She could clearly make out Fant's facial features. "I'm positive. That is Bob Fant." She knew Fant well and was elated at identifying a missing American.

Only upon returning home did the weight of the revelation sink in. If Fant was a confirmed POW, where was her husband Chuck?

When he first disappeared in July of 1968, she hoped he had survived. Radio Hanoi broadcast that an F-4 had been shot down on the same day as Chuck's disappearance and in the same area where his plane imploded. The radio announcer said that the pilot had ejected, parachuted to the ground, and been captured. There were two men in the plane. Who was captured? Now she knew.

The Navy informed her that Lieutenant Fant's family had received a letter from him in captivity. "Based on this letter, the status of the other member has been changed to captured. I regret that the letter contained no information concerning your husband. Therefore, no change in the status of Lieutenant Parish is indicated at this time." He was missing in action, still.

That first year, she firmly believed he was alive and in captivity in Southeast Asia. "But you know, you get to a point where one day you're waking up and you think, oh, he's there. The next day you're waking up…and you're thinking, oh, he's not there. What if he's not there? And then you're waking up and you say, oh, he's there." Chuck's parents never believed he survived. Should she? The vacillation was exhausting. Sometimes, she forgot to eat, and her weight dropped to 104 pounds. Though her days are filled with the energizing work of the National League, evenings were long and lonely, even with a boisterous toddler running around and the steady and unwavering support of her parents.

Then, Candy received a surprising invitation. "Dear Mrs. Parish, On Saturday, 31 January, at 1930 hours our Red River Rats and their wives are having a cocktail-buffet at the Commissioned Officers Mess, National Naval Medical Center, Bethesda, Maryland. We cordially invite you to join us that evening as our honored guest. If you can attend, and we certainly hope so, please let us hear from you. One of our couples will be contacting you to arrange to pick you up and bring you home."

The "River Rats," or more formally the Red River Valley Fighter Pilots Association, was an organization of combat pilots who had flown missions over the eponymous valley in Vietnam. Founded in 1966–1967, chapters existed at most Navy and Air Force installations around the country to support the families of POW, MIA, and KIA aviators. The River Rats had flown with many of the missing and captured men. They helped mothers with chores and car maintenance, acted as surrogate fathers—taking sons to baseball games and providing academic scholarships. And they threw parties like this one to honor Washington, D.C.-area POW and MIA wives.

It was one of the rare nighttime social events Candy had been invited to since Chuck went missing. "Women didn't go out to dinner together. You didn't go out to a restaurant together. You really didn't.... It wasn't done."

Enthusiastically, she accepted and bought a new dress. Her parents agreed to babysit. Her escort arrived on time as she was feeding Hunter. At the door stood a tall and smiling naval officer dressed in a smart business suit: Navy Lt. Bob Ellis.

The two had met briefly at a wedding reception where Candy was charmed by Bob's genuine and kind demeanor. He had been so easy to talk to. On the drive to Bethesda for the River Rats party, their banter was lively once again. Like Chuck, Bob was a Naval Academy graduate and F-4 aviator. Unlike Chuck, he survived two deployments to Vietnam, with more than 200 combat missions under his belt. Now, he was a "detailer," determining duty assignments of fellow aviators. Bob had many missing friends, some captured. And like Candy, Bob was active in the POW and MIA campaign, attending rallies, press conferences, and meetings. He wanted to do something, even if he felt a bit helpless.

Other MIA wives at the River Rats dinner were escorted by married couples. Candy was accompanied by the only bachelor. A few months later, Bob called her, announcing, "I have two tickets to the musical *Cats*. Would you like go with me?"

Candy accepted wondering if this was a date. "'Oh boy,' I remember thinking, 'You don't need to add more problems to your life.'" But it was so nice to socialize with adults, and someone her own age. They dined at one of Bob's favorite pizza restaurants in downtown Washington, and once again, Candy was at ease. They talked and talked, full of subjects to discuss and debate. They had so much in common. And they laughed. It was an emotional outlet she had not allowed herself in a long time.

Despite the obvious attraction, the relationship remained platonic. Candy lingered in marital purgatory. She was technically a wife, as she had no confirmation that she was a widow.

That is, until the day before Thanksgiving, when she received a letter from COLIAFAM, the Committee of Liaison with Families of Servicemen Detained in North Vietnam: "In response to the request for information about your husband which we made in January, we have just received word that he was 'never detained in North Vietnam.'...We are sorry to be the bearers of this news."

Never detained in North Vietnam.

A few weeks later, a telegram arrived from Swedish Prime Minister Olof Palme, in response to an inquiry from Candy. "Referring to your inquiry about your husband Charles Parish I wish to convey to you the information given to me by the government of the Democratic Republic of Vietnam that he has never been captured in North Vietnam."

Never been captured.

Chuck was not a POW. He *must* have died when his plane plowed into the ground on July 25, 1968. It was the only reasonable explanation.

One year later, Rear Adm. Jim Scott at the Bureau of Naval Personnel gave Candy a heads up about a status hearing. In the absence of remains or an eyewitness account of his death, the presiding men will likely be reluctant to declare Chuck dead. It would mean the government would no longer search for him. It would end Candy's income. She would be a widow, her son fatherless. But how long should she be expected to live in limbo? She is twenty-six and has a long life ahead. Hunter needs a father. Bob Ellis is patiently waiting. Chuck is dead, she believes. Declare him so.

Most wives in her position do *not* want what she seeks. The war is still raging in Vietnam and there is no full accounting of the missing from the North Vietnamese. But Candy is resolute.

After the meeting, Admiral Scott calls Candy. "I'm sorry to tell you that there was just no uniform decision." Chuck will remain an MIA for the foreseeable future.

"It was a light bulb moment for me," Candy remembers. "Who's got *my* best interest? Or Hunter's? *Us*. The living, *the living's best interest*."

Candy vents her frustration with Admiral Scott. She wants to move on with her life. She and Bob Ellis want to marry. In a hushed yet authoritative tone, he advises, "I'm going to tell you what your father would tell you. Live with him. Don't marry him."

DIVERGING PATHS (APRIL–MAY 1971)

President Nixon is worried. Several hundred POW and MIA wives are losing faith in him. And they are receiving outsized attention—from the media, the North Vietnamese, and from millions of Americans. How can he keep them in his camp?

President Nixon's aide H. R. Haldeman writes in a memo that "we've got to be doubly sure we are keeping the POW wives in line." Sen. Robert Dole, the chairman of the Republican National Committee, describes the POW problem as a "tender-box [sic] that is about to explode..." And President Nixon's aide, the newly promoted Brig. Gen. James B. Hughes, admits that "there is a strong possibility that there will be a unified effort from within the families, which could include the National League of Families as an organization, to protest the Administration's policies in Southeast

Asia. At this point, I gather that it would be a dignified protest, but certainly one with great visibility and certainly with serious impact for the Administration." He advises "efforts...will be devoted to keeping the families on the reservation in order to buy us time."

It is too late. President Nixon ran for president in 1968 promising an end to the war. Three years later, he *has* brought home more than 365,000 American troops. But almost 200,000 remained on the ground, fighting in Southeast Asia, and several hundred men were dying every month. More than 1,400 Americans were missing or captive. The ones imprisoned for seven years were the longest-held captives in the nation's history.

In an Oval Office press conference on April 7, President Nixon tries to convince Americans that his war strategy is working and that setting a total troop withdrawal date is a bad idea: "If our goal is a total withdrawal of all our forces, why don't I announce a date now? For ending our involvement for the difficulty in making such an announcement to the American people is that I would also be making that announcement to the enemy, and it would serve the enemy's purpose and not our own. If the United States should announce that we will quit, regardless of what the enemy does, we would have thrown away our principal bargaining counter to win the release of American prisoners of war."

Valerie Kushner disagrees. Aggravated that the League focuses on advocating for better treatment for the men and third-party inspections of prisons, she caustically jokes that this will "let them rot in comfort." Instead, she believes the League should demand their release. She believed the organization should press President Nixon to announce a firm date when all troops will be home. He should do it now. Convinced that her president has been exploiting the popularity of the POW issue to *prolong* the war—not end it, she has been making a lot of noise in the media. The once tight bond among POW and MIA families is fraying.

In May 1971, Valerie forms a splinter group called POW/MIA Families for Immediate Release. Membership in this organization surges to 300 families. In response to this dissension, the National League reiterates its humanitarian and non-profit position: "When we incorporated, it was believed that broad appeal was more important to us than partisanship."

She and her cohort no longer support that stance. They embrace a more overtly political position and put pressure on the White House. The new organization declares, "The prisoners have become political hostages. We feel our government's obligation to the prisoners should take precedence over its obligation to the Government of South Vietnam."

President Nixon and Henry Kissinger worry about these increasingly direct and public exhortations. At President Nixon's behest, Kissinger has been meeting every other month with the leaders of the National League. President Nixon wants Kissinger to determine the women's next steps and gauge their mood. The president warns, "We must not let them go off on a tangent here." Kissinger agrees: "That's why we've got to keep that residual force thing alive."

A residual force: he is referring to a contingent of American troops on the ground in South Vietnam to help defend its government from collapsing and to "protect our withdrawal." Even more important to the American people, President Nixon has promised that, as long there are POWs still in Southeast Asia, some troops will remain in Vietnam. He wants to use the residual forces as a "bargaining counter."

At the same time, President Nixon urges Kissinger to rein in the women: "…they've got to not fight on one of these withdrawal programs or something like that, you see."

Kissinger is not concerned: "I don't think they will."

President Nixon is not convinced: "Well, don't be too sure. Remember everybody is working on them."

The president is right. Many people are convinced that America is fighting this war just to get prisoners back. Everyone *is* working on the wives, trying to co-opt them for their own purposes. Their husbands have a cult following. The POWs, a tiny fraction of the total American casualties, are upstaging the men fighting and dying on the front lines.

CHAPTER THIRTEEN

OUT OF LINE

CRYING FOUL (JANUARY 1972)

Wisconsin Democratic Rep. Les Aspin rises from his seat on the floor of the House of Representatives, indignant. He waves a letter from the national coordinator of the National League of Families, revealing plans to solicit donations from Republican National Committee donor lists. Quoting, Aspin reveals: "Most importantly, no one will know that we are using the lists owned by the Republican National Committee."

The congressman is alleging an all-too-cozy relationship between the Republican National Committee, the fundraising arm of the president's re-election campaign, and the National League. In fact, he is accusing the RNC of *taking over management* of the League and its fundraising.

Although the National League is *also* using Democratic National Committee donor lists, Aspin ignores this fact. He believes this is a "a Republican coverup hiding the link between the Republican National Committee and the League. The GOP took over the fundraising activities for the league secretly without any notification to the general membership of the organization.... It was no mere coincidence that the position of the Nixon Administration and the league were identical."

Is it a coincidence? Given the significant financial support the administration has provided to the League over the last year, the question is valid. While the American Legion has been giving the wives free office space, the White House is supplying a free telephone line to cover the costs of long-distance calls and free military flights to and from meetings and conferences in Washington, D.C. Vice President Agnew is donating royalties from sales of watches bearing his name. Then there is the matter of the $25 million campaign sponsored by the Advertising Council, endorsed by the White House.

The non-profit Ad Council agreed to secure free newspaper space for the League, as well as radio and television network airtime for a series of public service announcements urging Hanoi to open prison camps to third-party observers.

The League and the Red Cross intended to pay for production of the ads, which would cost $125,000, but a New York advertising agency offered to donate time spent working on the campaign.

Each of the ads would also state: "Of course, we all want the war to end, and the prisoners released as soon as possible, but meanwhile there is no need for even a day's delay by Hanoi and its allies for answering this plea."

The Ad Council planned to include an appeal for Americans to help fund advertisements where North Vietnamese leaders might see them. The president of the ad agency asserted that the campaign would *not* be political, saying "If I were a prisoner of war in North Vietnam behind barricades where nobody is allowed to see what is going on, I'd be pretty bitter if the American people and the advertising business couldn't lend a hand."

Valerie Kushner, no longer a Nixonette, protested the ads.

"We're all in favor of free inspections, and we certainly want humane treatment for our husbands," she stated. "But the issue now is not how the men are being treated in the prisons; the issue if that they're still there, some for eight years, and they want to come home."

Valerie and *her* legion of wives in the Families for Immediate Release were determined to stop this ad campaign *or* to secure their own. They complained to the Federal Communications Commission, requesting equal airtime for ads demanding the administration set a withdrawal date. Valerie's reasoning: "Since the other side has agreed to identify and release all the prisoners, not just to talk about releasing them, but to release them, if we'll set a withdrawal date, we believe all our attentions and all our energies should be devoted to that end."

The FCC complaint placed the television campaign on hold. The National League leadership was incensed. "We are very surprised and shocked that anyone could disagree with these ads, and intimate that anyone would condone even one day's delay in emptying the prisons in Southeast Asia."

All their hard work, they believe, was being "sabotaged" by Valerie.

THE WIVES COMPETE WITH NIXON (JANUARY 2, 1972)

Under the glare of intense studio lights, seven women stare soberly at television host Mike Wallace. The ladies will precede President Nixon on national television and are keenly aware this is their chance to deliver a message directly to their president.

Wallace asks them about President Nixon's recent bombing campaign near the Demilitarized Zone (DMZ). After a three-year pause, the president has ordered air strikes against a buildup of enemy forces north of the DMZ. Critics say it is a strategy to cover for the failing South Vietnamese regime and recent military setbacks.

Wallace solicits opinions from the women: "The bombing of the past week, has it been wise or unwise. Do you understand the necessity of it?"

Forthright Valerie states what she *really* thinks about the prolonged war in Vietnam. "Oh, I can understand the necessity for it from the viewpoint of the administration, yes, certainly.... The CIA has been kicked off the Plain of Jars, Phnom Penh is surrounded and threatened. The ARVN troops in Cambodia are being whipped and sent in retreat, so I can certainly understand the administration's necessity for it, yes. And the benefit that would accrue to the government of South Vietnam. What I don't understand is any benefit it brings to this country, to the fighting, to the American men in South Vietnam or to the prisoners of war. Certainly, to them it's the greatest harm, if by the minimum it's increasing their number."

Wallace presses on: "What you seem to say is that we really have no stake in the survival of the government of South Vietnam?"

"No, I don't think so," Valerie concedes. "I think our commitment should be certainly more to American men. I think that the bulk of the country would certainly support me in this. We've been there for ten years. We've more than fulfilled what we said we would do."

Wallace: "If Laos falls, Cambodia falls, if the government of South Vietnam falls, so be it?"

Valerie is fed up political machinations. The war should end, even if it means disagreeing with presidential policies on national television. At peace with her convictions, she confirms: "So be it."

Wallace turns to Carole Hanson, who is more aligned with President Nixon. She is against setting a troop withdrawal date. She explains: "I know it's difficult and I think it's especially difficult for the families in a war such as this, where there isn't any national resolve to the whole Vietnam conflict. Prisoners are a side effect of a war, whether we like it or not. It's always been that way. I'm not trying to minimize my husband at all, and I don't mean that. But I don't want the prisoner issue to be resolved at the expense of everything else. I just can't bring myself to look at it that way."

After more than seven years of conflict and three years of a troop drawdown, the prisoner issue seems to be the *only* reason America has more than 100,000 troops deployed to Southeast Asia.

After the broadcast, the president and Kissinger talk privately by phone. The president is scheduled to be interviewed later that evening by CBS's Dan Rather in a live Oval Office appearance. President Nixon and Kissinger are anxious about the women and the primetime publicity they garner. The two commiserate.

"I just got a note from [Patrick] Buchanan which bore out my hunch on that POW thing." Buchanan serves as President Nixon's advisor and opposition researcher. "Mike Wallace had POW wives on his program *60 Minutes* tonight, most of whom have turned against the administration." Nixon wants Kissinger to gauge the interview's impact and asks him to find out exactly how many wives feel the same way.

Thirty minutes later, the two convene again by phone, "...from the report, it sounds—these are the standard questions with which these ladies always begin. They always have the idea that if we only set a deadline [for troop withdrawal]," Kissinger whines.

Minutes before President Nixon begins his television appearance, Kissinger defends his efforts to keep the women from criticizing the administration. The wives believe the Nixon administration isn't doing enough, and he is powerless to corral them. Kissinger asserts, "I have in the past always been able to turn them around on it. I am in correspondence with the [National League's] board of directors and I was in correspondence with them as late as two weeks ago."

The president interrupts.

"This has nothing to do with that, Henry. This has to do with the relationship with the bombing, you see."

The wives have set the president on edge. "You see that's what [Wallace's] questions were about."

Kissinger: "Yeah…I'm just speaking about their general mood."

President Nixon: "…well you see that was before the bombing, and that's what Wallace was [gigging] 'em on…by reason of the bombing, that's gonna make them more intransigent…. You know the same thing on Laos, that kind of argument, you see."

Kissinger: "Yeah."

President Nixon: "And [they may get through] with some of them on that point." *They*—the antiwar movement, the media, and Congress—are getting through to the growing contingent of dissident POW and MIA wives. And President Nixon is having a hard time drowning out the resounding chant from them to set a date for withdrawal.

Kissinger feels the president can still appeal to and manipulate the women to see things his way: "Well, Mr. President… I think the average person doesn't understand what the details are. If they see a president who is dedicated to bringing [the POWs] back, he can make all these others look like cheap shot [artists]."

President Nixon hangs up. In his interview that evening with Dan Rather, he congratulates himself for significantly reducing the number of troops and casualties in Vietnam. "We brought 400,000 home…and we have reduced the casualties from 300 a month last week to one, to an average of less than 10 over the past three months."

Rather asks if American involvement in Southeast Asia will end by election day 1972. That will depend on one thing, President Nixon replies: "Our situation with regard to our POWs."

Rather asks the president to repeat his promise to end American involvement in the war in 1972. President Nixon dodges. "Can [the president] withdraw all of our forces as long as the enemy holds one American as a prisoner of war? The answer is no." On the hot seat, President Nixon reiterates, "We have gone the extra mile as far as the POWs are concerned."

JUMPIN' JOE (MAY 1972)

Joe McCain, brother of POW John McCain and Carol McCain's brother-in-law, is attending a specially convened meeting of the National League of Families. Tensions are high. Dissension among the women has reached a crescendo. They huddle in "caucuses" to consider pushing the League to abandon its humanitarian mission for an overtly political one.

Joe is indignant at a POW wife, who is introducing a resolution condemning the president's Vietnamization policy, calling it a failure. How unpatriotic—even treasonous—for a POW wife to criticize the president's war strategy. Always fiery and impulsive, he jumps on his chair and shouts, "That resolution is aiding and abetting the enemy!"

Ever hawkish on the Vietnam War, Joe is a caricature of his older brother—a sparkplug with a beard. Like his brother, Joe attended the Naval Academy, but dropped out after his plebe year, enlisting in the Navy as a sailor. After a short stint at sea, he became a newspaper reporter in San Diego; that career was also short-lived. Only his brother's captivity seems to keep him motivated. He has become a vocal and unorthodox advocate for him, sometimes over his family's objections. Does he feel constrained by his family name? "Fuck no."

Sybil Stockdale called Carol McCain, complaining about her lack of involvement in the National League. Maybe Sybil was unaware of Carol's full-time rehabilitation. Or she just wanted the daughter-in-law of the commander of the Pacific Fleet to lend her weighty last name to the efforts of the National League. Carol deadpanned, "Well, you have Joe."

Joe goes to great lengths to garner publicity for the POWs. He arranges to be photographed in a bamboo cage, dresses in a prison uniform, and eats pumpkin mash and watery rice. He organizes a cross-country Pony Express-style horseback ride where he collects letters from Americans addressed to members of Congress protesting Hanoi's treatment of the prisoners. And he rolls out 26 million signatures in a half-mile-long petition on the street in front of the North Vietnamese peace delegation's building in Paris.

He is not about to let a one POW wife, a dissenter, change the mission of the National League. Joe and the leadership of the National League win the day, voting down the resolution to abandon the League's original charter in favor of a more politically oriented organization. For now, at least, the National League will remain, officially, non-partisan.

POLITICAL PAWNS (JULY 12, 1972)

In the glare of spotlights and a haze of cigarette smoke, Valerie is undaunted by the cavernous hall crammed with throngs of boisterous supporters and delegates at the Democratic National Convention in the Miami Beach Convention Center.

Thousands are holding campaign signs and sporting straw hats. The room is filled with way more beards (with sideburns), blue jeans, and Black people than in 1968. Eight years into the Vietnam War and four years into Nixon's Vietnamization strategy, the crowd is decisively antiwar.

Launching into her well-rehearsed speech, Valerie seconds the nomination for U.S. president of South Dakota Sen. George McGovern. Reflecting on recent policy changes for her gender, she begins with thanks: "Mr. Chairman, fellow Democrats, my participation in this convention is a tribute to the reforms instituted by the Democratic Party. For I am a woman, and I am under thirty."

She continues: "But I also represent an even smaller minority group at this convention. The wives of Americans missing or imprisoned in Southeast Asia."

Valerie has commandeered the attention of the crowd and continues her poignant remarks.

"Although my husband was captured in 1967, I was not active during the 1968 presidential campaigns. During the primaries that year, I was working on another, more personal project. And besides, both candidates promised to end the war. I knew my husband would only be home when the war ended."

Valerie pauses for effect. "Well, it's the election year 1972 and the personal project that kept me out of the 1968 presidential primaries is now four years old. And he has never seen his father." She lets the meaning of her words sink in.

Valerie has lost all faith in President Nixon. She wants to do more than get the men better meals and better treatment. It is time to get them home. And the only way they will return, she believes, is if all U.S. forces are withdrawn from Southeast Asia. President Nixon contends that the only way to incentivize Hanoi to release the POWs is to continue to hit military targets in North Vietnam. Valerie disagrees. The president's relentless bombing campaign, she argues, is just producing more POWs. She trusts Senator McGovern will end the war immediately and bring the men home. That's why she has signed on to campaign for him, traveling from New Hampshire and Wisconsin to California and New York, while her in-laws watch her children.

Valerie tells the thousands of delegates and politicos in the room, and millions more watching on television, "I examined the Democratic candidates. And I examined them carefully. When *you* vote, you will vote for a better way of life. But when I vote, I am voting *with* a life. That of my husband."

Valerie has become ardently antiwar. When Ann Compton was a rookie reporter at a TV station in Roanoke, she traveled with the Virginia delegation to Miami in 1972. "To be totally supportive of our president would have been difficult," she remembers. "The fabric of our country was shredded over Vietnam." Now a veteran ABC News reporter, she recalls Valerie as "the best combination of being the vulnerable, caring wife and mother of children who didn't know him, and also someone who had a spine—who would speak up with focus."

Tonight, Valerie's focus is on getting Senator McGovern elected. As antiwar as she has become, she remains a patriotic American and believes Senator McGovern shares that value with her. "...Not once did I hear George McGovern use the rhetoric of fear. Instead, he spoke of the hopes and aspirations, those things we have in common which unite us. He used words like peace and justice and freedom and human dignity. And it was called the 'new politics.' But to me, a Virginia Democrat, those words didn't sound so very new. For we will celebrate in George McGovern's first term the 200th anniversary of their use by the founder of our party, Thomas Jefferson." The audience whistles and claps. Practically shrieking into the microphone to be heard above the din, she concludes in a throaty baritone: "And he was called a radical, too."

Valerie's transformation from military housewife and schoolteacher to partisan political firebrand is complete.

CLARK'S CHARADE (AUGUST 1972)

POW brother Bob Brudno is waiting patiently in the small, nondescript reception room of syndicated columnists Robert Novak and Rowland Evans. In his hands is a secret recording of a conversation between former attorney general Ramsey Clark and a small group of POW and MIA wives. He is a little nervous about what he is going to propose. But he has thought the options through. He is not one to make decisions hastily.

Bob is the younger brother of Air Force Capt. Alan Brudno, a POW for nearly seven years and one of the longer-held American captives. An MIT graduate, Alan aspired to be an astronaut and Bob has no doubt that, but for the war, he would have succeeded.

Tall and wiry with a scholarly demeanor, Bob is a former naval officer with an MBA from the Wharton School. But his primary cause is his brother's.

"I wasn't particularly close to him growing up." He has grown closer to Alan since he has been in Hanoi. "He was, like me, a veteran and, for that reason, I was walking in his shoes."

Bob has devoted a quarter of his life to his brother's plight and currently serves on the board of directors of the National League of Families. A prolific editorial and speech writer, his columns are published in many outlets, and he gives speeches lamenting the inhumane treatment of POWs. "I knew enough to fear that many of the POWs might not survive until the end of the war."

His parents and Alan's wife Debby have received only twenty letters in seven years. They are disturbing. In code, Alan describes torture and mistreatment: "fags on the skin," or cigarette burns, and extended periods of solitary confinement.

Clark, back from a two-week trip to Hanoi by way of Moscow, has been making headlines around the world refuting Alan's claims of torture. He believes Hanoi is treating the POWs well. Invited by the International Commission for Inquiries into United States War Crimes in Indochina, Clark jumped at the opportunity to see for himself the impact of America's war in Southeast Asia on the North Vietnamese people.

Many antiwar activists have visited Hanoi. But this was the first former senior government official to do so. Clark carried 102 letters, given to him by the State Department and addressed to American servicemen believed to be held by the Viet Cong. Clark was also given 300 letters addressed to men known to be held in Hanoi. Clark traveled alone, wandering the city and heading by Jeep deep into rural villages and provinces, speaking to villagers and government officials—anyone willing to talk to a tall Caucasian. Allowed the freedom to roam, he took copious notes and photos, documenting the impact of President Nixon's renewed bombing campaign begun in April 1972. Intended to counter Hanoi's Easter Offensive and to interrupt her supply lines south, Operation Linebacker I was the first continuous bombing effort since Operation Rolling Thunder ended in November 1968.

"Whole villages had been wiped off the earth," Clark witnessed. "There was no conceivable military significance in those villages, or, for that matter, in Hanoi. There are only people."

While there, Clark also met a handful of POWs. He had requested a meeting with at least fifty POWs, including a few who had been held the longest. His request was denied. But he was allowed to visit ten captives in one wing of a prison.

Driven late at night to the meeting, Clark and a radio reporter from ABC spent two hours with the men in what he called a "bull session." The prisoners told Clark about their detention, and he toured their cells. Clark gushed to them about the North Vietnamese people: their devotion to freedom and their just cause. One captive called President Nixon's bombing campaign "idiotic," and Clark replied, "If McGovern were elected, the war would end on the day he came into office.... There can be no question that the prisoners would be returned immediately." ABC recorded the entire meeting.

Clark emerged from his encounter convinced the men were in good health, good spirts, and being well-treated. "If you worry about their health, it's better than mine," he told reporters.

"And I'm a healthy man."

Clark's comments enrage the National League of Families. Statements like these threaten the lives of the POWs, they believe. Clark *must not* go unchallenged. However, before publicly rebuking Clark, they request a private meeting where they hope to convince him of the truth about POW treatment so that he will temper future statements. Unbeknownst to Clark, they record the conversation.

POW wife Bonnie Metzger, MIA wife Evie Grubb, and League volunteer Lou Stockstill sit across from Clark's desk in his wood-paneled office. He nods toward bags sitting on the floor next him.

They contain 112 letters addressed to families of POWs from the captives in Hanoi. They ask if they can look for a letter from Bonnie's husband. Clark refuses. "No, you can't. You'll have to wait until Cora Weiss's group distributes those letters. They are going directly to her first." Stunned by his icy reply and denial, tears run down Bonnie's face.

The group asks Clark about the ten POWs he met. They note that eight of the ten are recent captures, held less than a year. The other two are frequently trotted out for Hanoi press conferences. Evie asks: "How could you possibly have assessed, from those ten, the reality of the condition of the hundreds of other POWs in Hanoi? Why not include some of the ones who have been prisoners for seven years or more? ...Visitors to Hanoi like you and Miss [Jane] Fonda see and hear only what the North Vietnamese government *wants* you to see and hear."

Coldly, Clark insists that the ten men he met were not "showcase" prisoners. He lectures the women that they will not be successful if they offend the North Vietnamese. "You're going to have to think about their [Hanoi's] suffering."

Clark's visit to Hanoi received extensive media coverage. Americans only heard a thirty-minute excerpt of the ABC radio recording of his meeting in Hanoi with the POWs. They have no idea what Clark has said to the families. *Bob Brudno is going to change that*. He wants to expose Clark as a mouthpiece for the North Vietnamese.

Bob is under no illusion. He knows the POWs will not come home until the war is over. What he does *not* understand is what he calls "the near enemy," the antiwar activists who attack U.S. policy but leave the treatment of the POWs unchallenged. Calling for humane treatment and demanding to know who is alive and who is dead will not jeopardize antiwar efforts, he reasons.

Bob cannot understand why those who oppose the war cannot find a middle ground. "While you're all fighting over how to end the war, how about saying something about our boys? They're *our* boys. I respect your antiwar views, but these are still *our* boys." His brother, like all the rest of the servicemen sent to Vietnam, went *because their country asked them to go.*

Novak's syndicated weekly column, "Inside Report" from *The Washington Post,* has readers in 300 newspapers all over the country. Since his column launched in 1963, Novak has broken many national news stories. Bob wonders, would he be interested in the secret recording of Clark's meeting with the families? Through a mutual friend, Bob is introduced to Novak's secretary who arranges an appointment.

Novak greets him in an ill-fitted suit with suspenders. He smiles easily, his face framed by dark bushy eyebrows. They shake hands and walk back to Novak's office. Newspapers and sheets of paper are stacked everywhere, crowding the desk. Ignoring the mess, Bob makes his pitch: "If I can get my hands on the entire recording of Ramsey Clark's own words to the families, will you listen to it?" Without hesitation, Novak agrees.

Without telling anyone else on the board of directors of the National League, Bob and his wife, Sheila, set up two cassette recorders next to each other on their dining room table. They play the original tape on one and record on the other.

Bob arranges to have the copy sent via courier to Novak's vacation home, a three-hour drive from downtown Washington.

Novak listens to the *entire* two-hour meeting. Then, he composes a pointed column about Clark, published on September 11, 1972 in hundreds of newspapers around the country. In it, he lambasts Clark's treatment of the families. But he reserves most of his indignation for Clark's behavior in Hanoi, specifically his meeting with the selected group of POWs he met: "Simply put, the August 10 meeting was a charade, giving the dubious impression of American POWs splendidly treated by their captors and infuriated by U.S. war policies."

TAKING SIDES (OCTOBER 15, 1972)

Carole Hanson is jolted awake by the phone ringing next to her bed. It is 3:00 a.m. Who in the world? she wonders as she turns on the light. "Hello?" She tries not to sound groggy.

Carole is hoping to get a good night's sleep before a long and momentous day at the National League's annual convention. Chairman of the board of directors, the organization's leader and spokesperson, she is presiding over the meeting. And she is under lot of pressure.

The voice on the other end is familiar. It is one of Carole's reliable contacts at the Pentagon, but she is still surprised he is calling her in the middle of the night. The caller has an urgent question: "Do you think, if the president appears tomorrow night at your banquet…the families are going to make such a scene that it would be embarrassing to the president?"

Without hesitation, Carole puts her reputation on the line: "No, I think we as a group wouldn't do that. He is the commander-in-chief of our husbands. He is the president of the United States and I think I can assure you that he will be received the way he should be."

She may not be able to deliver on that promise. More than 700 fired-up family members are attending the three-day conference, ready to share their opinions about the intractable war. They know they have leverage: the release of their husbands is central to the outcome of the peace negotiations.

For that reason, *everyone* is trying to influence the wives. Carole does not want anyone or anything to divide them. The growing faction in favor of setting a withdrawal date is making her job harder.

Carole doesn't buy the argument that announcing a withdrawal date will force the release of POWs: "…where does there exist any insurance for an adequate solution to the prisoner problem by immediate and total withdrawal? With this approach we would have to rely upon the 'good faith' of Hanoi for the return and accounting of our men. Most prisoner-of-war families find it impossible to muster that kind of faith."

She also rejects the idea that the Nixon administration is using the National League. The women are not blindly allegiant to President Nixon. They have no choice but to support their president, she firmly asserts. He is their commander-in-chief, and *he* has the power to end the war and bring the men home. But the National League had a rancorous meeting four months ago and the White House is understandably worried that President Nixon will encounter hostility the next day.

With Carole's 3:00 a.m. reassurance that he will be warmly received, President Nixon *does* make the last-minute decision to go. He promises once again to bring home the POWs and account for all the MIAs. The audience gives their commander-in-chief a standing ovation and many ask to pose with him for photos.

The timing of the photo opportunity could not be better, demonstrating support for the president from a critically important constituency—the face of the Silent Majority—on the eve of the election. And it helps White House efforts to put a lid on the brewing Watergate scandal.

The break-in at the Democratic National Committee offices four months ago has become a spreading stain on the presidency. Blamed on a rogue group of "third-rate burglars," the scandal is creeping ever closer to the Oval Office with each new media revelation. Just days earlier, *The Washington Post* published yet another damaging article, uncovering evidence of massive political spying within President Nixon's re-election campaign.

President Nixon needs some good publicity, and his aide H. R. Haldeman is pleased with today's results. In his diary, he writes: "[The president] did the POW [event] wives at the last minute this morning. We ran it in because we had no story to counter the espionage/sabotage story.... He had a great reception, gave one of the best talks he's given."

Privately exasperated by the lack of progress on getting the latest peace settlement draft signed, President Nixon and Kissinger discuss options. The president says, "This is the thing you've got to keep in mind: What would the country think? [The American people] don't even care, except for the POWs." With far fewer casualties compared to previous years, President Nixon believes the country has lost significant interest in the war—*except* for the plight of the POWs languishing in Hanoi. Yet his concerns about the influence of the wives persists. "As far as the POW wives, that will escalate as [the POWs] do not come back, and will be a continuing, nagging problem."

In truth, he does not need to worry about the National League and its leadership. On the eve of his re-election bid, most of them are still solidly in his camp. Finishing her term as chairman of the board, Carole passes the gavel to POW wife Phyllis Galanti and then publicly endorses the president for re-election: "Mr. McGovern's proposals would dishonor this country and abandon the men like my husband to the mercy of an enemy that has shown no compassion. I don't want my husband's sacrifice to have been in vain."

BETRAYAL (OCTOBER 3, 1972)

Cora Weiss is alleging American espionage. Holding evidence so reporters can see, cameras click furiously. The photograph of an extra-large tube of toothpaste sent in a care package from Bob Brudno to his brother, POW Alan Brudno, is plain for all to see. Cora is indignant as she describes her discovery: "Here is a tube of Colgate toothpaste which I myself personally squeezed and found a silver foil container in it….And inside that little foil container was an apparatus for receiving messages." A radio receiver.

A longtime activist, Weiss is older and more traditional in appearance than the younger generation of protesting the war. In suits, high heels, and gloves, she protests, banging on the doors of the Pentagon and staging a "die-in" in New York City, where she lies down on the street with a sign on her chest inscribed with the names of Vietnamese dead.

She is also the daughter of Samuel Robin, founder of the Fabergé cosmetics and perfume company, is married to American lawyer Peter Weiss, and the mother of three children. Weiss is not often home to perform traditional housewife duties. But she has a housekeeper who can stay the night. For the past decade, she has dedicated herself to creating "a more sensible world." In 1961, she formed the Women's Strike for Peace, a group advocating the establishment of an atomic test-ban treaty. In 1969, she set her sights on President Nixon and his inability to end the Vietnam War. "None of the last three presidents have been able to stir up support for the war in Vietnam. Nixon thinks he's found the way." She believed he was using the POWs to prolong the war. "Mr. Nixon and his Pentagon have been beating the POW issue to death lately. But I don't believe they really care about the lives or welfare of the captured men. I believe they are only interested in using a big lie to focus hatred on the enemy. I think they are mostly concerned with creating propaganda."

She also has a problem with the sympathy the POW wives are generating for their men. She told *Look* magazine, "The women are going around as if their men had been kidnapped. They were caught in the act of bombing, and you can't expect to have them sent home with flowers.... The men are getting food and clothing and medicine. The Geneva Convention doesn't say they have to be comfortable."

She does agree, however, they should get mail. In 1969, in collaboration with Hanoi, Weiss helped found the Committee of Liaison with Families Detained in North Vietnam, or COLIAFAM, to establish a channel of communications between North Vietnam and families of American POWs. Under rules dictated by Hanoi, COLIAFAM allowed the families to send one letter each month and one package every other. Mail to and from the captives were *only* distributed by COLIAFAM. Announcing this new arrangement to families, COLIAFAM was clear on its stance: "The only way to secure the eventual release of prisoners is through the decision by the United States to end the war."

Members of COLIAFAM travel to Hanoi once a month, delivering and collecting mail. On Weiss's most recent visit, she escorted three American pilots on their journey home from Hanoi, after being released by the North Vietnamese. All had been held captive for less than one year. Where are the men who have been held for seven or more years? Where are the men captured in Laos?

While she was in Hanoi last month, the North Vietnamese complained to Weiss about spying devices they have confiscated from mail for the POWs. In addition to the radio receiver in the toothpaste, they showed her two pieces of cellulose paper with instructions for writing secret messages, hidden in a candy bar and a bar of soap, as well as a hollowed-out peanut shell, cans of Carnation milk and Maxwell House instant coffee. All contained secret messages and instructions to the American captives.

Weiss is livid. She cannot believe that families would endanger the welfare of their men and keep them from getting packages. "It looks to us an unmistakably professional job."

The Pentagon denies involvement: "The charges are too ridiculous to dignify by trying to address them in detail. I know of no instance of such actions taking place and I think it is just another of the propaganda web that Hanoi is spinning to obscure the real facts concerning her intransigent position in refusing to negotiate meaningfully for all our prisoners of war."

Bob Brudno also denies the charges of espionage: "My family would never take part in such a thing.... We mail the packages... they are sent to New York, shipped to Moscow, and transported to Hanoi. Conclude from that what you want."

Besides, he reasons, few of the packages he sends reach his brother. Most are returned, unopened. Some are pilfered. And, despite Weiss's claims that the Committee of Liaison is successfully delivering hundreds of letters from the men to families, the Brudnos have not received a letter from Alan in six months. The family has only received twenty letters in seven years. Yet Weiss never questions Hanoi's motives, only those of Americans.

Bob is admittedly horrified by the photograph. He had sent the toothpaste to his brother Alan. "I could see my handwriting on the package." It was one of a few interesting items the U.S. military has asked him to include in the monthly package he and his wife Sheila mailed to Alan. He sent the toothpaste tube, a can of candy, and boxer shorts, given to him by Sergeant Clinebell, the intelligence official at the small unit, the 1127th Field Activities Group, at Ft. Belvoir, where its personnel analyzed and deciphered encoded letters from POWs, along with reams of raw data collected by both the CIA and DIA. Clinebell occasionally showed up at the Brudno apartment and said, "Put this in your next package to Alan." Bob never asked questions.

Why would Weiss expose these devices? Does she feel the U.S. government is "cheating" by trying to secretly communicate with American POWs? It's puzzling, yet families have had no choice but to collaborate with her and COLIAFAM if they wanted the mail to flow. Hanoi won't release or accept mail from anyone else, and certainly not the U.S. government. As Weiss says, "...we were doing what the government couldn't do, and that was enormously embarrassing for them. That's when I discovered that embarrassment is a good form of diplomacy." Weiss considers her work a worthy public service for the men and their families. Some Americans agree.

The POWs view Weiss through a different lens. In a very long poem Alan Brudno composed in his head and later recorded for fifty-two minutes, he waxed on:

"From home a few came seeking truth (?) –
perhaps fame;
To themselves they brought shame in our eyes.
So naïve to be sure – yes, they got the cook's tour;
Most were fools for the lure of the Red lies.
Though our plight would remain,
and the Reds would maintain
Propaganda to quell world suspicions,
The wind carried straws to plead for our cause,
And to press them for better conditions."

CHAPTER FOURTEEN

REUNIONS

THE LIST (JANUARY 28, 1973)

Bundled up in coats and gloves, Bob Brudno and his wife Sheila wince as the winter wind whips their faces. They walk hand in hand from the National League offices to the Army and Navy Club in downtown Washington, D.C., the last block of a seemingly interminable journey. This is the day Bob has been anticipating for more than seven years. By his calculation, he has spent a quarter of his life working for this moment.

The Paris Peace Accords, ending America's engagement in Southeast Asia, were signed yesterday and the Pentagon has a list of 591 POWs the North Vietnamese will release in the next sixty days. Before publication, officials have invited area POW and MIA families to see the list privately.

Along with a dozen other family members who volunteer in the National League office, the Brudnos loiter in the club's dining room. They have time to kill. Full of nervous energy, they try to make jokes.

Guided to a conference room, they file in to view an extensive list of names, arranged alphabetically, taped onto the far wall. There it is: the name "Edward Alan Brudno." Bob smiles, running his finger over the sheet of paper. He steals a glance at Sheila and squeezes her hand. They savor the moment.

Behind them stand several wives who cannot find the names *they* came to see. The Brudnos drew the lucky ticket. Alan is on the list of men coming home. But they cannot exult in this room where families with whom Bob have worked shoulder to shoulder have just been crushed by sad news.

He remembers, "For us, we were close to the end. For them, it was just the beginning." Bob and his wife quietly and quickly duck out.

FREEWHEELING (FEBRUARY 25, 1973)

Emilee McCarthy is a ball of nervous energy as she waits for her turn at the phone. It seems like a game of musical chairs. As one person finishes, everyone inches one chair closer. If she leaves the room, she will lose her place in line. This is the only location at the university where she can make a long-distance phone call. "It wasn't easy. It seemed like a laborious task to try and make a very simple phone call."

Living in Cholula, Mexico, Emilee's husband is earning a graduate degree in pre-Columbian art. The Vietnam War is over. The POWs are coming home. She feels an urgency to reconnect with Jon Reynolds. She was engaged to him for nearly three years. But it has been seven and a half since she has heard his voice. She feels responsible for having broken his heart and not waited for him. *Will he talk to her?*

In a letter to his parents, he had said he was not angry with Emilee for breaking off their engagement and marrying someone else. "It was probably for the best."

While waiting, Emilee desultorily picks up an English-language newspaper and instantly recognizes a face on the front page. There is Jon, grinning at a press conference at Andrews Air Force Base in Maryland. She is transfixed and her heart starts pounding. Looking more closely, she notices a jagged scar on his left cheek and along his jawline. It has changed the shape of his face. She runs her finger over the photo.

Now it is her turn to make a phone call. All she has is a home number for Mr. and Mrs. Reynolds. She knows it by heart. Will the call go through? Will anyone be home? Will they hang up on her? Her eyes dart around the room and she notes, again, with a bit of irritation that there is no privacy. The other dozen people will hear every word. But she *must* try to reach Jon. Today.

He is her link to the life she left behind. What would her life be like if she were still waiting for him in Philadelphia?

After nearly five years with her artist husband, her domestic life has become tenuous. His mood swings are unpredictable. It was not always like this. Or maybe, she just had not noticed, swept up in the freedom of their lifestyle and the intensity of their shared passion for art. She is beginning to question the union. Thank goodness there are no children. "The pill saved me," she admits.

Jumping on a motorcycle, they had traveled almost 9,000 miles to get to Cholula—traversing the southern states, across the border in Texas, and all the way to southern Mexico and around the country. While the artist taught and attended classes, she was free to spend her days exploring the unique color palette of this historic place. On the outskirts of the city, perched on a great pyramid, was the carrot-colored Iglesia de Nuestra Señora de los Remedios sanctuary, framed by a massive snow-covered volcano in the distance. The town was fiercely proud of its daily parade of children in whitewashed robes honoring one patron saint or another, mercados selling fresh food on Wednesdays and Sundays with a rainbow assortment of fruits and vegetables, and a dense collection of gilded religious art in its fabled 365 Catholic churches.

But, back at their small apartment, evenings can be somber and depressing, especially when Emilee's husband is out of sorts. Without a job requiring her to punch in at 8:00 a.m., she finds herself looking in the mirror and asking, "What am I doing? How much longer can I go on like this?"

Emilee approaches the desk and hands the phone clerk a Philadelphia phone number. He dials the black rotary phone. She sits beside him, staring at the wall. Her mouth feels dry.

The clerk hands her the phone. It rings and rings. She glances over her shoulder. A booming voice bellows, "Hello!" It is Cyril Reynolds, Jon's father. Wistfully, she recalls how magnanimous he always was to her—to everyone, really. But how will he react now?

"Mr. Reynolds," she says tentatively. "This is Emilee."

She can almost hear him smiling. "Well, you know, Emilee," Cyril says in his usual warm and friendly tone. "We just arrived from Andrews where Jon has gone through his physical. And we've just driven back to Philadelphia. We've just walked in the door and the phone was ringing. And I'm glad I got it. And I will put Jon on."

Mr. Reynolds sounds so welcoming. Is he preparing her for something? What did the physical examination reveal? How damaged is Jon? Her heart races at the thought of the unknown, and of finally hearing Jon's voice. "I promise I won't keep him very long. I just wanted to say hello."

Then, "Hi, Emilee." She is startled. His voice sounds just like the Jon of 1965.

At first, the conversation is awkward. Emilee is unsure what Jon has endured mentally or physically. He says he is doing fine. A clumsy silence ensues.

Soon, they find their way toward easier and more familiar banter. It is almost as if *nothing* has changed between them. But, of course, a lot has. "And I had to face these consequences."

Her mind drifts back to her wedding plans, and so does their conversation. It is a comfortable topic, one they had often discussed. Jon reminds her that they never exchanged wedding gifts. The Mikimoto pearls he purchased for her in Japan. The Steuben glass crown for him. Succumbing to nostalgia, they agree to mail the gifts to one another.

What's next? Emilee asks. "I'm going to travel for a while and then transfer to San Antonio this summer to get re-qualified as a pilot," Jon says. "Let's keep in touch, okay?" Of course.

Emilee reluctantly ends the call. Her heart is still pounding. She holds onto the receiver, unwilling to relinquish it to the next person. She jots down one more familiar phone number, and hands it to the clerk. Her father answers and gets her mother on the phone, so the three of them can talk. "I knew *they* knew Jon was back." She tells them about the conversation with Jon. Hesitantly, "Maybe I should come home?"

HOMECOMINGS (FEBRUARY–APRIL 1973)

Rubbing the sleep from his eyes, eleven-year-old Patrick Stratton stares at the television with its rabbit ears antenna. It is 2:00 a.m. on March 4 in California, and the networks are reporting live from Clark Air Base in the Philippines, the first stop of the POWs' journey home from Hanoi. Patrick tries not to blink. He doesn't want to miss one second. The C-141 Starlifter touches down and taxis to a roped-off area near the flight line. A crowd of more than one thousand people is cheering and waving miniature American flags. Friends and fans of these POWs who have been held captive—some for more than eight years—can barely contain their excitement. Patrick is glued to the black and white images as a ramp is wheeled into place and a red carpet unrolled. A military color guard standing at attention forms a gauntlet at the base of the ramp.

Patrick's father, Dick Stratton, disappeared six years ago while flying his A-4E over the skies of North Vietnam. It has seemed so long since his mother opened *Life* magazine to the disturbing photo of his father in prison pajamas bowing to his captors. The Stratton Incident horrified his mother and the U.S. government. It confused and scared Patrick. But at least he knew his father was alive. Since his mother received a telegram on January 28, listing Dick as one of the returnees, Patrick has known his father will be coming home. But it didn't seem real. Until now.

Sitting next to Patrick is Tom Foy, godfather and surrogate father. Protectively, he pats the boy's shoulders. They have spent a full day on the slopes of Tahoe with Tom's older children and then a few sleepless hours waiting to see the live homecoming on television. Tom and Patrick lean in toward the TV as Dick Stratton emerges from the hatch, smiling broadly. He rushes down the ramp to salute the receiving line of American military officers. Though young, Patrick remembers his father well. Now he sees him, live on television. He tears up and smiles, too.

The Stratton family in Oakland, California in 1973, just after Dick's repatriation. (*Photo courtesy of the Stratton family.*)

Answering the phone in Coronado, Sybil Stockdale hears her husband's voice for the first time in seven years. She is apprehensive, told by military briefers that the longest-held group of POWs in American history might be hostile to those they loved. His familiar flat Midwestern accent melts away some of her anxiety. Three days after his release, on February 15, she and three of her sons are driven by U.S. Navy officials to Naval Air Station Miramar to greet Jim's plane.

As he descends onto the tarmac, the family notices that Jim is limping badly. His gait is awkward, and he is unable to bend one of his legs. His hair is still thick and white as snow. His eyes look sunken and his uniform hangs loosely on his thin frame. But he is home! As Jim approaches his family, Sybil grips Stanford's and Taylor's hands, and Jimmy squeezes her shoulders from behind. Sybil breaks free and embraces Jim with so much intensity that they nearly topple over. Sybil is grateful they remain upright with all the media in attendance.

That evening, fourth son Sidney joins the family for a steak dinner in Jim's suite at Balboa Naval Hospital. The Stockdales stare at one another trying to comprehend the new reality. Having six of them together will take some getting used to. Asked to say "grace" on behalf of his family, Jim breaks into tears. "Syb, I just can't do it. I'm so happy." After dinner, Jimmy drives his younger brothers home, while Sybil remains with her husband, savoring each moment. After popping open a bottle of champagne, the couple moves pillows and blankets to the plush carpet at the foot of their bed, where they passionately rekindle their relationship.

Andrea and Donald Rander's reunion on March 27, 1973, is complicated. For seventy-two months, she has been dreaming of Donald coming home to her and the girls. Those dreams did not include hordes of photographers capturing every second of the reunion. Nor did she expect to share the limelight with his ex-wife and two older children. She is incensed that they plan to join her to greet *her* husband at Valley Forge General Hospital. Who invited them? It is a sore subject because she and Donald rarely spoke about his first family. He told Andrea that "he would not have anything to do with them because that was the past and it should have no reflection on our marriage." So, what are they doing here today?

Andrea has other things on her mind. How will Donald look and feel? She was aghast at the sight of the gaunt and pale men on television stepping off the plane at stopovers on the way home. Would Donald act like a changed man?

She has nothing to worry about today. She is first in line to greet him, while everyone else waits. Andrea is thrilled when her husband takes her face into both his hands, looks into her eyes "with love, lust, and happiness," and plants a big wet kiss squarely on her lips.

The moment is captured by a photographer and published in newspapers around the country. It begins months of unrelenting attention and publicity for Donald and the other returnees. Andrea hopes the couple can be alone. She does not want to share her husband with all of America.

Feeling elated and victorious about his brother's homecoming, Bob Brudno also knows Alan's wife must be first in line to greet him. While he has been advocating for his brother for several years, Debby Brudno has not. She stopped sending monthly packages because it was too hard, she admitted. She taught school in Germany while he was held captive. Informed of his homecoming, Debby flatly tells Bob, "He needs to know the war was wrong." Bob is stunned. "No, he doesn't, and certainly not from you," Bob retorts. Debby hangs up on him.

In deference to Debby, Bob lets her greet Alan on the tarmac first, knowing his brother would want to reconnect with his wife before his sibling. But the marriage that Alan has mythologized in his mind does not match reality. Initially euphoric about being home, Alan's depression returns.

Page Rander, 6, Andrea Rander, and Lysa Rander, 11, sit in the waiting room on March 27, 1973, at Valley Forge General Hospital, Pennsylvania, minutes before a reunion with Army Sgt. Don Rander. (*Photo courtesy of Andrea Rander.*)

Don and Andrea Rander, with daughters Lysa (L) and Page (R), together again after more than five years of separation. (*Photo courtesy of Andrea Rander.*)

One week after his homecoming, Alan attempts suicide. Debby tells no one, probably knowing that his mental illness would impair his aspirations of returning to the cockpit to chase his long-sought dream of becoming an astronaut. Several returning POWs, aware of Alan's periods of deep depression while in captivity, try warning the Air Force about his mental state, urging medical intervention. But post-traumatic stress disorder, or PTSD, did not have a name in 1973. Alan, the brilliant resister in captivity, is good at deception. The Air Force sends him home to his wife, someone unschooled in mental illness.

Four months later, Alan's second suicide attempt is successful. Wounded but not killed in Vietnam, he bleeds out at home.

Bob Brudno giving a speech honoring his brother in their hometown of Quincy, Massachusetts in 2017. Alan's name is etched on the city's Vietnam Veterans Memorial Clock Tower, a monument that pays tribute to all the Quincy men lost in the Vietnam War. (*Photo courtesy of Bob Brudno.*)

Valerie Kushner was not expecting her husband to be released in the spring of 1973. When Richard Nixon was re-elected by a landslide in November of 1972, she was disheartened and discouraged.

She was convinced this meant her husband would be in captivity for at least another four years. President Nixon had promised to end the war when he ran for president back in 1968. Four years later, the POWs were still in Hanoi. She despaired. "I don't think Richard Nixon will end this war and I don't think he wants to end it on any terms except a good old military victory," she told a reporter, with obvious sarcasm.

After placing her life and her family's life on hold for five years, traveling around the world, testifying before Congress, picketing the White House, calling the media, and campaigning for months for McGovern, she was done. "This is the end point," she had vowed in November of 1972.

She told a reporter at the time that she planned to move with her daughter and son from Danville, Virginia, to Daytona Beach, Florida. And, while she had no plans to divorce Major Kushner, she said in the media interview that she was going to think about dating. "I'm not going to sit down and plan it out. When it's time for it to happen, I will permit it to happen rather than prevent it from happening." Perhaps it was a cynical and impulsive comment, made in the frustrating aftermath of McGovern's crushing defeat.

One thing she felt certain about: Hal was no closer to being released than he was four years ago.

But he was. Five months later, he is on a plane out of Hanoi. And at a press conference after his release, on April 3, 1973, Hal Kushner is asked if he was aware of his wife's political activities during the war.

Five-year-old Mike Kushner waves an American flag as thousands of residents of Danville, Virginia, greet his family at the city's homecoming celebration for his father, Maj. Hal Kushner, April 5, 1973. (*Photo courtesy of Toni Kushner Nee.*)

He waxes poetic: "…I said to her that her devotion, her loyalty, and her love were my sustenance and surcease. She is perhaps the major reason that I survived. When so many stronger and better trained men did not. And I would like to publicly right here and now, honor her, for her indefatigable efforts on my behalf."

Did Communists use Valerie's activities to force an antiwar statement out of him, reporters want to know?

Hal hedges a bit: "I'll have to refer you to my opening statement and I'm not going to accept any more questions in this regard. I think you're intelligent enough to understand that."

A reporter presses on, "You already said you received one letter from your wife."

Hal: "I did. I received one letter in September 1972."

The reporter insists: "But you're not aware...of your wife's activities?"

Hal gives in a little: "I was, alright. In 1971 I saw a copy of *The New York Times*. It had a little article by my wife."

Valerie had penned an editorial on Christmas Eve of that year, an unabashed call for an end to the war. It captured the despondence many of the wives were feeling. "Must have an end to this war. I see no end. I cannot rejoice in the birth of the son of God. My son has no father. This Christmas Day we celebrate the birth of a son to Mary. This Christmas Day some other mother's son will die in Vietnam. That death takes away all that was taught by Christ's birth."

Reporter: "Was this [article] used to pressure you to make statements of any kind?"

Hal: "It was used to pressure me, yes."

Valerie vows to Hal that her political days are over.

Carol McCain assembles her three children. "Your daddy is coming home. He is out. They cannot get him anymore." With their long hair and surfer looks, fourteen-year-old Doug and ten-year-old Andy cheer.

Six-year-old Sidney is confused. With no memories of her father, she has no concept of one. But she does know how to take care of pets, since she has a house full of them: dogs, cats, fish, birds, and gerbils. Wondering aloud to her mother, she asks: "Where will he sleep? And what will we feed him?"

Carol believes she has managed to keep the news of her accident from her husband for four years. After twenty-three operations to repair her shattered legs, she has relinquished the wheelchair, but the former model is on crutches and walks with a pronounced limp. And like Jim Stockdale, one of her legs no longer bends.

Carol braces herself for her phone call with John, where she tries to gently break the news. "I already know," he says. "I know you had an accident." A military official at Clark Air Base, charged with debriefing John, has unwittingly told him, "Carol's been doing fine since her accident."

"John, it was really bad. You might be upset when you see me." Carol learns her husband's humor is intact when he quips: "Well, you know, I don't look so good myself. It's fine."

Then she reveals another surprise, one that also might upset him. "Now the other thing is, the boys have long hair."

While many of the returned POWs and their families are celebrating the men's homecoming, others are facing more uncertain futures.

Carole Hanson is attending a star-studded concert hosted by Ross Perot, flanked by recent returnees and former Navy POWs Jim Bell and Jim Hickerson. They had heard Carole's January 1972 *60 Minutes* interview, where she had defended President Nixon's strategy to end the war. Bell and Hickerson liked what they heard and wanted to meet Carole. Both men are newly free, in more ways than one. Their wives left them while they were in captivity.

Four months earlier, Carole had received definitive news that Steve was not among the 591 men who survived the war. A month earlier, she had learned that Steve likely did not survive the firefight that took down the CH-46A helicopter he was piloting on that fateful day six years ago.

Marine Corps Lance Cpl. Frank Cius, who was with Steve on the covert cross-border "extraction" mission into Laos, gave her the answers. After more than five years in captivity, Frank was released, and Carole sought him out for his eyewitness account. He told her that after picking up U.S. Army Special Forces and South Vietnamese troops, their helicopter came under heavy enemy small arms fire, veered out of control, and crashed into the basin of a bomb crater, breaking in half. Steve emerged from the wreckage alive and wounded. But he returned to the helicopter to retrieve his carbine and was never seen again. Frank doubted he survived the ensuing barrage of gunfire.

It was hard to hear. Harder still was the news in the telegram from the Marine Corps: "I deeply regret to confirm that the status of your husband, Major Stephen P. Hanson, has been changed from missing in action to deceased."

Governor Reagan seemed as saddened as Carole. He had worn Steve's bracelet for years. The condolence letter she received was typed but signed in ink "Ron." Tenderly, he told her, "This noon Nancy dedicated a display case in the corridor of the Capitol, which will be a memorial to all the men who were prisoners and missing in action. She placed the bracelet I have been wearing in the case. I've worn it so long I feel as though I had a personal knowledge and friendship with Steve. For some strange reason I have a feeling without the bracelet on that I, too, shall miss him."

Without remains, Carole has no real closure. But she does not want to continue to live in purgatory. It is time to move on. When she tells her mother about the homecoming party Perot is hosting in Dallas, her mother urges Carole, "Go!"

Perot entertains more than 415 former POWs before the men and their guests are treated to an Air Force flyover and a concert with Bob Hope as MC. When Tony Orlando breaks into song at the Cotton Bowl, it elicits a range of emotions. Hearing him belt out "Tie a Yellow Ribbon 'Round the Ole Oak Tree," Carole tears up.

Jim Hickerson, next to her, is touched by her sadness amid so much celebration. He can relate. Carole is surprised when "Jim leaned over and gave me a little kiss on the cheek."

Art Mearns is still missing, not on a list of detainees and not on a list of returnees. "I found myself getting angry," Pat reveals. "But I was still hopeful." POW lists are often unreliable. "You know, they had been ever since Art was shot down," she says. Surely, there could be more names. Watching on television as her friends—women she has been working with for years—jump into the arms of their husbands, she remains stoic. "I was so happy for them and for the men who got home. But I cried a lot," Pat admits. Sometimes, the pain becomes overwhelming. "I found myself wondering why they had Art fly the same exact route each day. They were sitting ducks. The enemy was just waiting for his plane so they could shoot it down," she says, shaking her head. Steeling herself for formal notice of what she fears most, she maintains her vigil, watching the news and waiting for the telephone to ring.

On May 24, First Lady Pat Nixon has tea with the POW wives, enthusiastically expressing her admiration for their work. That night the President and the First Lady host 1,300 guests: the returnees, their wives, a few mothers, and celebrities for a dazzling celebration with dinner, speeches, live music, dancing, and performances on the White House lawn. POWs bask in the glow of appreciation from their commander-in-chief. In his spiffy tuxedo, President Nixon is all smiles. "As all of you know, this is the largest dinner held at the White House.... But I know I speak for all of the American people when I say that never has the White House been more proud than it is tonight because of the guests we have tonight." The guests look radiant, their applause resounding throughout the grounds.

The wives of the POWs stand in their ballgowns and white gloves, savoring the limelight. It has been four years since they forced their government to change its long-standing Quiet Diplomacy policy. Silent no more, they have built a national organization, publicized their plight with national media, lobbied Congress, beseeched foreign leaders, and stared down the North Vietnamese. Pliant no more, this small band of women made the successful release of their husbands the sole remaining objective of the Vietnam War and the men's homecoming a national celebration. Once shunned by their president, these ladies are now being lauded by him as national heroes.

PART III

The Long and Winding Road (1973 – present)

CHAPTER FIFTEEN

MYTHMAKING

INTO THE JUNGLE (JULY 1973)

The signing of the Paris Peace Accords on January 27, 1973, and the subsequent live television coverage of the release of the longest-held group of POWs in the nation's history six months ago lifted the collective mood in America. It was a celebratory moment for the nation, after an endless war. The returning POWs were feted with homecoming parades, lifetime passes to Major League Baseball games, free cars and vacations, keys issued by the mayors of their hometowns, and a celebrity-studded White House dinner. In contrast, other Vietnam veterans were greeted at American airports with derision, accused of being "baby killers," spit on by fellow citizens. Americans did not seem to care about their service and sacrifices. *The POWs are seemingly the only heroes of this unpopular and divisive war.*

While the returned POWs and their wives revel in the lavish celebration, the wives of the missing were only able to watch the White House gala on television. They were not invited to Mrs. Nixon's tea nor the president's star-studded dinner in May. Pat Mearns purses her lips, "It hurt like hell."

Joan, Lea Ann, Michael, Marian, John, and Charlie Shelton in Louisville, Kentucky, 1973. (*Photo courtesy of the Shelton family.*)

What *about* the missing men? They have not been accounted for, including Marian Shelton's husband, Air Force Capt. Charles Shelton, missing since 1965. Who is searching for him now that the United States has withdrawn all troops from Southeast Asia? Marian is.

In a small plane above Laos, she drinks in the peaceful scene below. Surveying the patchwork of muddy brown and beige rice paddies, she notices the landscape seems covered by a thin, glistening layer of moisture. In the distance, lush hillsides glimmer. As the aircraft glides northeast, hills give way to mountains—dense and dark, and the vast paddies shrink into tiny squares carved into the mountainsides.

The little plane is heading toward Sam Neua, a provincial town in northeastern Laos near the North Vietnam border. This is where

Charles Shelton disappeared eight years ago. She believes he might still be alive, here.

Marian has spent the last six weeks in Southeast Asia on a pilgrimage to find out. She is going to the spot where Charles vanished. The odyssey has led her to faraway places she never expected to see while growing up in rural Kentucky: Tokyo, Taipei, Phnom Penh, Saigon, Bangkok, and Vientiane. VIVA, the organization behind the wildly successful POW and MIA bracelet campaign, is sponsoring her trip. Gloria Coppin, the wealthy Los Angeles socialite chair of VIVA's national advisory committee since 1966, planned the route. The goal is to meet with as many Communist party heads as possible. The fate of Marian's missing husband lies somewhere in these jungles.

She is not alone. Trailing her every move is a reporter from a Louisville, Kentucky, newspaper, and Edgar Buell, an agricultural advisor for the U.S. Agency for International Development, or USAID. Marian hopes Buell can help her dig up something, anything, about what happened to her husband. Buell has been living among the Laotian people since 1961 and has become a fierce ally of the Hmong highlanders, resistance fighters backed by the CIA in their battle against the Communist Pathet Lao. Buell, who the Hmong call "Uncle Pop," is also working closely with the CIA's airline, Air America, which ferries supplies to the Hmong. He may be just the right person to uncover facts about the husband who disappeared on his 33rd birthday in April 1965.

The day he vanished, Charles was flying covert photo reconnaissance missions over the mountainous jungles of Laos. Marian was managing the home front on U.S. Air Force Base Kadena on the Japanese island of Okinawa, raising the couple's five rambunctious young children. She was blissfully unaware of the risks associated with the Laotian missions her husband flew. Known for her naiveté, she questioned little. That is, until her husband went missing.

Growing up, it was best not to ask too many questions until Marian's father sobered up. The family home in Owensboro, Kentucky, a small, predominantly white town nearly one hundred miles southwest of Louisville, was tense. Marian Vollman was the youngest of seven children—six girls and one boy—born to Carl and Mary Catherine Vollman, both Catholic. Carl was a sheet metal worker and Mary Catherine a homemaker. They lived in a small house, where the girls shared bedrooms and menstrual cycles. Owensboro was notoriously the site of the last public hanging in the United States when a young Black man convicted of raping an old white woman was executed in 1936, in front of 15,000 spectators. Besides that gruesome milestone, the town had little of note: it produced furniture, cars, and electric bulbs, and processed tobacco. After high school, most kids went to work at one of the local manufacturing plants and settled down. Marian was the rare resident who left.

Marian was just thirteen when she fell in love with Charles Shelton. The couple met on a tennis court. Their attraction was instant. A hillbilly who lived outside town in a home with no plumbing, Charles was also one of seven children. Unlike Marian, he was a Southern Baptist. Not particularly tall, his trim and sturdy frame—like a tree stump, some said—was topped with sandy blond hair, green eyes, a square jaw, and an easygoing and reassuring smile. Also blonde and green-eyed, with an almost cherubic smile, Marian could have been his sister. She was seventeen and pregnant when she married Charles, soon after graduating from high school. The first in his family to attend college, Charles was leaving Owensboro for the University of Evansville. Then, he would train to be an officer and an aviator in the U.S. Air Force. The life of a military wife was much more exciting and adventurous than a future in Owensboro.

Marian had lost her only brother Buddy during World War II. A Navy sailor, he died when his ship was sunk in the Pacific. His remains were never recovered. Marian claimed meeting and marrying Charles helped her get over the loss. But had she considered the risks of Charles's chosen career?

The Shelton family (before youngest Joan was born) at Shaw Air Force Base, South Carolina, circa 1960. (*Photo courtesy of the Shelton family.*)

The couple embraced itinerant military life. More than a decade later, after tours in Germany, South Carolina, Colorado, and Texas, Charles was a seasoned aviator, on his second deployment to Southeast Asia, rotating in and out of Udorn, Thailand, every thirty days.

Captain Shelton spent Easter of 1965 with his family in Okinawa. Nine days later he was flying the lead plane on an aerial mission, a single-seater RF-101C "Voodoo" reconnaissance jet that held up to six cameras in its nose and could fly at low altitudes. The assignment: to capture photos of the Communist Pathet Lao headquarters. Not an easy task, as they were warehoused in a jumble of massive caves near Sam Neua. Passing over the target, Charles descended to 3,000 feet. As he was lining up to snap his first shot, he was hit by ground fire.

Back on Okinawa, Marian was sipping a cocktail at the squadron commander's home expecting Charles to walk in the door to celebrate his birthday. While the adults drank, the kids were sent to play in a bedroom where nine-year-old Johnny Shelton and eight-year-old Michael were transfixed by an extensive and colorful vinyl album collection. Wandering toward the living room, ostensibly to find the bathroom, Johnny caught a glimpse of his mother, surrounded by guests, crying and shaking in her flowery mu-mu. Johnny's eyes widened as he watched them try to comfort his mother.

Captain Shelton was forced to eject from his plane. His wing man saw a good "chute" and an F-105 pilot rushing to assist with the rescue spied Shelton on a steep, sloping hill about thirty to forty yards from his parachute, which was caught in a tree. Search and rescue (SAR) helicopters picked up an intermittent signal from his beeper—a device worn by air crews that emits an electronic signal to rescuers. However, the signal was weak, the weather was bad, and the sun was sinking. Those factors made it difficult to pinpoint his exact location. SAR crews vowed to return in the morning when the weather improved.

Johnny ran to tell his four siblings that their dad's plane had been shot down. Twelve-year-old Lea Ann, the oldest of the five Shelton children, did not believe him. "I told him to *git out*! And then he came back in and was telling me some more.... So, I thought there must be something to this story. I went into the front room where Mama was, to get her word on it. I couldn't even get to her. She was covered up with people, handing her drinks. And pills." Everyone was consoling Marian, but no one thought to console her children.

A team was expected to rescue Charles before midnight Okinawa time, Marian was told. She believed it. She *had* to. She could not face the prospect of another family member lost in war.

SAR helicopter crews searched for several days. But Captain Shelton seemed to have been swallowed up by the jungles of Laos. He was never heard from again.

Hmong guerilla fighters working with the CIA reported that Charles was captured by the Pathet Lao and held in a warren of caves near Sam Neua. But the American ambassador to Laos, William Sullivan, was reticent to authorize rescue attempts. Sullivan was running a clandestine war for President Johnson in this nation he called a "landlocked, lousy little place." And, while he was concerned about the American captives, he did not want to strain his meager search and rescue resources. Even less did he want to expose the covert war he was running, he admitted. "...I am consciously jeopardizing entire Air America [CIA] operation in this country and am risking severe embarrassment to both U.S. and Lao governments."

Embarrassing the U.S. and Lao governments is of no concern *now,* in August of 1973. Marian wants answers. She is not afraid to speak out. Neither a diplomat nor an intelligence professional, she is serving in *both* roles. Stepping out of the small plane, Marian and her companions visit one of many small villages where Buell and USAID provide food and medical support to refugees. Then, they board a helicopter that whisks them to an even more remote location, the mountain valley of Houayxay, where Buell wants Marian to meet families who have emigrated from Sam Neua, the last place where her husband was seen alive.

Thick white clouds hang over the mountaintops as the Americans walk through the village. Banana trees droop over muddy roads as ducks wander aimlessly. Marian and Buell drop onto straw mats around a table at a village home, where they are served a hot corn whiskey, called "lau lau." Marian proffers her hosts a picture of Charles. Buell interprets. The women draw blanks. No one recognizes her husband, but they have seen Americans in the caves of Sam Neua as recently as last year. Do not give up searching, one woman tells Marian. If Charles is alive, he will be in those caves. Marian hands her a POW bracelet inscribed with her husband's name.

The meeting produces no leads but Marian refuses to give in to disappointment. "This has been the best thing on the whole trip," Marian admits. "Just to get up here and see what's happening. I knew Charles went down in a jungle, yet I had no idea what kind of jungle it was. I can see why they can't get him out."

THE TROUBLE WITH LAOS (1973–1975)

President Nixon sits rigidly, speech and notes in front of him, a bright yellow satin curtain behind him. It is March 29, 1973. This is the eleventh time in the past four years that he has addressed the American people from the Oval Office, live, about ending the Vietnam War. Tonight is different. An accord has been reached. He has achieved his "peace with honor." For the families of Vietnam soldiers, sailors, airmen, Marines, and POWs, American men are on their way home.

President Nixon has cleared his schedule to work on this speech, but the Watergate affair constantly interrupts his day. His chief of staff H. R. Haldeman has spent the week managing the barrage of meetings about the grand jury investigation into the growing scandal, yet today's news stories are full of words like "sabotage," "espionage," "obstruction of justice," and "cover up." The president's ambitious domestic and foreign agendas have been derailed.

Tonight, President Nixon hopes to get back on track. "For the first time in twelve years, no American military forces are in Vietnam. All of our American POWs are on their way home." He looks proud.

But all the men are *not* home. More than 1,300 men were still missing. Are they alive or dead? Of those, 350 who were lost or captured in Laos have never been heard from again. Between 100 to 300 men were alive at their last sighting. "Last known alive," like Charles Shelton. Military intelligence knows that he was held captive *at one point*. What happened to him? Marian and the other families with MIAs lost in Laos will have to seek answers on their own.

President Nixon admits that the job is not finished: "The provisions of the agreement requiring an accounting for all missing in action in Indochina, the provisions with regard to Laos and Cambodia, the provisions concerning infiltration from North Vietnam into South Vietnam have not been complied with…."

It might seem that the homecoming of 591 men—a fraction of the 2.7 million who fought in Vietnam—would not warrant a live, prime time announcement. But as Henry Kissinger said two decades later of the negotiations he led in Paris: "There was no other single objective as important to us as the POWs." The last 6,000 U.S. troops in Vietnam were instructed not to withdraw until the last C-141 Starlifter carrying the last group of American POWs have left Hanoi air space, to ensure the DRV held up their end of the bargain.

As President Nixon makes his announcement, the families of those still missing feel betrayed.

What about the MIAs, especially those in Laos? Kissinger had hoped to receive a list of forty or forty-one prisoners to be released from there. At this point, the Pentagon still believes "the [Lao Patriotic Front] may hold a number of unidentified U.S. POWs although we cannot accurately judge how many. The American embassy, Vientiane, agrees with this judgment."

The release of this list became tied to a unilateral promise from President Nixon to North Vietnamese Premier Pham Van Dong. Henry Kissinger delivered a letter from Nixon detailing the economic aid the United States was prepared to give North Vietnam under Article 21 of the Paris Peace Accords.

Article 21: "The United States anticipates that this Agreement will usher in an era of reconciliation with the Democratic Republic of Vietnam as with all the peoples of Indochina. In pursuance of its traditional policy, the United States will contribute to healing the wounds of war and to postwar reconstruction of the Democratic Republic of Vietnam and throughout Indochina."

What did the United States promise the DRV that will heal the "wounds of war"? Although Kissinger had said publicly that Congress would be consulted before any financial commitments are made to North Vietnam, and that the ongoing discussions of war reparations would be discussed only after the Paris Peace Accords were implemented, President Nixon secretly committed to $3.25 billion in reconstruction aid over five years. Kissinger was set to promise this in writing to Le Duc Tho on January 30, in exchange for a list of American POWs held in Laos.

The list of POWs held in Laos was not produced, so Kissinger refused to hand over the aid letter.

Two days later, on February 1, the list *was* handed to Kissinger. In return, he handed over the promise of massive aid. The linkage between the two was clear. Kissinger refused, even decades later, to accept this notion: "My major concern was not to have people go around saying we owed them reparations and to avoid any possibility of their linking this thing together…. It was something to reassure the ladies that I have been meeting with for several years, to tell them that the release of their husbands could not be held up on the basis of any of these positions."

The coveted list of Americans Kissinger received from the DRV was disappointing, containing only nine American names and one Canadian. When Americans learned of the paltry number of men being released from Laos, there was outrage.

"Where Are Our MIAs?" blared full page ads paid for by VIVA in more than 150 newspapers. Gloria Coppin was incensed: "We know with modern ejection methods there is a great chance of pilot and crew survival when a plane goes down. This figure…is ludicrous." She was convinced that the Communists were holding onto Americans as bargaining chips.

The National League of Families sent an urgent letter to the White House with grave concerns. "...our members have become increasingly alarmed that the other side might erroneously conclude that the lists will go unchallenged by the American people. We cannot allow this to happen, and our organization does not intend to keep silent indefinitely."

The Pentagon privately recommended a forceful, plain, and personal demand from the American ambassador to LPF representatives: release the remaining POWs and provide a full accounting of those who may have died. Failure to do so could result in punitive actions.

But there was no appetite in America for a resumption of military operations in Southeast Asia.

So, the White House and the Pentagon stuck to the talking points.

The Pentagon's point man on Operation Homecoming, Dr. Roger Shields, echoed President Nixon. "We have no indications at this time that there are any Americans alive in Indochina," he asserts. While the statement is technically true, Dr. Shields knows the question of the missing men in Laos can only be answered by the Pathet Lao or the North Vietnamese.

At his request, DIA prepared a situational analysis of the conundrum over the missing in Southeast Asia, and in Laos in particular. In it, intelligence analysts cited the facts: 982 U.S. aircraft have been lost in Laos since 1964. Since many of the crash sites are near the DMZ or in Hanoi-controlled territory, it was reasonable to assume that Hanoi could provide answers.

Hanoi has no intention of doing so. In September of 1973, Hanoi says no information on missing Americans or remains of servicemen will be provided to the United States until all provisions of the Paris Agreement are met. No reparations, no list, and no remains.

Congress conducts its first of many investigations. After fifteen months presiding over the House Select Committee on Missing

Persons in Southeast Asia, Mississippi Rep. G. V. "Sonny" Montgomery concludes in 1976: "No Americans are still being held alive as prisoners in Indochina, or elsewhere, as a result of the war in Indochina."

In the ensuing months and years, Vietnamese refugees fleeing Southeast Asia disagree. They report having seen many Americans in captivity, and recently.

The stories grow in number and elaboration after Saigon falls in April of 1975. They are chilling. A firsthand account from May 2, 1975, describes two gaunt men, one Caucasian and one Black, with their hands lashed behind their backs hunkered in a sampan silently sluicing through the muddy waters near the village of Xeo Ro in South Vietnam. Several months later, two more emaciated Americans are seen near the same village. Other refugees talk of bedraggled Americans begging for cigarettes, and a small group of Americans in chain gangs building roads or being moved around the jungles of Laos and Cambodia.

With the Vietnamese invasion of Cambodia in 1979, some 64,000 Vietnamese flee their homeland in the month of May alone. The U.S. government is overwhelmed interviewing thousands of these refugees. Some have haunting stories, eyewitness accounts of Caucasians in captivity. Can all these refugees be wrong?

MARIAN'S MEGAPHONE (FEBRUARY 9, 1974)

The board of directors of the National League of Families is eager to meet Kissinger. It has been nearly a year since Operation Homecoming brought 591 POWs home. The National League is now mostly populated with families of the missing. They are still looking for answers.

After being feted nationwide with homecoming parades and free vacations, and deluged with media interviews, the former POWs are settling into their lives as military men, husbands, fathers, and sons. For the families of *those* men, the battle is won. They have drifted away from the National League and its work as national and international activists.

For the families of the missing, the battle continues. And for Marian Shelton, these are desperate times. Watergate is consuming the Nixon presidency and hardly any attention is being given to the missing men. She believes her husband Charles is still alive. Desperate times call for desperate measures. Marian circles the White House in a rented Winnebago plastered in signs. They lambast President Nixon's inability to secure a full accounting of the missing. They request a meeting with him. Marian's daughters Lea Ann and Joan are with her. The trio sits in the jostling camper, driving around the White House for a week.

The stunt makes headlines in *The Washington Post* and creates headaches in the White House. Kissinger aide Frank Sieverts drafts talking points for his boss for the potentially contentious National League meeting. "There are some 'dissident' members on the board who advocate actions such as the 'vigil' at the White House January 27.... Although this demonstration was not organized by the League of Families, several of the board participated in it...and [they] will be present Saturday.... Most of the families you will see Saturday hope you will support their strong dedication to the search of the missing. A few...are working quietly to bring the League to an honorable conclusion soon."

Sieverts advises Kissinger to be realistic with the families: there is no evidence any Americans are held in Vietnam, and there is little chance Hanoi will provide the U.S. government with information about the missing. Continued pressure on Hanoi about the missing "may divert our energy from other important aspects of the Indochina situation."

Kissinger follows the talking points and is blunt with the families on that cold and bleak winter Saturday morning. He says he is "very pessimistic" that American prisoners are alive, left behind in North Vietnam. There is a possibility, "but a remote one," that

Americans are alive in Laos, Cambodia, or South Vietnam. To date, he says, the North Vietnamese have declined to comment on any of the "discrepancy cases." These are cases of missing men who were, at one point, known to be alive and in captivity, like Charles Shelton. He warns against more public awareness campaigns, hinting that the public pressure the League applied to the White House *during the war* is not welcome *now*. But "world conditions could change, and the League should be prepared to take advantage of any such changes."

CHAPTER SIXTEEN

DESPERATELY SEEKING ANSWERS

IN PURSUIT (DECEMBER 1980–MAY 1981)

In a darkened room, the analyst leans over the light table, squinting through a magnifying glass. He scrutinizes images of a compound near Nhommarath, in central Laos, under construction since April of 1978. It has been occupied only in the last month. The photographs have been captured by an SR-71 Blackbird spy plane or the new KH-11 satellite circling the earth.

They show what resembles a large detention camp, with twenty-five buildings and two guard towers, surrounded by a bamboo fence. The analyst jolts upright. The figures milling about the camp do not appear Asian. Their shadows appear taller than most Asians', and the tools lying around seem too long for use by Asians.

Even more peculiar is what looks to be the number "52" matted in the grass inside the compound. Nearby is what looks like the letter "K." Each symbol, stamped into the ground, is about six feet wide and ten feet high, and only visible from above. Curious, the analyst tracks the symbols each time he receives a new set of images from the reconnaissance plane or satellite. Over a two-month period, they appear four times.

Are the symbols a natural anomaly or are they manmade, he wonders? What do they mean? "K" is the standard distress signal

American air crews use when stranded. *Could it be that Americans are sending an S-O-S? And could "52" mean the camp holds a B-52 air crew? Or fifty-two men?*

The images are the latest intelligence suggesting Americans might be held against their will in Southeast Asia, and the most unusual. In the seven years since 591 American POWs came home, the Defense Intelligence Agency (DIA) has received more than 1,000 reports of Caucasian "live sightings" from refugees. Three hundred are alleged *first-hand*, eyewitness sightings of live American POWs.

Many of the reports are dismissed by authorities. "I don't have any confidence in them," says Rep. Sonny Montgomery, who has traveled to Vietnam twelve times in search of information on missing Americans. He and many intelligence officials believe refugees make false or exaggerated claims to U.S. government authorities to ensure passage to America. "They might have seen Americans, but they might have seen them in 1967 or 1968. They might have even seen me. It has really got the families stirred up."

Further stirring things up is Robert Garwood, a Marine who was captured in 1965, but who did not return in 1973 with the other POWs. In early 1979, he surfaces in a hotel bar in Hanoi. Approaching a diplomat, he passed a note that read, "I am an American. Are you interested?" He claims he had been held against his will in-country. Former POWs who were held with him, including Dr. Hal Kushner, tell a far different story. Garwood, they allege, collaborated with their captors, not living among the POWs in their jungle camp in South Vietnam, but with the guards. He changed allegiances. Carrying a weapon and wearing the uniform of the Viet Cong, he guarded American prisoners and interrogated them. Garwood is a traitor—not to be trusted nor believed, they say.

Garwood's return makes international news, and his case torments MIA families. How many other Garwoods are in Southeast Asia? Is he to be believed? He claims he saw at least fifteen American men in Vietnam since 1973, although his details are inconsistent.

He does not get a hero's welcome. Garwood is court martialed and convicted in February 1981 of collaboration with the enemy.

The intelligence from the compound at Nhommarath is different. And it coincides with the claims of a source close to the Communist leadership in Laos who says up to thirty Americans are there. In addition, in intercepted radio chatter, a top Laotian military leader is heard ordering American POWs moved to central Laos.

DIA director Lt. Gen. Eugene Tighe, Jr., finds the information convincing enough to suggest a covert rescue mission. White House National Security Advisor Richard Allen agrees. "Let's get it going," he says in March.

Following on the heels of President Jimmy Carter's disastrous Iranian hostage rescue attempt, Operation Eagle Claw or "Desert One," a year ago, President Reagan proceeds with caution, authorizing a reconnaissance mission only. A full-scale rescue operation is ruled out until better intelligence is obtained.

In March of 1981, thirteen Lao mercenaries financed and trained by the CIA travel through Thailand and across the Mekong Delta. They slip into Laos aiming to determine if the images taken high in the sky are of American prisoners. Soon discovered by Laotian army patrols, they are forced to retreat. On their second attempt, they spend more than a month traveling forty miles from the Thai border through the treacherous jungle to the camp perimeter, close enough for first-hand observation.

News of the mission, codenamed Operation Pocket Change, is leaked to *The Washington Post*. Defense Department officials negotiate with the newspaper and secure an embargo on the story until the CIA team returns from its clandestine mission.

The team lies in wait, peering at the compound through binoculars, studying the camp's activities and taking photos. No Americans or Caucasians are observed.

If the CIA recon team returns with solid confirmation that Americans are in the camp, a rescue operation will follow. Army Lt.

Col. Lewis "Bucky" Burruss, Jr., one of the original members of Delta Force, is charged with planning and leading it. A seasoned officer, Burruss served two combat tours in Vietnam alongside indigenous soldiers and participated in the ill-fated Iran raid last year.

A full-scale mock-up of the camp is to be built in the South Pacific. Burruss assembles a team at Ft. Bragg in North Carolina to begin training. But, he admits, "we never got overly excited because there was no actionable intelligence. The degree of planning was not very deep."

Finding no evidence of American POWs, the Pentagon gives *The Washington Post* permission to run with the story. *At least they tried.* Published on May 21, 1981, the article states that "*The Post* learned about the secret, officially backed mission into Laos before it was launched and agreed to withhold publishing the information as long as there was any chance of Americans being identified and rescued. Top officials have now firmly concluded that there are no Americans in the camp in Laos, defense officials said."

MIA families are at a loss, once again.

The only winner is President Reagan, who claims that the return of any POW and MIA from Southeast Asia is America's "highest national priority."

President Reagan has been a staunch ally of MIA families since his interest was piqued as governor of California. Carole and Steve Hanson's three-year-old son Todd captivated him at a meeting of POW and MIA wives.

"Twelve of us flew up there to see the governor and we decided to take our children," Carole remembers. In the governor's quarters with the press in attendance, Todd wandered from his seat to the head of the table and tugged at the governor's coattails. As the cameras zoomed in, he looked up at the governor and declared, "Governor Reagan, I have to go to the bathroom." The governor chuckled, excusing himself to escort Todd to the men's room. Upon returning, Todd tugged again and asked earnestly, "Governor

Reagan, will you bring my daddy home?" For years, Reagan wore Steve Hanson's bracelet.

It appears this mission is to show the families of the missing that President Reagan *cares*. They know he also scores political points. Operation Pocket Change is the only official post-war rescue operation ever considered.

THE OVER-THE-HILL GANG (MARCH 1981)

Carol Bates is awakened by a bullhorn. Dawn has barely broken outside of the sparse cinderblock dormitory room where she has slept at an empty cheerleading camp near Orlando, Florida. The former VIVA volunteer and one of the creators of the bracelet campaign is here with MIA sister Ann Mills-Griffiths to meet a team of former special forces operators training for a private POW rescue mission to Laos. This one is neither sanctioned nor sponsored by the U.S. government.

Ann's brother, Navy Lt. Cdr. James Mills, has been missing since September 21, 1966. His F-4 disappeared without a trace on a nighttime armed reconnaissance mission over North Vietnam. Ann's father served as the executive director of the National League until he became ill, and Ann took over in 1978, moving to Washington, D.C., from her native California. Acerbic and wickedly smart, the thrice-divorced mother of three and grandmother rattles even the most outspoken critics with her raspy smoker's voice and penetrating gaze. She is a pit bull with no limits on tenacity. No one questions her dedication. Finding POWs and MIAs is her life's work.

Ann and Carol, who is now working for Ann, have been sent to the camp by the director of DIA, Lieutenant General Tighe, to keep tabs on the group's leader, former Green Beret Army Lt. Col. James "Bo" Gritz. Gritz is convinced dozens of Americans are prisoners in the jungle compound near Nhommarath.

As Carol rubs her eyes and peers out the window, she spies Gritz leading some of his men in a calisthenics routine. Among the group gathered here in Florida are veterans of SOG—an elite special operations military unit used for highly classified and unconventional missions in Vietnam, a Medal of Honor recipient, a Son Tay raider, a hypnotherapist, a psychic from Los Angeles, and Carol and Ann. A slew of reporters tags along, including one from *The Washington Post,* two from the *Orlando Sentinel-Star,* and two from ABC-TV News. Media have agreed to hold their reports until the mission is completed.

The oddball team assembles for a pep talk from Gritz. A trim, compact man with slicked-back hair who looks fit enough for duty, Gritz is a highly decorated combat veteran with charisma enough to charm even the most skeptical critics. Having served in the Army for twenty-two years, including four in Vietnam, Gritz is dedicated to rescuing American POWs he believes were left behind in Southeast Asia.

He claims the DIA's deputy director ordered him to retire from the Army in 1979 and take on this mission as a private citizen. In a memo of questionable authenticity that was kept under wraps until 1984, Army Gen. Harold Aaron writes: "…It is too bad we have to proceed this way, but the Administration will not face up to the problem.…Keep your government contacts limited to those with an absolute need to know." Gritz's rescue attempts will be paramilitary and privately funded. General Aaron is also clear that Gritz's chain of command in this clandestine mission must not be revealed: "This thing is so sensitive it could result in a real inquisition if word leaked out that we were proceeding unofficially." In addition to General Aaron's directive, Gritz also claims that businessman Ross Perot has encouraged him on these missions.

At today's meeting, Gritz tries to inspire the assembled team members: "I have been picked by God to rescue the POWs and you are my disciples."

Gritz has seen the DIA overhead images of the prison camp, he says, but will not produce them for the team. He proffers no large-scale maps of the region. Instead, the psychic from Los Angeles conjures a drawing of the prison.

The psychic closes her eyes and explains what she sees in her mind: a compound surrounded by barbed wire with a building in the center. Under the building is a tunnel that holds a group of cells. Each cell door has a dog tag affixed to it, to identify the occupant. She claims the POWs spend their days in the nearby jungle, digging up bamboo.

Her map will be their navigational guide.

Gritz says he has lined up interesting equipment, including an AR-180, a silent machine gun with a laser to pinpoint the target. It supposedly can cut a car in half. The "probe-eye," an infrared optical system, can discriminate between human and animal forms, and between armed and unarmed men. Finally, there are the "inflatoplanes," 250-pound neoprene-rubber airplanes, with a hand-cranked drone engine, which fit into a fifty-five-gallon drum. Inflated with a compressed air bottle or a generator, they can carry two people 250 miles and sustain seven bullet holes before losing air. The only problem is Gritz has no plan to get this state-of-the-art equipment to Laos, along with radios and other necessary weapons—other than vague references to a media crew smuggling them in.

The scheme to rescue the POWs is complicated. Led by members of the Lao resistance, Gritz and his band plan to cross into Laos on foot to the location he calls Fort Apache, where he believes twenty-nine or thirty American men are being held.

Gritz envisions a small reconnaissance unit advancing on the compound 200 to 300 meters ahead of the assault team of eight to ten Americans, plus up to ten Laotians. They will find the POWs. Then the plan grows even more convoluted.

Gritz will radio team members at a base station in a Bangkok hotel. They will call Ann, who will be standing by in Washington.

Ann will call high-level contacts at DIA and request helicopters be sent from ships in the Seventh Fleet that are reportedly seven days away from the operating area. The helicopters will hoist up the POWs and bring them home. Gritz envisions a celebratory parade on Fifth Avenue.

What if they are caught? Gritz says he will issue cyanide tablets, wired to their teeth—so all they have to do is bite down. That's right: if captured, the entire team is expected to commit suicide.

Gritz's cloak-and-dagger scheme stretches credulity. But his wartime credentials are bona fide, enough to convince many to go along. MIA family members, like Ann, are allies—for now. As she says more than a decade later, "To the vulnerable people we were at the time, and to the uninformed populace, Gritz can be very persuasive."

But Ann and Carol are livid at the presence of reporters and disillusioned with the motley crew Gritz has assembled. They don't seem able to mount a serious effort. Heavy-hearted, they catch a plane back to Washington. One of the ABC reporters, calling the group an "over-the-hill gang," also departs.

Gritz estimates the mission could cost upwards of $250,000. All funding will come from the private sector, he boasts. Federal Express founder Fred Smith and other major corporate benefactors are rumored to be providing money for the mission. MIA families also contribute $30,000.

In reality, Gritz is having trouble securing enough cash, putting the mission in peril. Then, the *Sentinel Star* reporters break the embargo with a story that runs on March 26 in the *Chicago Tribune* that owns the *Sentinel Star*. Gritz and his group vacate the cheerleading academy and scatter like cockroaches.

In the article, Gritz defends the mission, saying that he has the blessing of POW/MIA families because "even if one came out alive, it would be worth it."

The operation cancelled, Gritz is undeterred. He sends a reconnaissance team to Thailand six months later. This attempt, dubbed Operation Grand Eagle, will prepare ground reconnaissance units for a rescue operation later that winter. Gritz recruits a mercurial figure who makes wild claims about his background, expertise, and contacts. His name is Scott Barnes.

THE "MYSTERY BOX" (OCTOBER 1981)

"We had come up on a knoll and started unpacking the apparatus and then looked down. There, in fact, was, cut basically in a jungle clearing, a detainee camp." Scott Barnes made this wild claim to a congressional investigation a decade later.

It is broad daylight, but Barnes and Mike Baldwin are well hidden in thick shrubs at the top of a mountain in central Laos. For the past few days, they have been bushwhacking through dense forest, brush, swamps, and creeks with Laotian indigenous forces, trying to avoid detection by Communist soldiers.

Barnes has broken away from Gritz's mission, to which he was invited, after telling Gritz that Gen. Vang Pao, a former Lao Army general living in exile in the United States, was a good friend who would vouch for him.

Upon arriving in Thailand to join Gritz, Barnes embarks on his own, separate, reconnaissance mission with Baldwin, who regales Barnes with tales that two admirals from Washington have ordered him to find American POWs.

Youthful and affable, Barnes sports a beard, a Gilligan-style boat hat—soft and floppy, and a slight paunch. He is not the stereotypical chiseled, weathered special operator. But he seems to know *just enough* about clandestine operations, mixing fact and fiction seamlessly, to make it difficult to discern the truth.

As he unspooled his yarn years later, Barnes claimed that from his hideaway in the shrubs, he and Baldwin spied on a triangular camp with several guard towers not much higher than the perimeter fence.

They unpack waterproof cameras with long lenses, a tripod, and a listening device that looks like a satellite dish mounted on a small stand, connected to a battery pack and a recorder. With this gear, they look and listen…and spot two Caucasians! The men are being escorted from one side of the camp to the other. They are thin, balding, and dirty, according to Barnes, "the worst condition of a living human that was still alive that I've ever seen, and I've been in a lot of places and I've never seen anybody that looks physically in that bad a condition, that was alive. It was sad."

As they watch the two captives, a guard strikes one of the POWs in the elbow with the butt of a gun and the prisoner reacts angrily, "Shit, you mother fucker!"

They are Americans!

Barnes grew emotional, as he recalled the sight to congressional investigators: "I cried, I mean, I really did. It was a very upsetting situation and I said, 'I can't believe we would leave them behind.'"

Barnes and Baldwin take hundreds of photographs of the two captives. They must get these to U.S. government officials ASAP. They retreat, trekking through the jungle for two days, crossing the Mekong River in a sampan, where a waiting vehicle takes Barnes on the final leg of the adventure: to the post office.

As instructed by Baldwin, Barnes wraps the precious rolls of film in a shoebox and mails them—without a return address, to a CIA handler in Vienna, Virginia.

Back at his hotel, he reconnects with Gritz team members who wonder where he has been. They hand him a "telex" from the Department of Energy. Decoded, it says that Colonel Gritz has been fired from the mission, as he can no longer be trusted. Most disturbing, it says that "If merchandise confirmed, liquidate."

Barnes is dumbfounded. "Merchandise" refers to POWs. "Liquidate" means destroy. What? Is he being ordered to kill the two POWs he has just discovered? “No way!” Although he is exhausted, Barnes is fired up. “Is this a setup? What’s going on? I’ll have no part in this!”

The others shout at him. An order is an order. A scuffle ensues and someone punches Barnes in the face. Now fearing for *his* life, Barnes hightails it back to the United States.

Gritz and others on the trip say Barnes’s story is a fairy tale. He did go to Thailand with the team, but their Lao contact did not show up, the mission was called off, and everyone went home. Barnes did not trek into Laos, and he did not photograph POWs. It never happened.

Gritz regrets inviting Barnes, who is, in his opinion, a fraud and a fake. He calls him “would-be do-gooder, who brings a new dimension to the term Walter Mitty.”

This is but one of many tales Barnes has spun. Over the years, he has claimed to be a former Green Beret, Navy SEAL, military intelligence analyst, and on the CIA’s payroll. In truth, Barnes only served three years stateside in the Army. He dodges queries by claiming that his military records were mysteriously altered.

He fooled many people. For a while. Peter Jennings fell for him. Ross Perot did, too. Ted Koppel and Jack Anderson did not. Marian Shelton was a lamb to the slaughter. She mortgaged her home to help pay his bills.

CHAPTER SEVENTEEN

TURNING A CAUSE INTO A PROFESSION

THE RISE OF ANN MILLS-GRIFFITHS (SEPTEMBER 1982)

It's a steep climb up a massive stone bluff. Ann Mills-Griffiths is laboring, but undaunted. She has waited a long time to reach this limestone cave, one of more than 480 connected chambers in the cliffs of Viengxay near Sam Neua. This mammoth, labyrinthine city hid housing, a school, a hospital, offices, and even a theater. During the war, it headquartered the Communist Pathet Lao. And, according to Ann's Laotian escorts, it was also the prison that held several American POWs captured in Laos.

The dank, humid cave beckons Ann and the others: an MIA wife and two MIA fathers. The first room is spacious: twelve to fifteen feet wide with a fifteen- to twenty-foot ceiling. Cement reinforces the floor. POWs lived here, in this space, say the Laotian escorts. Off to the left is a concrete structure, a water supply, they explain. The back of the cave opens into a second area, half the size of the first. Visitors must duck to enter. There, it is darker, damper, more dismal. Water drips, drips, drips.

Hunching in the murk of the cave on this steamy September day in 1982 is the first group of Americans escorted by Laotian officials into these caves, where American POWs were last known to be alive. Some, like Charles Shelton, have been unaccounted for since 1965—seventeen years. Shelton is the only missing man officially listed as a POW, a symbolic gesture made by President Reagan to show his resolve and dedication to the issue.

Ann has been instrumental in making this trip happen. She and the National League initiated it. Executive director of the National League of Families, Ann's star power has risen during the presidency of Ronald Reagan. The president's national security and diplomatic advisors consider her the expert on the issue of missing men from the Vietnam War. The National League, and Ann specifically, has a seat on a high-level POW/MIA governmental committee. Her security clearance gives her access to all classified intelligence the government collects on the missing men. She is the only non-government member with both. She is on a first-name basis with admirals, generals, diplomats, and the president's national security advisor. When Ann calls, the Pentagon, the State Department, and the White House pick up.

Peering into the gloomy interior, Ann notices a slit in the wall, beyond which is a staircase. She motions to one of her companions and, before their Laotian escorts can rush them back outside, the two women slip through the wall and dart up the stairs, hoping to find clues of Americans' presence. Climbing along an angular crevice, they reach the top of the stairs and enter another large room that looks more like a vault. Wiring dangles, so they assume the space was a communications center. But nothing indicates Americans lived there.

Outside the cave, the Americans press their official Laotian host, Col. Khamla Keophitoune. Was Charles Shelton held captive in this cave? Glancing at a folded piece of paper he pulls from his pocket, he says, "That sounds like it." He claims Charles and Air Force Capt. David Hrdlicka died of malnutrition in 1968 and are buried nearby. The colonel guides the group a short distance. He points to a large bomb crater, now a pond filled with murky water. American bombs destroyed the men's graves and killed a witness to their burial, he says. Truth or propaganda?

The State Department calls the trip a "major breakthrough." It is the first time representatives from the Lao People's Democratic Republic and the United States have discussed the fate of American men lost in Laos during the Vietnam War. Professional diplomats did not make it happen. Family of the missing did. Once again.

THE REAL RAMBO (OCTOBER–NOVEMBER 1982)

Despite mixed reviews, an unsettling movie about a Vietnam veteran is a smash hit at the box office. The hero is a despondent drifter on a walkabout to visit war buddies. Released less than a decade after the end of the war, *Rambo*: *First Blood* plays on every stereotype of the Vietnam veteran: disturbed, misunderstood, violent. Sylvester Stallone cements his fame as John Rambo, former Green Beret, POW, *and* a Medal of Honor recipient, an unlikely combination only seen in Hollywood fantasies.

Rambo's propensity for violence persists throughout the film. Perhaps it is an indication that he is suffering from PTSD at a time when the term is not commonly used and not well understood.

The sequel, *First Blood II,* released three years later in 1982, mirrors real life: a POW rescue mission. Rambo, out of prison, is recruited by his old Army commander to embark on a Southeast Asian adventure, sanctioned by the U.S. government, to retrieve a small group of POWs in enemy hands.

While Stallone enthralls moviegoers, the "real Rambo," Lt. Col. Bo Gritz, is trying once again to get into Laos to retrieve American missing men. He dubs this latest attempt Operation Lazarus, for the biblical character Jesus raises from the dead.

This time, Gritz is sure the mission will succeed. He has congressional support from Bob Dornan, now U.S. representative from California. "I told Gritz I would bring this up with President Reagan, which I did December 27 [1981] aboard Air Force 1. But I didn't talk to Reagan about anything specific. I told the president I didn't want him to lose interest in the POWs and he assured me he wouldn't."

Gritz also has financial backing from Hollywood. William Shatner has paid him $10,000 for movie rights. Clint Eastwood has given him $30,000 and promised a meeting with President Reagan at his Santa Barbara ranch if Gritz locates missing soldiers. Gritz believes this "back door" channel to the president will ensure safe evacuation of American POWs.

Once again, Gritz is planning to bring sophisticated electronics equipment and weapons. He expects to pick up 400 to 500 Lao guerillas, enough manpower—in his opinion—to start a small war and more than adequate to rescue a few Americans.

Looking like a movie star soldier, Gritz brandishes an Uzi submachine gun as he stands on the edge of the Mekong River wearing night vision goggles, carrying a rucksack. With a rousing cheer, Gritz orders his fifteen commandos aboard rocking sampans to cross the mile-wide murky river: "It's a good night to die. Fuck it. Let's go!"

It's not exactly George Washington crossing the Delaware.

Disembarking on the Laotian side, the group treks southward and then east, struggling under their heavy load in the dense jungle terrain. They hump at night, and rest during the day. On the third day, they are ambushed from behind. As rounds of fire come at them, they scatter, hightailing it back to the Mekong River. But there are no boats. They must swim. The swift current flings them back on the Thai side, several miles downstream. The men crawl out of the river far apart.

One by one, the team retreats to Bangkok. Mission aborted. Again. This time, Gritz is arrested by Thai authorities and put on trial for illegal possession of high-powered radio equipment and given a suspended sentence.

Gritz's cross-border adventures generate earfuls of complaints for U.S. diplomats meeting with Laotian government representatives on the POW/MIA issue in Vientiane. Colonel Keophitoune warns, "If you continue to send Green Berets into Laos and at that time we arrest them then our talks will become extremely difficult. If the Green Berets are captured by us, they will be considered as 'war criminals.'" U.S. officials assure him that the U.S. government has not sent Green Berets and has neither supported nor condoned this activity. Colonel Keophitoune shakes his head and asks, "Why can't the U.S. government do something about this fellow?"

Undeterred, Gritz is already planning his next rescue. This one will be Operation Lazarus Alpha. "If I and my people don't do it, I don't know anyone in Washington who will. It takes action, and both Teddy Roosevelt and John Wayne are dead."

MINDSET TO DEBUNK (SUMMER 1985)

Tom Brooks, newly minted Navy rear admiral, arrives at the Pentagon in June. A career intelligence officer, Brooks has spent more than two decades in the profession—including a tour in Vietnam as commanding officer of a Naval Investigative Service unit from 1969 to 1970. Then, he investigated sailors and Marines accused of criminal activity. Now, he is tasked with finding the missing.

Director of collection management for the DIA, he is given a second, part-time assignment to run the agency's office dedicated to the POW and MIA issue. He is told the office team basically "runs itself" and little supervision is needed.

Rear Admiral Brooks is surprised at the three small, windowless rooms buried in the inner rings of the Pentagon. No wonder Carol Bates, now one of twelve analysts working at desks so jammed together that the chairs knock against one another, calls it the "rabbit warren." Under harsh fluorescent lights, Carol and her co-workers mostly work by hand. When she asks for a typewriter, she is issued a 1960 IBM. At least it is electric. There is one 1970s-era punched card sorter to store and process information. Old maps and charts and notes are thumbtacked to the walls.

Brooks is taken aback.

The disarray is stunning. Basic analytic procedures—intelligence collection 101—are not being followed. Files are sloppy, incomplete, and mixed up. Activity logs are incomplete and outdated. Requested, indeed required, follow-ups take years to complete. There is not enough staff and existing analysts spend an inordinate amount of time responding to congressional and public inquiries.

The U.S. government is not walking the talk. President Reagan repeats publicly that the POW and MIA issue is of the highest national priority. Brooks feels the claim is disingenuous at best and an outright lie at worst.

Most disturbing is that he senses a collective bias of doubt among the analysts. Thousands of reports of live sightings have deluged the office in the last decade. After years of chasing down bogus claims, the analysts have a "mindset to debunk."

He drafts a memo to his boss, Army Brig. Gen. James Shufelt: "I'm afraid we are in for some troubled times. We have not done our job as well as we should have in days past, and we will not withstand scrutiny very well."

The memo, intended for one set of eyes, is leaked to the press in 1992 and the "mindset to debunk" becomes a rallying cry for the families of the missing.

LOOSE CANNON (MAY 6, 1987)

Ross Perot is crestfallen. The Oval Office is full of people. He was expecting a private meeting with the president to report on his recent trip to Hanoi and give his recommendations.

A man of tremendous financial resources with bold and unconventional ideas to break through the paralysis he feels plagues the government surrounding American hostages overseas, Perot is putting his money and ingenuity to work for the Reagan administration. A Marxist terrorist group kidnaps an Army general in Italy in 1981: Perot sends $500,000 ransom. White House national security staff in 1986 asks him for $1 million to free American hostages in Lebanon: he wires the money. Most famously, he commissions a private mission into Iran in 1978, led by Son Tay Raider Col. Bull Simons, to rescue two of his EDS employees from jail. It succeeds.

Perot is convinced that the U.S. abandoned American POWs in Vietnam in 1973. Some, he believes, are alive. Government officials "have covered up, dissembled and finessed this issue for 20-some-odd years." When did it start? "We ransomed our prisoners out of Hanoi." He's referring to President Nixon's 1973 promise of reparations. "But we never wrote the check. And that's what caused the people to be left in Hanoi." That, and, of course, Watergate.

Immediately after the war, Perot sent loyal and savvy aide Tom Meurer and Colonel Simons to Laos on a private search. They paid to track down leads and for a team to trek into remote villages and interview inhabitants. After two months, they came up empty-handed, reporting to Perot that no live POWs were left.

Ross was not satisfied, telling Meurer, "I do know the Communist mind.... If they have some [POWs], you'll never know about it." Ann Mills-Griffiths said: "People kept calling Ross.... Every nutcase, everybody claiming to have information found their way to him"—feeding his worst instincts, his penchant for believing conspiracies.

Years after the fruitless private search, in a receiving line at a White House reception, Perot told President Reagan that he wanted to help find the missing. "Do I have your promise that if I bring hard evidence to you, you will follow up?" he asked. "Yes."

Perot remembered President Reagan telling him to "dig into" the POW and MIA issue: "...go all the way to the bottom of it and figure out what the situation was." He believed President Reagan wanted him to report back with recommendations. According to him, it was a presidential assignment.

Perot got to work. At the request of Vice President George H. W. Bush, he scoured classified files at DIA and agreed to front $4.2 million for a 240-minute videotape that allegedly showed Americans mining for gold in Southeast Asia. The tape never materialized. Perot said Vice President Bush promised to reimburse him but reneged. Vice President Bush insisted he had never asked Perot for money.

DIA asked Perot to serve on a POW/MIA task force. He declined. We don't need any more studies, he says. "I told [Vice President Bush] I did not want to because I knew that we had left men in Laos and I did not need to make a study to prove that, and that I had real concerns whether or not our government would do anything if I did make a study and proved it again."

Perot believed that President Reagan and Vice President Bush were giving the MIA issue lip service, just as Presidents Nixon, Ford, and Carter did. "Spasmodic, temporary, no organized, sustained effort to get it done," was his summary.

He told Vice President Bush he was not getting the cooperation he needed and was "getting out of it." He told him he was cancelling his donation to the Reagan library. Vice President Bush wrote, "He feels he has been badly treated by all (although he didn't say so, I think he means me too)."

A day after announcing to Vice President Bush that he was quitting, Perot hopped a plane to Vietnam to meet with Foreign Minister Nguyen Co Thach. Perot claimed Thach asked him, "Why did your government declare these men dead immediately after the war? After all these years, how can you expect us to take you seriously about looking for live Americans?"

Back home, Perot wanted to brief President Reagan one on one and make concrete recommendations he has laid out in a seven-page memo.

Walking into the Oval Office, Perot feels ambushed. This is not a private meeting. Around the president are chief of staff Howard Baker, national security advisor Frank Carlucci, and deputy national security advisor Colin Powell.

"Once I saw those national security guys there, I knew it was a waste of time." Perot is convinced that President Reagan's team is thwarting his efforts. He believes they are misleading the president on the issue of missing men.

Perot takes a seat next to the president. Referring to talking points on index cards prepared for him by Carlucci, President Reagan thanks Perot for his efforts, then brusquely tells him that the United States needs *one* foreign policy, and only one. Perot reads his memo, urging President Reagan to consider a "broader relationship" with the Vietnamese, to which the president responded, "We'll NEVER have a 'broader relationship' until they return our boys."

Perot listens politely, seething in silence. Then he informs the men in the room it is "probably time for me to get out of this and go back to my business." No one responds.

LOST CAUSES (OCTOBER 4, 1990)

Gently, Marian Shelton lays the .22 caliber Colt pistol on the dining room table. It is eerily illuminated by the bright chandelier. She picks up a pen, staring at the blank piece of paper. It's afternoon. She has been drinking all day and most of the previous evening. All night she stayed up talking to friend, confidante and fellow MIA activist, Navy Chief Warrant Officer Michael Clark. He frequently pulled all-nighters at this table listening to her troubles as she drank herself to sleep. This time, he left for work at 5:00 a.m.

Sometime before lunch, Marian called her son Michael to bring her vodka. He refused and noticed her voice sounded weak. He could tell she was depressed.

Marian starts writing. The note to her five children is brief. She loves them. She has done the best she could to find their father. And she pens an apology. Then she sets the pen down, removes her necklace of St. Jude, patron saint of lost causes, and the Charles Shelton POW bracelet she has been wearing for twenty years, and picks up the shiny little gun her brother had given her for self-defense. Her blood alcohol content was at .30. She stumbles out the back door and climbs to the top of her terraced garden overlooking the Rancho Mission Canyon in San Diego. Finally, she places the barrel of the revolver in her mouth and pulls the trigger.

Charles went missing twenty-five years ago. Seventeen years ago, the Paris Peace Accords were signed, and 591 POWs came home. Presidents Nixon, Ford, Carter, Reagan, and Bush all assured Marian they were working to bring Charles home. She heard many other things: her husband was dead, he was teaching English in Haiphong province, he was living in California in the witness protection program. She died believing that her Charles was alive, abandoned by the country he dedicated his life to defend. She was tired of the "distraught widow" moniker, of charlatans trying to extort her to stage rescues, profiteers offering information for money. She was weary of the government's empty promises and worn out from fighting bureaucracy.

This year, Charles was promoted by the Department of Defense to the rank of colonel even though he had disappeared a quarter of a century ago. Because he was not declared dead, Marian still received his paycheck and benefits. Charles is the only military service member officially listed as a prisoner of war from the Vietnam War. It is a symbol, President Ronald Reagan asserts, of the high national priority he places on the MIA issue.

Small consolation for a broken woman.

POW hunter Scott Barnes calls Marian's son. He is at Marian's house with two sisters of MIAs. "Michael, I can't find her." Michael hurries to his mother's house. He finds the suicide note but the house is empty. Strangely, the sliding glass door to the backyard is locked from the inside. As they scour the garden, they discover Marian in a secluded spot. Her blue dress is askew, her left knee buckled under her. Her body is covered in ants. The coroner tells Michael that she died instantly.

Marian's funeral is held at Arlington National Cemetery. In his eulogy, her friend Chief Warrant Officer Michael Clark describes the pressure and the burden of being the wife of the last POW. "She was a wife, a mother, a grandmother, and a symbol. It was being that 'symbol' that was the hardest for her to live up to. But she tried her best."

CHAPTER EIGHTEEN

POW POLITICS

"SHUT UP AND SIT DOWN!" (JULY 1992)

This is an election year. The Vietnam War has been over for nearly twenty years, but the National League of Families still wields influence in Washington. President George H. W. Bush, running for re-election this year, is addressing their meeting. President Bush exuberantly remarks to 600 people: "We live in a marvelous time of tremendous opportunity. We've seen the end of the Cold War and the collapse of imperial communism and a new birth of freedom from Moscow to Managua. America's courage, America's vision, America's values have indeed changed the world."

He is right. During President Bush's four years in the White House, the Soviet Union collapsed, and the Berlin Wall fell. He has triumphed over Saddam Hussein, pushing the dictator back within the borders of Iraq, freeing Kuwait from Hussein's forces. Maybe he's even overcome Americans' aversion to overseas military involvements and redeemed the nation after its seemingly irredeemable loss in Vietnam. The president is basking in the glow of these successes, which he predicts will assist his re-election bid. He does not expect a renewed battle over a war that officially ended almost two decades ago.

The Paris Peace Accords concluded American combat operations in Southeast Asia. But make no mistake, the Vietnam War is far from over. The fate of the missing men from that war *still* haunts the nation and plays an outsized role in this presidential election.

One year ago, in July of 1991, *Newsweek* magazine published a faded photograph of three smiling, middle-aged, well-fed Caucasians with mustaches. They were standing in a wooded setting holding a sign with a date: "25-5-90." Could the mystery photograph be of three Americans held captive in Southeast Asia as recently as May 25, 1990? After so many dashed hopes, could this be *real* photographic evidence?

The same month the *Newsweek* photograph was released, a *Wall Street Journal* poll indicated that 70 percent of the country believed the North Vietnamese were holding Americans prisoner.

Some National League members believe President Bush symbolizes the U.S. government's failure to account for their missing husbands, fathers, brothers, and sons. Attestations from Presidents Carter, Ford, Reagan, and Bush that no credible proof exists of live POWs in Southeast Asia hold no sway. American prisoners are alive. No one can convince the League members otherwise. They have lost faith in their nation's leadership. President Bush's words do not inspire them. To the contrary, the room boils over with anger.

A man jumps up and approaches the podium to shout: "This is symptomatic of the issue. This is our twenty-third meeting. Gosh darn it, why can't you get on a plane and negotiate? The Vietnamese have everything we want. We have everything they want."

A handful of family members stand, raising their fists, waving photos of their missing loved ones. They chant: "We won't budge! Tell the truth! We won't budge! Tell the truth!" Some turn their back on the president in protest with their hands clasped behind them.

Embarrassed, moderator Ann Mills-Griffiths tries to quell the unrest. She orders the dissidents to sit and asks the media not to pay them any attention. The rancor carries on for more than five minutes before President Bush, flustered and irritated, assumes control of the podium: "*Would you please shut up and sit down?*"

Conspiracy theories compounded the crowd's distrust. The media has been reporting allegations that Ronald Reagan's campaign negotiated with Iran in the fall of 1980 to delay the release of sixty-six American hostages in Tehran until after the election. President Bush feels the need to disprove them. These are the sort of disgruntled Americans who might believe them.

He addresses the issue head on: "To suggest that a commander-in-chief that led this country into its most successful recent effort would condone for one single day the personal knowledge of a person held against his will, whether it's here or anyplace else, is simply totally unfair. Now, to say I understand the agony that I've reheard here today is true. I do. But I do not like the suggestion that any American anywhere would know of a live American being held somewhere against his will, whether it's here or the allegation being over in the other part of the world. Iran, the suggestion was made that we left people being prisoner in Iran so to win an election. Now, what kind of an allegation is that to make against a patriot?"

The question is not entirely rhetorical. The allegation is not without precedent.

In 1971, President Nixon calculated that he could use the POWs held in Hanoi as a negotiating chip. He made the fate of 591 men, a tiny fraction of the 58,000 fatal war casualties and an even tinier fraction of the 2.7 million men who fought in the war, a strategic priority. By agreeing to the demands of the wives, he made them *de facto* hostages.

In April 1971, President Nixon told the country that he was increasing the rate of American troop withdrawals in Southeast Asia but refused to set a date for a *complete* withdrawal: "If the United States should announce that we will quit regardless of what the enemy does, we would have thrown away our principal bargaining counter to win the release of American prisoners of war."

His Democratic nemesis, Senator George McGovern, disputed that notion. He believed the *only* way to get the POWs released was to set a withdrawal date. He sponsored legislation with a December 31, 1971, withdrawal deadline.

Which should come first? Withdrawal date or a promise of the release? The chicken or the egg?

The McGovern–Hatfield "end the war" amendment, requiring withdrawal of all forces by the end of 1971, was defeated fifty-five to forty-two in the Senate in June 1971, handing President Nixon a win for his emphatic refusal to set a withdrawal date.

Privately, President Nixon and his national security advisor had another reason for keeping troops in Vietnam: Saigon could fall before the election if there were a complete withdrawal beforehand. Henry Kissinger reminded his boss that it would be disastrous for his presidency. "We can't have [South Vietnam] knocked over—brutally—to put it brutally—before the election," Kissinger advised. President Nixon agreed: "That's right." He did not want voters to think him responsible for losing the war.

For that reason, Kissinger told White House chief of staff H. R. Haldeman he favored a continued winding down to a pullout in the fall of 1972 so that "any bad results would be too late to affect the election." Haldeman agreed that it made sense.

These people might believe that Nixon played politics with the war. And, by keeping troops there until after the 1972 election, he condemned Americans to two more years in captivity. They believe that subsequent presidents have covered up the existence of Americans still in captivity in Southeast Asia, almost twenty years later. How unreasonable, then, would it be to believe that President Reagan or Bush would delay the release of American hostages in Iran to influence an election?

President Bush tries reassuring the skeptics. "I know there's doubt here, and I know people are saying, as this gentleman said right from the heart, 'Go over there and bring them back.' Do you think if I knew of one single person and where he is and how it was, that I wouldn't do that? Of course, I'd do that."

He gets booed by the crowd. In her diary that day, Barbara Bush blamed Ross Perot: "Darn that Ross Perot. He has really hurt these people by making them think that their loved ones are alive and that their government has not done everything to find them." Richard Childress, who served on the national security staff under President Reagan, was in the audience that day—sitting in the front row. He, too, was convinced that Perot got the audience "sparked up," even though it was a small minority who protested.

A few days later, Ann published an apology to President Bush in *The Washington Post* for the "disrespectful behavior" of a few of the attendees. The statement said that President Bush had called Ann after the meeting to reaffirm his commitment to the issue of the nation's unaccounted-for MIAs.

As he concluded in his speech to the families: "So, all I'm asking, all I'm here to say is I am the President, and I am the Commander in Chief. Some of you believe it and some of you may not, but we are going to get this job done, and we are going to account for every single person who is missing. I'm going to keep on it. I don't care how long it takes."

THE OUTSIDER (OCTOBER 13, 1992)

Sybil Stockdale has a clear view of Jim. Her beloved husband is center stage behind a podium, wearing a conservative business suit and big, tortoise shell-rimmed glasses that show off his piercing eyes, as azure and arresting as they were during the war. Retired from the Navy, his hair is white as snow and has not been sprayed into place. He still walks with a pronounced limp.

Jim is talking to the American electorate, introducing himself as the number two on a presidential ticket. Flanking him are two politicians, decades younger, with full makeup and hair that does not move. Polished and practiced, Vice President Dan Quayle and Sen. Al Gore debate each other, talking over and around Jim. He feels as if he is watching a game of ping pong.

It has been almost two decades since Jim returned home from Vietnam to a joyous nation and a grateful family. For his leadership and heroics in the Hanoi Hilton, he was awarded the nation's highest military honor: the Medal of Honor. In recognition of Sybil's leadership and work on the home front, she received the Navy's Distinguished Public Service Award, the service's highest award for a private citizen. She is the only wife of a military officer to receive this award.

It is now Jim's turn to make his opening remarks: "Who am I? Why am I here?"

It is a Socratic question, posed by an academic, a distinguished fellow at the Hoover Institution at Stanford University, someone well versed in the philosophy of ancient Greek Stoics. But Vice Adm. James Stockdale is not lecturing a roomful of students at Stanford University nor is he speaking to naval officers at the Naval War College, where he once served as president.

Unschooled in philosophy, the audience does not understand and breaks into laughter.

Jim is surprised by the response, but he continues: "I'm not a politician, everybody knows that. So don't expect me to use the language of the Washington insider. Thirty-seven years in the Navy, and only one of them up there in Washington. And now I'm an academic. The centerpiece of my life was the Vietnam War. I was there the day it started; I led the first bombing raid against North Vietnam. I was there the day it ended, and I was there for everything in between. Ten years in Vietnam, aerial combat, and torture. I know things about the Vietnam War better than anybody in the world. I know *some* things about the Vietnam War better than anybody in the world. And I know how governments, how American governments can be, can be courageous, and how they can be callow. And that's important. That's one thing I'm an insider on. I was the leader of the underground of the American pilots, who were shot down in prison and North Vietnam. You should know that the American character displayed in those dungeons by those fine men, was a thing of beauty. I look back on those years as the beginning of wisdom. Learning everything a man can learn about the vulnerabilities and the strengths that are ours as Americans. Why am I here tonight? I am here because I have in my brain and in my heart, what it takes to lead America through tough times."

Why is Jim on the presidential ticket? Because Ross Perot asked him for a favor.

It had seemed simple. Perot had said: "Would you let me put your name as a stand-in candidate, and then as soon as I can get a real politician to join me, I'll let you know, and we'll erase your name?" Jim could not turn down Perot. Sybil had gushed over how helpful Perot had been to her and all the wives during the war.

Perot dropped out of the race in July and Jim figured the game was over. But Perot reentered the race on October 1 and accepted an invitation on Jim's behalf to participate in the vice-presidential debate.

That's why Jim is on the national hot seat in a live televised debate unrehearsed and without briefing books. "I never had a single conversation about politics with Ross Perot in my life—still haven't."

COMPROMISING POSITIONS (OCTOBER 25, 1992)

Ross Perot is making history. Pushed into the race for president as candidate for the Independent Party and ascending through grass roots efforts, his anti-Washington, populist stances on the issues are resonating. He leads in polls against both President Bush *and* Governor Bill Clinton in early summer. He is the most serious independent challenger to the two-party system in modern American history.

Telling Lesley Stahl on *60 Minutes* that the risks to his family are not worth it, he abruptly drops out of the race in July, stunning his supporters. Why?

The Bush campaign was planning to embarrass Perot and his family in front of the American public, Perot tells Stahl.

"I have a daughter, Carolyn, who was getting married on August 23rd and I received multiple reports that there was a plan to embarrass her just before her wedding."

MIA adventurist Scott Barnes is behind those reports. The alleged plot is a doozy. According to Barnes, the GOP was going to release to the press fake photos of Perot's two daughters in "compromising lesbian-related situations." Barnes claims to have seen thirty-five of these photos, set in a parking lot at a country club where Perot and his family regularly socialized. "Here I have this wonderful world-class daughter, she's getting married, it's one of the biggest days in her life. To have her smeared because I am in the middle of a political campaign for something that is completely untrue for political purposes…."

There's more. Perot believes someone tried to wiretap his phones and planned to disrupt the wedding in person. *And someone obtained a copy of his office floor plan*. Barnes has fueled Perot's fears claiming he was summoned to a lengthy meeting in Dallas with a Bush campaign operative and to a clandestine meeting in Mexico. Perot found this suspicious and disturbing.

Barnes and Perot were introduced in 1984, when Perot heard that Barnes had attempted to rescue American POWs in Laos and had snapped photos of Americans in captivity. Marian Shelton's suicide drew them closer together.

Perot fell under Barnes's spell. The stories Barnes told Perot confirmed his suspicions of a massive government plot with CIA involvement to cover up the existence of live POWs. Perot hoped President Bush was not personally involved: "My hope is that a bunch of zealots were doing stupid things."

But Perot does not have a lot of hope that President Bush is doing the right thing regarding MIAs from the Vietnam War. He has lost faith in his president and is convinced that President Bush could have done more to find missing Americans when he was director of the CIA in the 1970s.

He always thought President Bush was "weak." Now, he believes President Bush is corrupt. That he has betrayed the men languishing in Southeast Asia and that he will not do what it takes to bring them home because elements of the government are embarrassed over their lies, are feckless or, worse yet, involved in narcotics trafficking in the region.

Perot's anger over this failure is at the heart of his bid to unseat President Bush.

Lesley Stahl suggests in the interview that Barnes has scammed Perot. Authorities believe Barnes is a chronic fabricator, she says. "I do want to ask you. And hope you'll answer. Why would you listen to Scott Barnes at all?"

Barnes admits it *was* a big hoax. "It was a lie," he says in 1997. A whopper—with the goal of causing President Bush to lose to Ross Perot. The plan backfires. Perot fails to carry a single state, but receives 18.9 percent of the popular vote, the best showing by a third-party candidate since Theodore Roosevelt's campaign with the Bull Moose party in 1912. By splitting the Republican vote, Perot ensures that Bill Clinton ousts George Bush. He also ensures that most Americans will remember Jim Stockdale more for his unusual vice-presidential debate speech than for seven years of heroic leadership in the Hanoi Hilton.

SPARRING (AUGUST 11, 1992)

Sen. John McCain looks annoyed.

The white-haired Vietnam veteran is a member of the U.S. Senate Select Committee on POW/MIA Affairs, along with fellow

Vietnam War veterans Sen. John Kerry and Sen. Bob Kerrey. The committee is charged with determining if Americans are being held against their will and if the U.S. government has been neglectful or malfeasant in failing to bring them home.

The largest congressional investigation into the fate of MIAs from the Vietnam War and the most comprehensive has held hearings for ten months.

Senator McCain's patience is running thin. In his opinion, many of the witnesses whose testimony he has endured are delusional, con men, or *victims* of con men. Or family members who *believe* the con men. At times, the hearings resemble a circus.

McCain has credibility. A POW for more than five years, he sees no reason why Hanoi would continue to hold American men. "The Vietnamese could be cruel, but I never knew them to be capricious. There was nothing in it for them to keep any guys after the war."

Can the Vietnamese government account for the missing men? Probably. Though it would be hard for them to know what happened to every downed or injured American serviceman, they have more information than they have released. But rumors, sightings of Americans toiling in chain gangs, held in cages, and carving coded messages in fields? McCain is offended and irritated at the charlatans perpetuating these myths, preying on MIA families.

Across from McCain is a myth maker with a big megaphone: Ross Perot.

McCain is having a tough time disguising his contempt, and Perot is having a hard time disguising *his*.

McCain acknowledges that Perot, as a private citizen, did more for the POW and MIA families than most. He is grateful that Perot assisted Carol in getting the best care after her accident, although McCain has yet to personally thank him. Perot has continued to take care of POWs after their homecoming—with parades, jobs, college scholarships for their children, and medical care. Perot opens his wallet and his heart to many, many of McCain's friends. But

McCain's personal relationship with Perot has deteriorated, especially regarding MIAs. McCain believes that Perot is delusional. Publicly, McCain will eventually call him "nuttier than a fruitcake."

At the hearing, Perot is lecturing McCain and other senators on how to secure the release of the POWs he is convinced are in Southeast Asia. He is giving McCain a "101 lesson on negotiations" with the Vietnamese. "The Vietnamese, if you would spend time listening to them, just listen, listen, listen.... They are so sensitive. And they are so, you know, they are so angry, and they are so frustrated. And they so desperately want to be a part of the world community—all of the pieces are there to get this thing resolved. But I think we really have not gone into what I'll call long-term, intensive negotiations with them. I believe that if they ever felt that it was to their advantage, to clean this up, they would. Laos has no incentive at all. They've got full diplomatic recognition. And what, you know? We'd have to really sit down and come up with a good plan on to get Laos's attention."

McCain *has* been listening. He has been working since 1986 to improve relations with the Vietnamese, co-sponsoring a resolution to open diplomatic offices in Washington and Hanoi. It was unpopular with the Reagan administration, many of his fellow former POWs, veteran's groups, and the National League of Families—who want to keep Hanoi diplomatically and economically isolated.

McCain has had enough today. His notorious temper gets the best of him as he lashes out: "Mr. Perot, since you've brought it up again. I don't believe I was ransomed out of Vietnam. I believe B-52s got me out of Vietnam. And I think that it was clear that after the North Vietnamese grossly, blatantly, outrageously violated the Peace Accord—Paris Peace Accords—which clearly mandated that they do not invade and conquer South Vietnam. After they did so, that the American Congress and people very justifiably were not prepared to provide any money, nor am I at this time as a result of their invasion and conquering and subjugation, of South Vietnam.

So, we have a difference of opinion, clearly as to what brought the Americans home."

Perot sits in front of the committee for eight hours. His hearing is one of many that McCain and the rest of the committee endure during the investigation. After interviewing 1,000 people, taking 200 sworn depositions, and holding 200 hours of public hearings, the Senate Select Committee on POW/MIA Affairs issues its 549-page report in January 1993. "While the Committee has some evidence suggesting the possibility a POW may have survived to the present, and while some information remains yet to be investigated, there is, at this time, no compelling evidence that proves any Americans remain alive in captivity in Southeast Asia."

IT IS TIME (OCTOBER 1994)

All five Shelton children gather on a sunny fall day in Arlington National Cemetery for a solemn ceremony amidst thousands of white crosses. Four years ago, they buried their mother, Marian Shelton, who died by her own hand. Today is their father's funeral, although there is no body, and there are no ashes. They are trying to bury a burden. "It was for our own sanity, for our own futures," says John Shelton. "It's hung over us for so long."

At the children's request, the Air Force has changed their father's status to Killed in Action/Body Not Recovered, a change their mother did not want and successfully fought to prevent. Until today, Charles Shelton has been the sole missing man classified by the U.S. government as a prisoner of war.

It may have done more harm than good, the Shelton children reflect. The "legend" of their dad, promoted to colonel over the years, has grown exponentially with time. It is difficult to know what to believe. Some of the Shelton kids believe he is alive. Some believe he is dead. None has the answers.

Now officially orphans, the Shelton children hold it together when the color guard proffers a folded American flag. They are stoic as fighter jets streak overhead, standing still during the gun salute. But when the bugle plays "Taps" the tears flow.

CHAPTER NINETEEN

THE TRAILBLAZER (JUNE 1986)

Picking her way through the trip hazards on the deck of the USS *Yellowstone* on this hazy June day, Alice Stratton is eager to hear from the crew about their work and their families. Onboard the impressive destroyer tender docked in Norfolk, Virginia, the work pace is brisk. Longer than two football fields, the deck is a floating complex of more than seventy workshops to repair gear and equipment as large as underwater propellers and engines. Onboard, the crew can roll sheets of half-inch thick steel. This ship can resupply others—including aircraft carriers and ballistic missile submarines—with power and fresh water.

This afloat maintenance facility with its 1,600 crewmembers allows combat ships to be repaired and resupplied without returning to port. It also offers women rare opportunities to go to sea, as they are still prohibited from assignments aboard warships.

The first Deputy Assistant Secretary of the Navy for Personnel and Family Matters (DASN P&FM), Alice has traveled to the ship with her boss, the Assistant Secretary of the Navy for Manpower and Reserve Affairs (ASN M&RA) Chase Untermeyer. The ship's public address system officially alerts everyone onboard the ship that a senior official from the Pentagon has arrived. Dressed in functional pants, her face framed with button clip-on earrings and shoulder length, curly salt and pepper hair, Alice steps from the brow onto the quarterdeck, where the commanding officer greets her. Fumes of paint thinner mix with the smell of food cooking. But Alice is eager to get to work. She is especially keen to learn from the crew what their lives are like when they step ashore after long days at work.

Alice Stratton's official portrait as the first Deputy Assistant Secretary of the Navy for Personnel and Family Matters (DASN P&FM). (*Photo courtesy of the Department of the Navy and the Stratton family.*)

At the obligatory meet-and-greet with the commanding officer, he whines about the instability of his crew and their many pregnancies. "You know," Alice mentions offhandedly, "some shore commands offer sex education programs to help prevent pregnancies. Does *Yellowstone* have such a program?"

"Well, no," he replies. "In fact, I have never thought about it until now."

It is why she is glad to be onboard. Women form a vital part of the Navy workforce, and Alice wants to give attention to both lingering and emerging issues—not just pregnancies. Over time, she has developed a deep interest in how military families cope with separation, transition, and loss. In her role, she is empowered to examine those issues and make policy recommendations. Thoughtfully, she considers where and how to assign couples who both serve in the military, the lack of childcare, and how to address dilapidated military housing.

Since the end of the draft in 1973, the military has struggled to recruit and retain skilled sailors. The Navy is no exception. Military leaders have only just begun to understand the enormity of personnel problems and have been tackling those at a glacial pace. The 1981 recession financially squeezed military families, making it even harder to keep people in the military.

Recognizing the well-being of a sailor's family contributes to the crew's productivity and longevity, officials agree with Alice that the health and happiness of crew families are vital to the Navy's future. She knows firsthand that sometimes it's difficult to stay above water. While her own husband was a POW, she had to get creative when she faced a seemingly impossible obstacle when attempting to buy a new car. The dealership insisted on having her husband's signature. A notarized signature from a prisoner in enemy territory? With a coy smile, Alice took the documents, snuck away for a cup of coffee, forged Dick's name, and returned with all requirements having been met. Now, she's interested in hearing directly from the crew about the obstacles they face.

She and Secretary Untermeyer wend their way through labyrinthine passageways, descending ladders to the mess deck. Four dozen chief petty officers, the senior enlisted leaders onboard, tell them they do not earn a pay differential like sailors on combatant ships because of a technicality. *Yellowstone* is at sea for less than thirty days—the minimum needed to qualify for combat pay.

Chief petty officers complain about high crew turnover and the relentless disruption to watchstanding schedules. They don't agree on the reasons for this: some attribute disruption to pregnancies and the many single parents onboard. Others say the women are among the most motivated workers of the crew. The only consensus is that no one knows how to fix the problem. That is why Alice's position was created. And it is why she is out in the field engaging sailors and soliciting their perspective.

As she absorbs each detail, the next group files in. They are primarily female, single parents who are noticeably unsettled. Trying to break the ice, Alice speaks to them calmly and informally, trying to make a connection as a fellow member of the military family community—not as a high-ranking Pentagon official. The wife of a former POW, she understands the pressure of being a single parent. She can relate to their fear of speaking out. Back in 1970, she noted, "The influence of public opinion can have a great impact on the situation," and she has never forgotten that mantra. She tells the sailors they do not need to suffer in silence. Quietly, she tries to reassure them that she is their advocate at the Pentagon, and their conduit for policy change. They remain reluctant to speak.

Alice is patient and even-keeled. Her experience listening to others as a social worker, therapist, and mother of three boys pays off. She learns why they are reticent: their cover has been blown. Until now, most shipmates were unaware these women were parents. They had hoped to maintain secrecy lest their superior officers and shipmates wonder whether they were distracted at work. The sailors have juggled their personal lives to keep supervisors oblivious to their parenting struggles and limited support networks. Exposed, they worry about repercussions. This revelation is why Alice seeks face-to-face meetings and why Secretary Untermeyer supports her travel plans. Answers will not be found inside the Pentagon.

Secretary Untermeyer is also struck by their challenges: "One very articulate young woman said that she wanted to have a Navy career, but policies that made life difficult for single parents might drive her out of the fleet. Some married parents said the same thing." He is surprised that it took two senior leaders from the Pentagon to get this level of honesty and forthrightness from the crew.

In 1986, single parents are still something of an anomaly in military service. Alice is aware some face a Hobson's choice: place their children in the legal custody of another adult or get out of the Navy. Some leaders believe single parents cannot achieve mission readiness. Alice steadfastly believes the opposite. *Taking care of family issues* equates *to readiness. Time for a sea change.*

It is just one of the bold assertions she has been making during the six months she has been in her role, the culmination of her life's work. After creating the position of DASN for personnel and family matters, Secretary Untermeyer went in search of a candidate. Former POW and the Navy's Chief of Naval Personnel Vice Adm. Bill Lawrence unequivocally said, "Alice Stratton's the one."

She was an unorthodox choice. The head of political personnel at the Pentagon presumed Untermeyer would have selected a "white-gloved admiral's wife." Alice was something different. The position was also expected to be given to someone with political connections, or who had worked on political campaigns. Alice was not that person, either. But she became a DASN, the Navy's first appointee at such a senior level, with an office on the coveted "E" ring of the Pentagon. She had the ear of the Secretary of the Navy, a testament to the priority the service was now placing on family members.

Alice was a familiar face in the Navy, the wife of former POW Capt. Dick Stratton, a celebrated hero who had survived seven years of brutal captivity in Hanoi. His homecoming and reunion with his wife and their three boys became a Navy-wide cause for celebration. But her road to leadership had been bumpy.

After hearing firsthand from POW releasee Doug Hegdahl what her husband endured, she felt she had no choice but to "share with the world the true facts of Hanoi's POW treatment, especially since so many of the antiwar activists were insisting the released men's stories were fabrications."

Tentatively, Alice began her advocacy efforts, gradually building confidence in her ability and authority to buck the "keep quiet" policy. Encouraged to speak up by a call from the San Francisco Bay area wife of a missing aviator and Sybil Stockdale's leadership in southern California, Alice started meeting with POW and MIA wives in northern California. At the first meeting, "Someone was talking about Ho Chi Minh. I am ashamed to say I did not even know who the hell that was!"

Sybil asked the Bay Area ladies to initiate letter-writing campaigns to the foreign minister of North Vietnam, American newspaper editors, and legislators. Alice was at first afraid to make speeches, having been admonished to keep quiet when Dick first went missing. She did it for her husband, her kids, and the other POWs. She wrote up the raw and painful account of the inhumane treatment Dick was subjected to by the North Vietnamese. Wobbly-kneed, she gave her first speech in October 1969 to an empathetic audience, at her church in Palo Alto. It was uncomfortable for the reserved and private Alice.

Next, she spoke in front of a like-minded audience: military wives. Each time it got easier. She read her speech to anyone in the Bay Area who would listen, Kiwanis and Rotary Clubs, schools, colleges, and service organizations. To keep her emotions in check and appear calm, her delivery was a bit flat. Yet her underlying passion captivated audiences. A Toastmaster advisor smiled, shaking his head. “I don’t understand it, but that monotone is still effective.”

Once-shy Alice morphed into an accomplished crusader and lobbyist, participating in press conferences, collaborating with other wives on marketing campaigns. Though none of these skills came easily, her persistence paid off—and the camaraderie with other wives further bolstered her confidence.

When the war ended, Alice combined her professional expertise with her personal experience as a POW wife to help others. She advised Navy leadership on the need to institutionalize the family support she and other POW and MIA wives had developed *ad hoc*. She was in the vanguard advocating for policy changes, budgetary allocations, and for the Navy leadership to support Navy *families*. The adage that, “If the Navy wanted you to have a wife, they would have issued you one in your seabag!,” was tired. Alice tried a different approach, mentoring others and sharing useful information at a grassroots level long before Navy leadership recognized the need for change.

At the 1978 Navy Family Awareness Conference, Chief of Naval Operations Adm. Thomas Hayward proclaimed family matters would be a crucial Navy tactic. He told the crowd, “It’s the right thing to do,” and asked the Navy to develop a formal family support program. Alice, reputed to be an accomplished critical thinker and trainer, was asked to assist in hammering out the blueprint for what became the Fleet Family Service Center concept. She was all in.

Alice was motivated to learn metrics and statistics and obtained a second masters’ degree, in Military Family Studies. Already knowledgeable about naval operations, Alice could now gather hard data to support her research. The combination made her skillset unbeatable.

When Dick transferred to the Naval Academy in 1979, Alice offered to conduct a needs assessment for the Academy's superintendent, Vice Adm. Bill Lawrence. Her analysis demonstrated that Academy families wanted the same things as POW families: an easy way to find resources and referrals. "This was the core concept of the Family Service Centers," writes Alice.

She oversaw the implementation of Family Service Centers across the country, where the Navy offers counseling, referrals, programs on parental effectiveness, managing finances, and child abuse prevention programs. In recognition of her efforts, the Navy named the Family Service Center in Annapolis, Maryland, "The Captain Richard and Alice Stratton Family Service Center."

Dick and Alice Stratton in front of the eponymous Navy Family Service Center in Annapolis, Maryland. (*Photo courtesy of the Stratton family.*)

As she steps off the brow of the *Yellowstone* today, Alice is aware there is lots of work ahead. Having found her purpose in helping others, she's up for the challenge. During the remainder of her four-year appointment, she will visit eighty-four ships and bases.

Dick is immensely proud of his wife, feeling that Alice was ideally suited to lead the charge on behalf of Navy families. Her prominent appointment tickled him: "I woke up one morning and found that my wife now outranked me by two and a half pay grades."

CHAPTER TWENTY

RESOLUTION

BACK TO SON TAY (DECEMBER 1995)

Jon Reynolds immediately recognizes his prison cell. One of the bars on the window is still bent. Despite the passage of twenty-five years, the prison camp outside the village of Son Tay has not changed that much—except for the damage from the famous, failed 1970 raid. Out the window is a familiar sight: Ba Vi, the three-peaked mountain, covered in jungle. A navigational aid to American air crews during the war, the mountain is now a national park and game refuge.

The mountain, "a reminder of a better life, far from the prison wall and Vietnam," sparked fierce summer thunderstorms. With luck they would rise from the peaks and roll down the valley over the camp to cool off the prisoners.

Jon found that better life after seven and a half years in captivity, when he reconnected with Emilee. After leaving her first husband in Mexico, Emilee had planned to drive home, and get a quick divorce and a job in Atlanta. But first, she stopped in San Antonio to see Jon.

The long drive gave her time to think. "I was able to separate myself from Mexico by driving back. Driving through San Antonio. Spending some time with Jon. Reestablishing who we were, with each other. But without any obligation. Knowing that I needed to do something, and he needed to." They were both smart enough to recognize that he needed some time. And so did she.

"But there was an idle curiosity on both of us, that you know, he wanted to see me. I wanted to see him. You know?"

Jon and Emilee Reynolds with their children Andrew and Elizabeth on their first overseas tour to China, in Tian Tang, Beijing, 1985. (*Photo courtesy of the Reynolds family.*)

Eighteen months later, Emilee put her engagement ring back on. Nine years to the day from when it was first planned, she had her storybook wedding to Jon.

The next twenty years took the couple to Colorado Springs, Washington, and Beijing—twice. Jon now works as a vice president for Raytheon in China, having retired from the Air Force a decorated brigadier general. Emilee and Jon are on Christmas vacation in Vietnam exploring Hanoi with their two college-aged children, Elizabeth and Andrew, and a Vietnamese tour guide.

President Bill Clinton is normalizing relations with Vietnam, with the help of Sen. John McCain. Jon is insistent: he wants to go back to Son Tay with his family. He had promised himself long ago that he would return some day. They head outside the city in search of the prison Jon and fellow POWs called "Camp Hope." Jon is excited about the adventure, almost exuberant.

Forty-four kilometers west of Hanoi, they drive up and down the small alleys of Son Tay, asking where the prison camp is. Blank stares. One man old enough to remember the sights and sounds of the Son Tay raid, the explosions, and the helicopters, agrees to take them to the site.

The prison at Son Tay where Jon Reynolds was held captive May 1968–July 1970. (*Photo courtesy of the Reynolds family.*)

Inside the camp, Jon looks around with a wan smile. The buildings, with their corrugated tin roofs, still look dilapidated. The tree that the assaulting helicopter sheared is still missing its top. The dry well that Jon dug is still dry. The "tank," the outhouse where he was holed up in solitary confinement, is intact.

The hut where Jon was held in solitary confinement at the Son Tay prison compound, near Hanoi. (*Photo courtesy of the Reynolds family.*)

Emilee is struck by how cramped and unforgiving the cells are, with stone walls and clay floors that absorb both the heat and the cold. Jon tells her and Elizabeth that the doors and windows were frequently covered with bamboo mats to block out light and fresh air. Now Emilee understands how hard sleeping and even breathing was for the POWs—especially in stifling summers.

A diminutive woman with an armband arrives, waving her finger. A local politician, she shoos them out of the compound. The van treks up one of the three peaks of Ba Vi, the mountain Jon saw through his prison cell window all those years ago. At the top, Jon and Emilee look down at the camp, which seems so far away and so, well, inconsequential.

Was it emotional going back to Son Tay? "No, it wasn't," Jon flatly responds. He shrugs. One-two-three, he counts in Vietnamese. Sitting in that cell in 1970, looking longingly at those three mountain peaks, did he ever imagine that he would be standing on that mountain top with Emilee and their children?

In December 1995, Jon and Emilee Reynolds and their daughter Elizabeth trekked back to the Son Tay Prison, where Jon was held for twenty-six months and where the infamous Son Tay Raid was conducted. (*Photo courtesy of the Reynolds family.*)

Although Jon is not reflective, Emilee is. "I think the most fortunate thing in my life, and I'll always be thankful for it, is that Jon came back, and we were able to get back together. Because that is what I really wanted," Emilee emphasizes. Other experiences—graduate school, pursuing a career, living in two worlds, and straddling two generations—have given her an awareness that many women her age do not have. "If you haven't experienced it, maybe you don't miss it."

REMAINS OF THE DAY (1977 AND 2000)

Pat Mearns has a jam-packed schedule, typical for late September. A pediatric nurse working for the Los Angeles County Unified School District, she sees students throughout the day. Some come for medical attention. Others come with questions, paperwork, or to reconnect with their friend, the school nurse. Administration officials have cautioned her to be on the lookout for signs of gang activity. Her office at Franklin High School is sparsely decorated; on the wall a poster urges vaccination for measles and smallpox. With a stethoscope draped around her neck, Pat hasn't stopped since 7:00 a.m. Charting patient notes, she hears the girl working the switchboard call her name. "I'm transferring a call back to your phone," she says with urgency.

Pat picks up the receiver of the black rotary phone and her heart skips a beat. She wants to absorb every detail of what the Pentagon official has to say. It has been so long without news of her husband: eleven years. The time in limbo has affected everyone in her life: "My daughters, my sister-in-law Betty, our friends, family, neighbors, and my compatriots at work endured these years of no news right along with us."

The United States, frustrated by Vietnam's failure to give a full and final accounting of missing American servicemen, had vetoed the country's membership application to the United Nations. But in 1977, the Carter Administration softened its stance and instead of blocking Vietnam, abstained from voting, allowing Vietnam to be admitted on September 20, 1977. Within days, Vietnam repatriates twenty-two sets of remains to the United States, remains that they had clearly been warehousing for years.

The U.S. military suspects Art's remains are among them, the official says. A U.S. Air Force Casualty officer says the remains are being sent to the military's Central Identification Laboratory in Honolulu. She will hear from them in about a month. For a moment, Pat thinks about Art and the film reel of their life in Japan plays in her mind. Caught off guard by the call, "I didn't think to ask where he had been found, or how he died," she says.

Pat calls her younger daughter Frances with the news. It's a solemn conversation. Elder daughter Missy, away at college in Hamilton, New York, is probably in class. Pat makes a note to call her later that day.

In mid-October, the second call comes. Some of the remains were identified as Art's. Pat shares the dreaded news with her mother. Next is old friend Bob Dornan, now a congressman from California, who offers to help with funeral arrangements. She wants a caisson and a bagpiper, and Dornan to read the poem *High Flight*. She wants to bury Art on Veteran's Day, eleven years to the day after he disappeared.

The news is, in some ways, anticlimactic. "I felt sort of empty," she remembers. It isn't the homecoming she hoped for, but she isn't surprised either. "You knew these things were going to happen. For a long time, I was waiting in the back of my mind for the other shoe to drop." Now it has.

Carole Hanson Hickerson is also still waiting and hoping for closure. It is a new millennium, the year 2000, and this just may be the year she gets some. The government had never given up hope of recovering Steve's body and repatriating his remains. If they could be found. In February 1999, the U.S. government at last gained access to the crash site where Steve was last seen alive.

Steve Hanson is still a member of her family, but he *is* a distant memory. Carole made a conscious effort, in 1973, to move on with her life. A visit to the Vietnam Wall in the late 1980s reminded her why.

Carole and her husband Jim Hickerson (the guy who gave her that memorable kiss at the Cotton Bowl in 1973) were hurrying past the vendor's table, en route to pay respects at the engraving of Steve Hanson's name on the Vietnam Wall. The table was one of several that lined the pathway to the memorial. The POW/MIA flag, with its silhouetted profile of a POW, was emblazoned on everything from T-shirts to cigarette lighters to belt buckles to coffee mugs. Also on the table were brochures and a place to make donations to support the enduring mission: bring home our POWs, still languishing in Southeast Asia.

A young man ran after her: "Mrs. Hanson! Mrs. Hanson!"

Carole had not been Mrs. Hanson for many years, not since she married Jim in 1974. "Do you remember me?" the young man asked. In his late twenties or early thirties, he was about the same age as her older son Todd, but she could not place the face. He reminded her: he was the son of an MIA wife. His mother was active with Carole in the National League of Families during the war. He had taken the reins from his mother. "He is still at it," she thought to herself, more than twenty years after the war has ended.

Seeing this young man saddened her. "I did not want Todd to end up like him."

She had long ago walked away from her role as an international activist. "We scattered after the war. We just needed to get on with our lives." Besides, Todd needed a father and Jim was willing to step into that role. He adopted Todd and the couple adopted two more children. Todd attended the Naval Academy and served in the Navy, just like his stepfather. Todd, too, had moved on.

But now, Carole has been told that an excavation team has retrieved several sets of remains from the crash site—including teeth. One was Steve's.

On the day before he is interred at Arlington, on September 29, 2000, Carole arrives at the funeral parlor for a viewing ceremony. "The whole event was just a blur in my mind," she admits. Her father had died a few months prior, and now she is burying a husband who died thirty-three years ago. Steve's casket is open. She is not sure how much she can stomach.

Her friend from the 1970 round-the-world trip, fellow MIA wife Patty Hardy, is there for support. "It's okay," she reassures Carole.

Tentatively walking toward the casket, Carole winces and peers inside. There, resting on the fluffy white satin lining is a crisply ironed Marine Corps officer's black, blue, and red dress uniform. Laid on top of the smooth fabric is a tooth: Steve's molar.

TO THE WEST WING (JANUARY 21, 1981)

Ronald Reagan stops dead in his tracks and smothers her with a big hug. "Carol, can you believe we are here?"

The day after the presidential inauguration, Carol McCain is wandering the West Wing. She does not know her way around the White House. And, no, she cannot believe she is here. "Four years ago, if you told me what I'd be doing now, I would have told them they are dreaming."

Four years ago, she was married to Navy Capt. John McCain, the admiral's son and former POW whose celebrated homecoming catapulted him into the national spotlight. It will help launch his storied political career. Four years ago, she was going to physical therapy for several hours a day to improve her mobility.

She is now divorced from McCain. He married a much younger woman six weeks later. It has been a difficult time for her, but also one of tremendous professional growth. "I owe a lot to people like Mrs. Reagan who helped me through that period." Now, she is taking on the job as the new director of the White House Visitors Office, savoring the victory, as she was instrumental in helping Ronald and Nancy Reagan reach the White House. One of the first twelve employees on the campaign, she was on the road for a year as Mrs. Reagan's scheduler and press assistant. She also played a lead role in planning the Republican National Convention and the inauguration.

She was not certain she would be hired. She and John had become social friends with the Reagans when he spoke at the governor's prayer breakfast in Sacramento back in 1974. As he told of his harrowing experience as a prisoner of war for five-and-a-half-years,

Nancy Reagan could not stop crying. Governor and Mrs. Reagan were enthralled with the McCains. Carol headed Reagan's 1976 primary campaign for three Florida counties. The couples became close. Could Carol transition from friend to employee?

After a few trial trips together in the fall of 1979, Mrs. Reagan offered her the position. "I didn't know whether to take the job or not because I knew my marriage was going to break up and I really, almost, couldn't make decisions. And, I thought, well, if I do that, then I'm just admitting defeat."

A good friend, Ursula Meese, convinced her to take the job. Her husband, Edwin Meese, was also going to be traveling on the campaign. She called Carol: "Listen, bring Sidney to California. I'll take care of Sidney while you and Ed work on this campaign. It'll keep you real busy. It's probably a really good thing to do."

Carol and thirteen-year-old Sidney moved to San Diego. "I literally left our house [in Alexandria, Virginia] and went to California with Sidney. And John, while I was gone, moved out."

The 24/7 campaign was a grind even for an able-bodied person. Carol, 110 pounds, with a pronounced limp, uneven knees, and one leg that did not bend, found it grueling. Her legs swelled like balloons from long days and nights on her feet, on the road, and on the plane. But the work "held my life together. It was something I could be dedicated to twenty-four hours a day, which was really a blessing."

One of the hardest days on the campaign was May 17, 1980, when Carol was feeling blue, watching the rain pour from the campaign bus window. Noticing her mood, male reporters broke into song, belting out the barbershop medley "Wedding Bells Are Breaking Up That Old Gang of Mine." Her ex-husband was remarrying that day.

The friends she made that year have remained lifelong supporters, professionally and personally. And Ronald Reagan's landslide victory ensured her a political appointment. "I received a call from

Mike Deaver, and he said, 'I want you to be the director of the Visitors Office. It's the perfect job for you.'"

Carol thought for a minute and said, "What exactly does that do?" She learned quickly. During the course of her six-year tenure as director, she hosted up to 6,000 members of the public daily—some 1.5 million a year. She expanded and livened up the White House Easter Egg Roll, where the wooden eggs she had signed by celebrities and sports figures became coveted keepsakes. And she was the brainchild behind the White House Christmas ornament campaign that raised money for the White House Historical Association to refurbish the White House. Mrs. Reagan loved the idea but wanted to approve the design in what became a First Lady tradition. The first one? An image of the Mt. Vernon weathervane, topped with a dove. The campaign has become an extraordinarily successful fund-raiser, and the ornaments are collectibles.

But this morning, her first day on the job, she is lost and tired. She had returned home from the Inaugural Ball at 3:00 a.m. and was awakened by a call from the White House at 10:00 a.m. Where was she? "I didn't know where to go and I was scared." Report to the East Gate. Her son Doug drives her to the entrance, where she gives her name to the guard. "Oh, we've been expecting you. Come on in." She waves to Doug, and limps into the West Wing.

DISCORDANT (1993)

Andrea Rander is on edge. She is in divorce court. Again. This is not how she envisioned her life when Donald returned home in 1973, after seventy-two months in captivity. But he is determined to leave because, as he tells tortuously explains, "I love you so much, so I have to leave you."

Andrea is stunned. She loves her husband and does not want a divorce.

Perhaps she should not be surprised. In 1973, Donald came home a different man—more impatient, angrier, less tolerant of his family. The differences popped up soon after their passionate homecoming embrace was captured by photographers.

On a television appearance on *The David Susskind Show,* he called himself "a P.O.W.: a prisoner of wife." That stung.

He was still a prisoner, but *of the war,* tied to the bond he had forged with his fellow prisoners. Even under the best of circumstances, even right after stepping off the plane home, focusing on the marriage was a tug of war. She had waited five long years to be reunited, yet it felt as if he was a million miles away. Each day that he was gone during the war, she kept Donald's high school ring close, a gleaming gold and ruby talisman. Sometimes, she wore it dangling on a chain, sometimes she carried it in her purse. Then, upon hearing the news of his impending homecoming, Andrea had impulsively mailed the ring to him for his POW debriefing in Hawaii, to lift his spirits. Though she sent it care of the U.S. Army, it was lost forever.

On a trip that was designed to be a romantic getaway, things did not go as planned.

In a suite at a lavish Colorado lodge with her husband for an all-expense paid vacation, one of many hosted for former POWs and their families, signs of their passion, including tousled sheets and his and hers suitcases, surrounded Andrea. Her husband's initial welcome was warm. Twenty-four hours later, something seemed amiss.

Donald had slipped out of their hotel room, telling her he was going to find other former POWs at the lodge for a smoke. Understandable, but annoying. Her husband seemed to be more comfortable hanging out with *them* than reconnecting with *her*. She just wanted to spend time with him, she thought, longingly. Donald was missing in action. Still.

He could be mercurial. And critical. He did not like her clothing, the way she wore her hair, how she ran their household. She thought he would be impressed with how, in his long absence, she had managed the family, the household, and her career. She believed he would be in awe of her landmark activism and how hard she had searched for him. But, since his homecoming, it appeared five years of going it alone had made her too independent, at least for Donald.

There was rage just underneath the surface of his skin that would rear its ugly head. In retrospect, Andrea is convinced he was experiencing post-traumatic stress disorder.

"He was not trying to put this marriage together. He was all over the place and trying to catch up," Andrea said. The couple married in October 1964 and Donald deployed to Vietnam in 1967. He was gone longer than they had been together.

"We had had our ups and downs before he left, but the marriage wasn't the same after he came home." Andrea chalked it up to the impact of the war. "He had to get used to the way we did things after being away for so long. We had our own routine, the girls and I. But for Donald, things had changed so much, and he had to figure things out," she recalls. "His homecoming was an adjustment for the entire family." Perhaps that was why Andrea tried so hard to please her husband. Could being less independent and more docile have helped their relationship?

To complicate matters, she also confessed to a reporter that she dated "platonically" while Donald was held captive. But now that Donald is home, *he* was her focus and she wanted to be *his*. "I want some attention. That is what I was putting in my heart and my head. But I wasn't getting it." Sitting alone in their well-appointed hotel room, the minutes ticked by. Andrea became even more annoyed. Vacillating between self-pity and rationalization, she checked her wristwatch. *Where was he?*

Impetuously, she climbed into the dry bathtub, fully dressed, with her arms crossed. She hoped Donald would barge in, realize she has been *oh so patient*, and scoop her up in his arms. But he was a no show. Examining her nails, she waited in the empty tub, mulling over her husband's behavior. "I was trying to get him to recognize me as his wife." It was lonely when he was captive. In some ways, this was even lonelier.

Donald seemed to relish the limelight from the publicity surrounding the POWs' release, atypical for someone working in Army intelligence. "It was almost a conflict," Andrea notes.

Stretching out her legs, she sat back in the tub and waited. For *two hours*. Exasperated, she dragged herself out of the tub, heading out the door in search of her husband.

Despite the difficulties, divorce never crossed her mind. "I didn't even think about divorce. I said, I can't. There's no way I'm going to ever divorce this man and he's never going to divorce me. It's never going to happen."

Never say never.

Almost two decades later, the search for her husband—the one she knew in 1964—has ended. Reluctantly, she signs the divorce papers and starts a new chapter of her life. On her own. Again.

GETTING ANSWERS (OCTOBER 2017)

"Yes," the tiny old man says. "I remember Colonel Shelton very well." He smiles and nods. Souvanthone Nolasin is ninety years old, missing most of his teeth, but spry and with a fairly good memory.

Fifty years ago, he served in the Pathet Lao Army and was working near the massive cave complex near Sam Neua when Charles Shelton's plane was shot down and his parachute descended from the sky. It snagged a tree, leaving the pilot dangling with a broken leg. Nolasin claims he and a detachment of Pathet Lao cut Shelton down from the tree and took him to the caves, where he was a prisoner for several years until he died of dysentery, malaria, or malnutrition.

American Jeff Clark and Nui, his much younger Thai wife, are interviewing Nolasin in his home in the village of Ban Na Then of Laos. Jeff, seventy-five, is the brother of Michael Clark, the close friend of Marian Shelton who was with her the night before she killed herself. How did Jeff and Nui find the hamlet of Ban Na Then and this eyewitness?

It started online. Jeff met Nui on Facebook in 2016. Intrigued, he flew to Bangkok to meet her. He never went back to his family in San Diego. He remembered enough about the Shelton case to know that he was captured in Sam Neua province and was held in caves near Vieng Xai. With Nui's language skills and his connection to the Sheltons, could the two of them go in search of Charles? Nui was game.

In October of 2017, Nui's son Peter drove them eight hours to the tiny town of Vieng Xai. The Lao Army followed, posting a sentry outside their hotel room.

They met Win, a tour guide, who took them to the famous caves, once the home of the Pathet Lao. Are there any Pathet Lao who served during the war still alive? they asked. "Yes," Win replied, "my father. Would you like to meet him?"

At Nolasin's home, Nui directs the conversation. She wants to appeal as a friend, not an interrogator. Jeff is Colonel Shelton's cousin, she lies. He is not a member of the U.S. government. He wants to pay his respects, she explains.

The old man is wary. "Are you sure you don't tell USA?" Nui shakes her head. "I told him: 'I promise, I won't tell.' That's why he started talking to me. And people are still angry with the American Army, who killed their people."

Jeff and Nui show Nolasin a photo of Colonel Shelton and he begins to open up. He squints at the photo and smiles. Pointing to the sky, he says, "He came from up high." He tells them his memories of Charles's capture and time in captivity.

"Would you like to see where he is buried?"

Jeff is incredulous: "This is just too much to believe. To come 13,000 miles, meet a man in a town I'd never even heard of. Nui and I say, 'We'll go.'"

Nolasin and Win lead Jeff, Nui, and Peter to an open area not far from the road, with rice paddies and high brush. They stop at the middle of a ravine. Boulders of all sizes are scattered in the wake of nearby mining blasts. The mouths of large caves—hundreds of them, some 200 feet high—gape in nearby slopes.

Nolasin points to a large boulder. There, he says, several bodies were buried during the war, including Charles's. He did not witness the burial, but his brother did. He claims that the area was heavily bombed shortly after Shelton's burial. Jeff and Nui place a small, whitewashed cross at the site, surrounded by daisies.

Despite their promise to Nolasin, they share this information with U.S. government officials, who find Nolasin's intelligence credible. The site also matches the location Ann Mills-Griffiths was shown in 1982.

A joint American and Lao recovery team excavates several times, the latest in August of 2019. The team lays out a grid, the way archaeologists do. A mechanical excavator digs up 192 square meters of sediment, grabbing four feet of soil at a time, to an average depth of forty-five to fifty-five centimeters below surface level (cmbs). Each batch of soil is laid on a tarp and passed through a ¼-inch wire mesh using high-pressure water flow. In between, an explosive ordnance technician delicately searches unexploded ordnance. Numerous photographs are taken of everything.

The recovery team spends three painstaking months at the site. It seems promising, this latest of numerous investigations, site surveys, and other excavations conducted since 1992 in search of Charles Shelton's remains. It uncovers bomb fragments, bullets, shell casings, pottery shards, batteries, and medicine bottles. And they also find "possible osseous material."

John, Charlie, Michael, Joan, and Lea Ann Shelton, Christmas 2021 in Louisville. All five of the children have migrated back to Kentucky. (*Photo courtesy of the Shelton family.*)

A LONG TIME COMING (2017)

On a hot August day in Austin, Texas, Hunter Ellis signs for delivery of a small UPS envelope. It has taken two days for the package to arrive from a U.S. Navy mail facility in Tennessee. But it has been twenty-three years since he learned of the existence of its contents, and forty-nine years since his mom, Candy Parish Ellis, has seen it: his father's military identification card.

Navy Lt. Charles Parish did *not* survive the shootdown of his aircraft in July of 1968. Candy received eyewitness confirmation from Chuck's RIO Bob Fant in 1973, when Fant returned home after enduring four-and-a-half years in captivity. Fant ejected from the burning plane. Chuck did not. His status was officially changed to KIA/BNR, "Killed in Action/Body Not Recovered," in April of 1973.

Hunter was three weeks old when his father died, but Chuck never disappeared from the family. "I've always felt like he's been here." The only dad he has known is Rear Adm. Bob Ellis, the man his mother married in 1972. Bob adopted Hunter and raised him as his own, and Candy and Bob had two more children. But Chuck Parish always had a seat at the Ellis dinner table. "And he still does." Hunter feels so fortunate that he has a family that talks about the war, and its casualties. Like his father.

Candy and Hunter never received Chuck's remains. After Fant told them that the plane plowed into the ground and burst into flames, they didn't expect to. But his ID card? Hunter explains, "My mom said he would always fly with his ID card in his thigh pocket. So, it was sandwiched between two layers of Nomex." Nomex, the flame-retardant material used in aviation flight suits, protected the laminated card.

During an occasional review of the Charles Parish case file, the Ellis family was stunned to learn of the existence of the ID card. They had never been informed.

Somehow, the card ended up in a military museum in Vinh, Vietnam, where it sat on display for years. Hunter was busy following in the footsteps of his grandfathers and fathers, pursuing a career as a Navy F/A-18 pilot, then a stint as a FedEx pilot. An appearance on the reality show *Survivor* led him to a successful television career.

In 2016, Hunter, married with two young children, started asking questions about the ID card. "It's always bothered me it was over there." At a periodic family briefing hosted by the Defense POW/MIA Accounting Agency, or DPAA, the government organization whose mission is to account for *all* of America's missing servicemembers, Hunter pushed the issue. Could DPAA get the ID card returned? Relations between the United States and Vietnam had warmed significantly since 1993. An official told Hunter he would try. "For a family that never had closure, that never had any physical evidence, this was the only thing that was there. So, for me, that was the closure we needed."

Now, here it is, in his hands.

But he is not ready to look inside the envelope. Not quite. Hunter stuffs the package underneath his workout clothes at the bottom of his bureau, where he can see it each time he gets ready to go to the gym.

Four months later, on a holiday trip to Washington, D.C., Hunter takes his wife Meredith and their daughter Parish and son Bourne to the Vietnam Wall. "I always go visit the Wall every time I'm in DC." On his first visit, in 1983, he used a pencil to rub an etching of his dad's name from the black granite wall onto a piece of paper. Then he took it and walked to the steps of the Lincoln Memorial, where he sat for a while looking at it and gazing at the Mall. Candy remembers that Hunter was unusually quiet that day.

On this visit on New Year's Day 2018, it is twenty degrees Fahrenheit. The children plead: "Dad, can we go? It's *so* cold." No. Not yet.

Hunter takes the UPS envelope and tears it open. Inside a plastic pouch is a small, laminated card typed with his dad's name, service number, and an expiration date: INDEFINITE. It is all crisply legible. Even his dad's signature. *His handwriting.* And his faded photo. Faded but not erased.

"It was so raw," Hunter remembers, tearing up. Not just the weather, but emotions for a man he never met.

Hunter Ellis; daughter Parish, 8; and son Bourne, 6, at the Vietnam Wall, New Year's Day 2018. (*Photo courtesy of Hunter Ellis.*)

CHAPTER TWENTY-ONE

ONE LAST DIVE (AUGUST 14, 2018)

Ann Mills-Griffiths, leader of the National League of POW/MIA Families, in her office. She has held this position for more than forty-five years. (*Photo courtesy of the National League of POW/MIA Families.*)

"You gotta be shittin' me." Ann Mills-Griffiths is almost speechless. Almost. She is sitting at her desk in Falls Church, Virginia, on a sweltering summer day, across from three DPAA officials. They had called her this morning, asking to see her in person. "I didn't think anything of it because I talk to them all the time."

They have news. They have retrieved a few tiny bone fragments from the shallow, muddy waters off the coast of the fishing village of Quynh Phuong, north of Vinh. Using DNA samples she has given DPAA, they confirmed that the osseous material is her brother's, Navy Cdr. James B. Mills.

It has been fifty-two years since he disappeared during an armed reconnaissance mission, his seventh mission of his second deployment to Vietnam. Mills, a radar intercept officer (RIO) and his pilot, Capt. James Bauder, were flying an F-4B Phantom when they disappeared from radar in the dead of night. No flak, missiles, nor anti-aircraft artillery were in the area. No explosions were seen or heard. Search and rescue aircraft saw nothing. Bauder and Mills had vanished.

Ann was at the home of her parents in Bakersfield, California, when she received the news. A chaplain and the local high school football coach, also a Navy reservist, knocked at the Mills's front door in his uniform. Ann, twenty-five, escorted them inside. "I looked at them with dread. And they said, 'Yes, it's about Jimmy. But he's only missing.'" Jimmy and Ann were eleven months apart, Irish twins. "We were very close."

Only missing? Not knowing what happened to her older brother for five decades has been her driving force. Uncertainty is so much worse than death. It is a lifetime sentence. Yet, she is also realistic. "I knew the possibility of finding his remains was remote."

Staring at the DPAA officials, Ann admits, "I never expected to get this news."

Between 1993 and 2003, the case of Bauder and Mills was investigated fifteen times. Then, in 2006, in the shallows of the South China Sea, a fisherman's net snagged on something solid. Squinting over the side of his sampan, the old man saw a large piece of metal wedged in the muck. The scrap might be worth something, if he could figure out how to get it ashore. What he pulled out of the water was a large canopy frame of a plane.

Five underwater investigations were needed to find the rest of the wreckage. After that, DPAA sent divers four separate times looking for remains. They found some, of Captain Bauder, in 2017. But none of Jimmy.

"When Bauder's remains were recovered in 2017, I knew my brother was there. I knew he had died and where." But DPAA would not give up. Driven in part by the movement spawned by the National League to leave no one behind and to account for those missing during the war, DPAA insisted on *one last dive*. "This is the last time," Ann insisted. "I don't want any more resources spent on my brother's case."

Tasked with the mission to find and repatriate all missing men, DPAA vows to stay the course until the mission is complete. On their twentieth search, a diver emerged from the murky waters, with buckets of sediment. Working from a nearby barge, forensic archeologists poured the muddy silt through a sieve, hoping it would catch what has been hiding in this watery grave for half a century. And it did. One of the specialists held up a tiny piece of osseous material. It was a rib bone belonging to Mills.

With full military honors, Ann buried her brother at Arlington National Cemetery in June 2019. Ann is still serving as the leader of the National League, forty-five years after taking the helm. Because it was never just about her brother.

Before her brother disappeared, and before there were 2,500 Americans missing from the Vietnam War, and long before there was DPAA, there was the U.S. Graves Registration Service, established in 1917. This unit was responsible for identifying remains *after* the war's end and burying them, using mostly dog tags and the accounts of fellow soldiers.

But those who were missing in war were just left missing. Until the Vietnam War, when a small group of women changed all that. The women—Ann Mills-Griffiths, Carole Hanson Hickerson, Valerie Kushner, Pat Mearns, Candy Parish Ellis, Andrea Rander,

Marian Shelton, Sybil Stockdale, and Alice Stratton, *just to name a few*—took matters into their own hands. They made the fate of the missing a national priority.

Ann Mills-Griffiths, alongside her sister, Judie Mills Taber, during the funeral for their brother, Navy Cdr. James Mills, at Fort Myer Memorial Chapel, Virginia, June 24, 2019. Mills was accounted for by DPAA in August 2018, fifty-two years after his disappearance. (*U.S. Army Photo by Sgt. 1st Class Kristen Duus, DPAA.*)

After the war's end, the National League pressured the Pentagon to create a permanent government organization whose sole task was to resolve the still-lingering issue of the more than 2,500 missing men in Southeast Asia. That organization, established in January of 1973, was named the Joint Casualty Resolution Center. After many name changes, the JCRC became DPAA. The organization boasts an annual budget of $130 million, a highly skilled staff of 700 professionals, and the tagline "Fulfilling America's Promise"—a promise made to a handful of military wives more than fifty years ago.

This same group of women also fundamentally altered how the United States considers prisoners of war, who now have national value. Consequently, the United States fights its wars in ways to minimize the potential of capture by the enemy. It was no accident that the United States ended its longest conflict in 2021, in Afghanistan, without a single POW or MIA. The nation can still tolerate those killed in action (KIAs) but not POWs nor MIAs.

Likewise, this policy shift has also influenced other countries around the world. The families of missing and captive servicemembers in Kuwait, Israel, and Australia have all loudly pressured their governments to follow the American lead, and "leave no man behind." And Vietnamese families, having witnessed the substantial media coverage American missing men have received, have demanded their government do the same for *their* wartime missing.

As of this writing, there are 1,584 husbands, fathers, sons, and brothers still missing from the Vietnam War. Their wives, mothers, fathers, brothers, sisters, daughters, sons, and now grandchildren continue holding the U.S. and foreign governments accountable for determining the fate of each man. While the mission stipulates the United States will make every conceivable effort to leave no man behind, the reality differs. The toll of the missing men will never be zero. The job will never be finished.

But the effort is noble, uniquely and quintessentially American, and the return of long-lost servicemen always celebrated and commemorated. It's all thanks to a handful of women, like Ann Mills-Griffiths, who has no plans to retire. She believes *her* job is to keep the government honest. Keep on keeping on. She has taken the tragedy of her brother and turned it into her life's work. Her mother always told her to "Make a purse out of a sow's ear."

Signing off every email, she hails: "As ever and onward."

CAST OF CHARACTERS
(in alphabetical order)

Carol Bates Brown – A college student during the Vietnam War, and member of Voices for a Vital America (VIVA), she and others sought meaningful ways to support U.S. troops, which led to the development of the ubiquitous and highly successful POW/MIA bracelet campaign.

Rose Bucher – When USS *Pueblo* was captured in 1968 by North Korea and accused of spying, it became a diplomatic crisis and instantaneously thrust Rose, wife of *Pueblo* commanding officer Cdr. Lloyd Bucher, into the media spotlight.

Madeline Duckles – Wife of a university music professor in northern California, she was an associate of Cora Weiss and a peace activist with the Women's Strike for Peace and the Committee of Liaison with Servicemen Detained in North Vietnam.

Candy Parish Ellis – The daughter and daughter-in-law of admirals, she was barely twenty-three and the mother of a three-week-old son, Hunter, when her husband, Navy Lt. Charles "Chuck" Parish, was reported missing in action in 1968.

Carole Hanson Hickerson – Carole was a tall and lively brunette, a schoolteacher, and mother to nine-month-old Todd, when her husband, her college sweetheart, Marine aviator Capt. Stephen Hanson, was shot down in Laos, a place where the U.S. did not officially admit combat operations were taking place.

Valerie Kushner – Feisty and impatient, Valerie was a native New Yorker who moved to the small southern town of Danville, Virginia, when her husband, Army flight surgeon Maj. F. Harold "Hal" Kushner, deployed to Vietnam. He was captured when the helicopter ferrying him crashed into a mountain during a storm in December 1967. At the time, she was pregnant with their second child.

Carol McCain – Born and raised as an only child in Philadelphia, the savvy and tall brunette swimsuit model was the mother of three young children when her second husband, the admiral's son Navy Lt. Cdr. John McCain, was shot down, gravely injured, and taken captive as a POW in 1967.

Emilee McCarthy Reynolds – Born and raised in Miami and Trinidad, she was a high school art teacher living in the Philadelphia suburbs with the parents of her fiancé, when she answered the door three weeks before their wedding to be informed that Air Force Capt. Jon Reynolds had been shot down over North Vietnam earlier that day.

Mary Ann "Pat" Mearns – Raised in Burbank, California, Pat was a nurse and airline stewardess living in Japan with her husband, Air Force Maj. Arthur Mearns, and their two small girls, when he was shot down on Veteran's Day 1966, while flying a bombing mission over North Vietnam.

Ann Mills-Griffiths – Sister to MIA Navy Cdr. Jim Mills, missing since 1966, Ann became the face and leader of the National League of Families after the war ended, a position she still holds more than forty-five years later.

Andrea Rander – A poised mother of two little girls, Andrea's second husband, Army Sgt. Donald Rander, was captured when his military intelligence unit was overrun during the infamous Tet Offensive in January 1968. She is one of the few Black POW and MIA wives, and one of even fewer who were active in the campaign.

Marian Shelton – When the Air Force officials came calling to base housing on Okinawa on April 29, 1965, they shared encouraging news. Her husband, Air Force Capt. Charles Shelton, had survived ejection from his reconnaissance plane over northern Laos and had radioed that he was safely on the ground.

Sybil Stockdale – Raised on a dairy farm in Connecticut, Sybil had been married for nearly two decades to Navy Cdr. James Bond Stockdale when he was shot down over North Vietnam and captured in 1965.

Alice Stratton – Born and raised in the suburbs of Detroit, Alice was a clinical social worker, living with her three young sons near Naval Air Station Lemoore, in northern California, when her husband, Navy Lt. Cdr. Dick Stratton, was shot down and taken captive in January of 1967.

Cora Weiss – A vocal and early antiwar demonstrator, she is the founder of Women's Strike for Peace and the Committee of Liaison for Families of Servicemen Detained in Vietnam.

WHERE ARE THEY NOW?

Learn more about the characters in this book at www.unwaveringbook.com.

THE MISSING MAN TABLE

A crisp white tablecloth drapes the table, symbolizing a soldier's pure heart when answering the call to duty. A lemon slice and scattered grains of salt represent the bitter fate and tears families shed waiting for loved ones to return. A black napkin serves as an emblem for the sorrow of captivity, and the overturned water glass is a reminder of the meal that will remain untouched. A white candle symbolizes peace and a red rose in a vase tied with a yellow ribbon represents the hope that those missing will someday return or be accounted for.

Sometimes, the Missing Man Table holds a military cover, or hat, from each branch of the services and an empty chair for each. Often, a Bible is added to demonstrate the importance of faith when a loved one is missing. Although the setup varies, the meaning remains poignant. The table is set at U.S. military ceremonies around the world, when a narrator recites a script explaining its symbolism. A Missing Man Table is sometimes left set up throughout the year at mess halls and cafeterias on military bases.

While no one can pinpoint when the Missing Man Table was first staged, some say the idea originated with the River Rats, U.S. military air crews who flew combat missions over the Red River Valley in North Vietnam. Forming an organization in 1966–1967 called The Red River Valley Association, its first mission was to raise awareness for air crews missing in action or captured by the North Vietnamese.

According to informal history, they held their first reunions while the POWs were still imprisoned in Southeast Asia, setting a table for those they knew were missing or dead. Ever since, the practice of incorporating the remembrance table into military ceremonies has become a tradition adapted to military ceremonies. A meaningful tribute to the missing, the ritual has also found its way into civilian ceremonies.

ACKNOWLEDGMENTS

"I long to hear that you have declared an independency. And, by the way, in the new code of laws which I suppose it will be necessary for you to make, I desire you would *remember the ladies* and be more generous and favorable to them than your ancestors. Do not put such unlimited power into the hands of the husbands. Remember, all men would be tyrants if they could. If particular care and attention is not paid to the ladies, we are determined to foment a rebellion, and will not hold ourselves bound by any laws in which we have no voice or representation."

—Abigail Adams in a letter to her husband dated March 31, 1776

After two decades of research and writing about the *men* who still are the longest-held group of POWs in our nation's history, receiving an email from one of them, Navy Capt. Dick Stratton, in January of 2015, was a pleasant surprise. He advocated *for the ladies*: "What folks do not realize is that during the Vietnam War, the wives and families had it far worse than we did.... Our families from one day to the next did not know if we were okay or not; they had no confidence that our government gave a damn about us or would ever bring us home...."

He was right.

Theirs was a fifty-year-old story about a handful of military wives who made the fate of the captive and missing men a national priority. It was a stark departure from how our nation's military and diplomats treated the POW and MIAs during other wars. By moving from the sidelines to the frontlines, the women set in motion a wholesale shift in military policy, especially as it pertains to the missing. *Today, we as a nation continue to feel the impact of their work.*

We crafted our book with the assistance, insight, and experiences of many people who were generous in sharing their expertise, recollections, and personal and professional referrals—pointing us to specific sources and research across the country.

We thank our Post Hill Press acquisitions editor and champion Alex Novak, as well as managing editor Heather King; cover designer Cody Corcoran; our brilliant and highly visual storyline editor, Stephanie "DeeDee" Slewka; and of course, our diligent, bibliophile literary agent, Leah Spiro. Thank you for taking a chance on us and the ladies.

It is the narratives of the MIA and POW wives—and their families—that sustained our passion for more than seven years. They are our inspiration. Our gratitude and admiration go to Candy Parish Ellis, Carole Hanson Hickerson, Valerie Kushner, Carol McCain, Pat Mearns, Ann Mills-Griffiths, Andrea Rander, Emilee Reynolds, Marian Shelton, Sybil Stockdale, and Alice Stratton.

We also thank the many other wives and family members who advocated during the Vietnam War on behalf of America's missing men, working the phones, writing letters, and courageously assuming atypical roles for military family members.

POW brother Bob Brudno deserves special recognition. His personal experience, historical insight, and longitudinal perspective helped educate us as to why this story matters, elevating the significance of the work these women did more than fifty years ago.

Special thanks also go to POW sons Patrick Stratton and Dr. Jim Stockdale II for their invaluable guidance. Their eyewitness accounts and vantage points lent both gravitas and youthful perspective to the project.

Naturally, we owe a special thank you to the POWs, a group of men who endured the unthinkable, returning home with honor. To those who never made it home, your sacrifice and the dedication of the women who love you have catalyzed how our nation treats our missing.

There are countless others whose insight, interest, and in some cases, front-row seats to history assisted in the development of our book. They include, but are not limited to: the Hon. Everett Alvarez, Jr., Amy Argetsinger, the Hon. Richard Armitage, the Hon. Will Ball, Capt. Dale Bosley, Rear Adm. Tom Brooks, Carol Bates Brown, Sheila Brudno, Steve Bull, Lt. Col. L.H. "Bucky" Burruss, Richard Capen, Dwight Chapin, Richard Childress, Rear Adm. Ernie Christensen, Leslie Carpenter Christensen, Peggy Cifrino, Jeff and Nui Clark, Michael Clark, Rear Adm. Tony Cothron, Nancy Cuddy, Christine Cugini, Dennis Dalpino, Elinda Deans, Rep. Bob Dornan, Rear Adm. Bob Ellis, Hunter Ellis, Katie and Pat Foy, Steve Frank, Capt. Frank and Linda Gamboa, Lysa Rander Hall, Col. Mike Harrigan, Todd Hickerson, Judy Holliday, Phyllis Watt Jordan, Susan Katz Keating, Teddy Kunhardt, Ben Kushner, Kali Mason, Joe McCain, Sid McCain, the Hon. Robert McFarlane, Capt. Marty McCullough, Paul Mather, Joan Shelton May, Sid McCain, Frances Mearns, Missy Mearns, Tom and Tanya Meurer, Toni Kushner Nee, Elizabeth Reynolds Peltz, Art Pine, Adm. Joe Prueher, Merle Pribbenow, Dave Rosenau, Scott Russell, Charlie Shelton, John Shelton, Lea Ann Shelton, Michael Shelton, Geraldine and Walter Sherman, Dr. Roger Shields, Bradley Taylor, Craig Timberg, Pat Twinem, the Hon. Chase Untermeyer, and Harriette Will. A special thank you to our beta readers, Victoria Bond, Dory Codington, Steve Newborn, Kate Keith Pearsall, Mark Silverstein, Ted Weinstein, and George Wilkens. There are others who played smaller but vital advisory roles, providing details and documents. We remain grateful to each of you.

It was both challenging and rewarding to craft this book, taking great care to weave in cultural, military, and socioeconomic context into the personal narratives. We thank our husbands and families profusely for reading early drafts, listening to us read an occasional paragraph aloud, making suggestions, supporting our pre-dawn and late-night retreats into many iterations of our manuscript, or offering *le mot juste*. None of this would be possible without their good humor, coffee-brewing skills, tolerance of voluminous stacks of paper and uneaten meals, and vacations spent mostly at the computer or on Zoom meetings. We would also like to thank our friends who graciously offered encouragement and laughter as we shared tidbits about the book, trying to tantalize them with small details of chapters as we wrote them. Finally, here's to our parents and supportive brothers for imbuing us with a love of writing and history, and an interest in serving our country. We count ourselves lucky to have a tribe of forthright and reliable supporters.

As women and military veterans, we are honored to document the history, bravery, and persistence of a small group of ladies who against all odds, forever changed the way our nation regards and recovers our missing. Finally, we must credit Capt. Dick Stratton, a.k.a. "The Beak," who first urged us to write about the ladies.

Remember the ladies.

SELECT BIBLIOGRAPHY

BOOKS

Abramson, Rudy. *Spanning the Century: The Life of W. Averell Harriman, 1891–1986*. New York: William Morrow and Company, Inc., 1992.

Allen, Michael J. *Until the Last Man Comes Home: POWS, MIAs, and the Unending Vietnam War*. Chapel Hill: University of North Carolina Press, 2009.

Alvarez, Everett, Jr., and Anthony S. Pitch. *Chained Eagle: The Heroic Story of the First American Shot Down Over North Vietnam*. Washington, DC: Potomac Books, 2005.

Bell, Garnett "Bill," with George J. Veith. *Leave No Man Behind: Bill Bell and the Search for American POW/MIAs from the Vietnam War*. Madison, WI: Goblin Fern Press, 2004.

Blakey, Scott. *Prisoner at War: The Survival of Commander Richard A. Stratton*. Garden City, NY: Anchor Press/Doubleday, 1978.

Bradley, Mark Philip, and Marilyn B. Young, Editors. *Making Sense of the Vietnam Wars: Local, National, and Transnational Perspectives*. New York and Oxford: Oxford University Press, 2008.

Burkett, B. G., and Glenna Whitley. *Stolen Valor: How the Vietnam Generation Was Robbed of Its Heroes and Its History*. Dallas, TX: Verity Press, Inc., 1998.

Clarke, Captain Douglas L., USN. *The Missing Man: Politics and the MIA*. Washington, DC: National Defense University Research Directorate, January 1979.

Davis, Vernon E. *The Long Road Home*. Washington, DC: Historical Office of the Secretary of Defense, 2000.

Diplomatic Conference for the Establishment of International Conventions for the Protection of Victims of War. Geneva Convention Relative to the Treatment of Prisoners of War, 1949.

Ford, Harold P. *CIA and the Vietnam Policymakers: Three Episodes, 1962–1968*. Washington, DC: History Staff, Center for the Study of Intelligence, Central Intelligence Agency, 1998.

Foster, Gary Wayne. *The Hanoi March: American POWs in North Vietnam's Crucible*. Ashland, OR: Hellgate Press, 2022.

Franklin, H. Bruce. *M.I.A. or Mythmaking in America: How and Why Belief in Live POWs Has Possessed a Nation*. New Brunswick, NJ: Rutgers University Press, 1993.

Frazier, Jessica M. *Women's Antiwar Diplomacy During the Vietnam War Era*. Chapel Hill, NC: The University of North Carolina Press, 2017.

Gittinger, Ted, editor. *The Johnson Years: A Vietnam Roundtable*. Austin, TX: Lyndon Baines Johnson Library, Lyndon B. Johnson School of Public Affairs, the University of Texas at Austin, 1993.

Graff, Garrett M. *Watergate: A New History*. New York: Avid Reader Press, 2022.

Gritz, James "Bo." *A Nation Betrayed*. Boulder City, NV: Lazarus Publishing Company, 1988.

Grubb, Evelyn and Carol Jose. *You Are Not Forgotten: A Family's Quest for Truth and the Founding of the National League of Families*. St. Petersburg, FL: Vandamere Press, 2008.

Guenon, William A., Jr., *Secret and Dangerous: Night of the Son Tay P.O.W. Raid*. East Lowell, MA: King Printing Company, Inc., 2002.

Haldeman, H. R. *The Haldeman Diaries: Inside the Nixon White House.* New York: G. P. Putnam's Sons, 1994.

Harris, Carlyle "Smitty," and Sara W. Berry. *Tap Code: The Epic Survival Tale of a Vietnam POW and the Secret Code That Changed Everything.* Grand Rapids, MI: Zondervan, 2019.

Howes, Craig. *Voices of the Vietnam POWs: Witnesses to Their Fight.* New York and Oxford: Oxford University Press, 1993.

Hunt, Richard A. *Melvin Laird and the Foundation of the Post-Vietnam Military 1969–1973.* Washington, DC: Historical Office, Office of the Secretary of Defense, 2015.

Johnson, Lyndon Baines. *The Vantage Point: Perspectives of the Presidency, 1963–1969.* New York: Holt, Rinehart & Winston, 1971.

Keating, Susan Katz. *Prisoners of Hope: Exploiting the POW/MIA Myth in America.* New York: Random House, 1994.

Kissinger, Henry. *Ending the Vietnam War: A History of America's Involvement in and Extrication from the Vietnam War.* New York: Simon & Schuster, 2003.

Kissinger, Henry. *White House Years.* Boston: Little, Brown, and Company, 1979.

Lee, Heath Hardage. *The League of Wives: The Untold Story of the Women Who Took on the U.S. Government to Bring Their Husbands Home.* New York: St. Martin's Press, 2019.

Mather, Paul D. *M.I.A.: Accounting for the Missing in Southeast Asia.* Washington, DC: National Defense University Press, 1994.

McCain, John, with Mark Salter. *Faith of My Fathers: A Family Memoir.* New York: Random House, Inc., 1999.

McMaster, H. R. *Dereliction of Duty: Lyndon Johnson, Robert McNamara, the Joint Chiefs of Staff, and the Lies that Led to Vietnam*. New York: Harper Perennial, 1998.

McNamara, Robert S., with Brian VanDeMark. *In Retrospect: The Tragedy and Lessons of Vietnam*. New York: Vintage Books, 1996.

Moïse, Edwin E. *Tonkin Gulf and the Escalation of the Vietnam War*. Chapel Hill and London: The University of North Carolina Press, 1996.

Patterson, Charles J., and G. Lee Tippen. *The Heroes Who Fell from Grace*. Canton, OH: Daring Books, 1985.

Plaster, John L. *SOG: The Secret Wars of America's Commandos in Vietnam*. New York: ONYX, 1997.

Posner, Gerald. *Citizen Perot: His Life and Times*. New York: Random House, 1996.

Pye, Anne Briscoe, and Nancy Shea. *The Navy Wife*. New York: Harper & Brothers, 1945.

Rochester, Stuart I., and Frederick Kiley. *Honor Bound: American Prisoners of War in Southeast Asia 1961–1973*. Annapolis, MD: Naval Institute Press, 2007.

Rusk, Dean, as told to Richard Rusk and edited by Daniel S. Papp. *As I Saw It*. New York: W. W. Norton & Company, 1990.

Salisbury, Harrison E. *Behind the Lines—Hanoi, December 23, 1966–January 7, 1967*. New York: The New York Times Company, 1967.

Salter, Mark. *The Luckiest Man: Life with John McCain*. New York: Simon & Schuster, 2020.

Schemmer, Benjamin F. *The Raid: The Son Tay Prison Rescue Mission*. New York: Ballantine Books, 2002.

Stockdale, Jim, and Sybil Stockdale. *In Love and War: The Story of a Family's Ordeal and Sacrifice During the Vietnam War*. Annapolis, MD: Naval Institute Press, 1990.

Sullivan, William H. *Obbligato 1939–1979: Notes on a Foreign Service Career*. New York: W. W. Norton & Company, 1984.

Swerdlow, Amy. *Women Strike for Peace: Traditional Motherhood and Radical Politics in the 1960s*. Chicago, Illinois and London, England: The University of Chicago Press Ltd., 1993.

Timberg, Robert. *John McCain: An American Odyssey*. New York: Free Press, 2007.

Timberg, Robert. *The Nightingale's Song*. New York: Simon & Schuster, 1995.

Townley, Alvin J. *Defiant: The POWs Who Endured Vietnam's Most Infamous Prison, The Women Who Fought for Them, and the One Who Never Returned*. New York: St. Martin's Press, 2009.

Van Atta, Dale. *With Honor: Melvin Laird in War, Peace, and Politics*. Madison, WI: The University of Wisconsin Press, 2008.

Veith, George J. *Code-Name Bright Light: The Untold Story of U.S. POW Rescue Efforts During the Vietnam War*. New York: Dell, 1998.

UNPUBLISHED WORKS:

"Cora Weiss Oral History Project: The Reminiscences of Cora Weiss," Columbia Center for Oral History, 2014.

Garrett, Dave L., B.S., M.Ed., "The Power of One: Bonnie Singleton and American Prisoners of War in Vietnam." Thesis presented to the Graduate Council of the University of North Texas in Partial Fulfillment of the Requirements for the Degree of Master of Science, Denton, TX, August 1999.

Koenigsamen, Janet Lee, Ph.D., "Mobilization of a Conscience Constituency: VIVA and the POW/MIA Movement." Dissertation, Kent State University, 1987.

Meurer, Thomas E. *The Wild, Wild East: Adventures in Business from the Cold War to the War on Terrorism*. Washington, DC and London: Academica, 2022 (forthcoming).

Smith, Steven L. "The Reluctant Sorority: Stories of American Wives of Prisoners of War and Missing in Action, 1965–1973/Lessons in Exercising Leadership in the Absence of Power." doctor of education, University of San Diego, May 2006.

ABOUT THE AUTHORS

TAYLOR BALDWIN KILAND

Taylor has written, co-authored, ghost-written, or edited twenty-one books, including two about our nation's Vietnam POWs: *Lessons from the Hanoi Hilton: Six Characteristics of High-Performance Teams* and *Open Doors: Vietnam POWs Thirty Years Later.*

A former naval officer—the third generation in her family to serve in the Navy, Taylor was raised in Coronado, California, and Alexandria, Virginia, where she grew up with many of the Vietnam POW and MIA families. She lives with her husband and daughter in Old Town Alexandria, Virginia.

JUDY SILVERSTEIN GRAY

An award-winning journalist, Judy has written numerous military profiles and feature articles about women leaders for news outlets, including *The Tampa Tribune,* publishing six books for young readers—five on military topics—with her work appearing in two literary anthologies. Judy has worked as a public information officer in both the private and non-profit sectors and teaches public health communication and marketing on the graduate level.

The third generation of her family to serve in the military, she is a retired Coast Guard Chief Petty Officer who worked in public affairs. Throughout her pursuits, she has drawn on her fascination with storytelling to craft narratives about innovators and unlikely trailblazers. She lives with her husband in Tampa, Florida.

NOTES

PART I—TO THE FRONTLINES (1964–1970)

Chapter 1: Tea in Paris (October 4, 1969)

The bill for their travel and accommodations: Jim Stockdale and Sybil Stockdale, *In Love and War: The Story of a Family's Ordeal and Sacrifice During the Vietnam War* (Annapolis, MD: Naval Institute Press, 1990), 318.

One two-hour shopping excursion: Candy Parish Ellis, interview with the authors, August 9, 2016.

Tempers flare: Stockdale and Stockdale, *In Love and War,* 320.

"I looked up to her": Andrea Rander, interview with the authors, December 16, 2020.

They were shown photos of North Vietnamese officials: Candy Parish Ellis, interview with the authors, August 9, 2016; and Stockdale and Stockdale, *In Love and War,* 319.

"It wasn't a very convincing demonstration": Stockdale and Stockdale, *In Love and War,* 320.

"She was on her way to a nervous breakdown": Candy Parish Ellis, interview with the authors, January 14, 2022.

Xuan Oanh: He was assigned in 1968 to work in Paris as a member of the delegation of the Government of the Democratic Republic of Vietnam, where he "made a significant contribution to the formation and the powerful growth of the American people's antiwar movement that opposed the war in Vietnam inside the United States itself." In 1972, he was transferred back to Hanoi where "he was the Deputy Group Commander responsible for American proselytizing operations targeted on American airmen prisoners of war." Source: Vietnam Union of Friendship Organizations, 1 April 2010, accessed 27 September 2022 at *http://vufo.org.vn/Tien-biet-Nha-doi-ngoai-nhan-dan-lao-thanh-Do-Xuan-Oanh-25-516.html?lang=vn.*

Enigmatic looking: Sybil Stockdale's handwritten notes taken after the meeting on October 4, 1969, Dr. James Stockdale II's personal collection.

He asks her to write down the specifics: Sybil Stockdale's handwritten notes taken after the meeting on October 4, 1969.

"...he seemed warmer than the others, at least to me": Candy Paris Ellis, interview with the authors, February 4, 2017.

"But I had to say who I was...They must wonder, she thinks, how did *she* get involved?": Andrea Rander, interview with the authors, January 31, 2017.

"They just sat there...": Victoria Mares, "Trip fails to end wife's 3-Year Wait," *Newsday* (Melville, New York), October 8, 1969, 15, accessed on July 11, 2022, www.newspapers.com.

Sybil blinks... "We think you should direct your questions to your own government": Stockdale and Stockdale, *In Love and War,* 322; and Sybil Stockdale's handwritten notes taken after the meeting on October 4, 1969.

"You don't really know what trouble is...so the Americans can be well fed": Sybil Stockdale's handwritten notes taken after the meeting on October 4, 1969.

The women hand over a thick stack of letters: Candy Parish Ellis, interview with the authors, August 9, 2016.

"The napalm was horrific": Candy Paris Ellis, interview with the authors, February 4, 2017; and Dr. James Stockdale II's personal collection.

She blots her lips: Sybil Stockdale's handwritten notes taken after the meeting on October 4, 1969.

"to prove I was there": Andrea Rander, interview with the authors, July 13, 2022.

"What will you do now...Ohhhh, yes": Stockdale and Stockdale, *In Love and War*, 323.

"We felt very dejected": Mary Ann "Pat" Mearns, interview with the authors, March 14, 2017.

Pat is convinced that "Glasses" knows her husband...the wives have been unable to schedule an audience with their own president, Richard Nixon: Pat Mearns, interview with the authors, March 14, 2017; and "Hanoi men end meeting POW kin," United Press International in the *Windsor Star* (Windsor, Ontario, Canada), November 6, 1969, accessed October 27, 2022, *www.newspapers.com*.

"To force the prisoners...in such an arrangement": Stockdale and Stockdale, *In Love and War*, 323–324.

Chapter 2: Risky Business

How Many Are There? (January 1969)

Top aides take notice and so does the president: Steven L. Smith, "The Reluctant Sorority: Stories of American Wives of Prisoners of War and Missing in Action, 1965–1973/Lessons in Exercising Leadership in the Absence of Power," a dissertation submitted in partial fulfillment of the requirements for the degree of doctor of education, University of San Diego, May 2006, 213.

"Please remember those who have offered so much for our country...in Paris": Telegram from Pat Mearns to Richard Nixon, January 20, 1969, from the personal collection of Pat Mearns; Telegram from Richard Nixon to Mrs. Charles Parish, January 30, 1969, from the personal collection of Candy Ellis; and Letter from

Sybil Stockdale to Pat Mearns, February 12, 1969, from the personal collection of Pat Mearns.

Sybil had no experience with the Navy, except...Memorial Day weekend in 1935: Stockdale and Stockdale, *In Love and War*, 37.

"What is more, they must learn to wait patiently...The Navy doesn't particularly care for a wife who is too obviously carrying her load": Anne Briscoe Pye and Nancy Shea, *The Navy Wife* (New York: Harper and Brothers, 1942), 187 and 192.

Woolley had served: Benjamin Pollard, "The life and career of Mary Emma Woolley, one of Brown's first female graduates," *The Brown Daily Herald*, April 8, 2021, *https://www.browndailyherald.com/article/2021/04/the-life-and-career-of-mary-emma-woolley-one-of-brown-s-first-female-graduates.*

"I assure you that the subject of their release and welfare will have an urgent priority in our talks in Paris." Grubb and Jose, *You Are Not Forgotten*, 101.

I appreciate your message and fully share: Memo; William P. Rogers to President Nixon; Subject: Response to Prisoner of War Telegrams; January 27, 1969; folder 1: 3-D Prisoners of War (All); Box 2; White House NSC Files: POW/MIA; Richard Nixon Presidential Library and Museum, Yorba Linda, California.

It's a refrain he will repeat often: Smith, "The Reluctant Sorority," 216; and Dwight Chapin, interview with the authors, August 12, 2022. Chapin was President Nixon's appointments secretary 1969–1973.

Gathering Forces (October 1966)

"I could understand their fear": Stockdale and Stockdale, *In Love and War*, 145.

But they are isolated from one another, for fear the knowledge could be manipulated by the North Vietnamese: Tape 10 Transcript of Video Interview with Sybil Stockdale, 29750110001. Vietnam Center and Sam Johnson Vietnam Archive. No Date, Box

01, Folder 10, Phillip Daniels Collection, Vietnam Center and Sam Johnson Vietnam Archive, Texas Tech University, accessed September 9, 2021, *https://www.vietnam.ttu.edu/virtualarchive/items.php?item=2975011000l.*

She offered postage: Stockdale and Stockdale, *In Love and War,* 143.

Acknowledging the elephant in the room: Stockdale and Stockdale, *In Love and War,* 145–146; and Heath Hardage Lee, *The League of Wives: The Untold Story of the Women Who Took On the U.S. Government to Bring Their Husbands Home,* (New York: St. Martin's Press, 2019), 64–65.

Keep Quiet – That's an Order! (May 1965)

The following citations are the sources for this scene:

Dr. James Stockdale II, emails to the authors October 17, 2020, and November 19, 2020.

"Advise [sic] to potential prisoner of war families," notes typed by Sybil Stockdale, undated, Sybil Bailey Stockdale papers, Box/Folder 11:15, Hoover Institution Library and Archives.

Letter from Jim Stockdale to Sybil Stockdale, August 5, 1965, Sybil Bailey Stockdale papers, Box 2/folder 1, Hoover Institution Library and Archives.

Sybil Stockdale diary, May 1965, Sybil Bailey Stockdale papers, Box 11/folder 15, Hoover Institution Library and Archives, and email to the authors from Jim Stockdale II, October 17, 2020.

The Doorbell Rings (September 1965)

The sources for this scene are the following:

Stockdale and Stockdale, *In Love and War,* 119–120.

Dr. James Stockdale II, "Collateral Damage," Lecture to Mercersburg Academy Alumni, May 2020.

Chapter 3: Premonitions, Proof and Policy Changes

Proof of Life (April 1967)

The headline on the April 7 issue blares: *Life* magazine, April 7, 1967, front cover.

...an image that will continue to haunt her: Scott Blakey, *Prisoner at War: The Survival of Commander Richard A. Stratton,* (Garden City, New York: Anchor Press/Doubleday, 1978), 154-155.

Their bond is unshakeable...sit in stunned silence: Pat and Katie Foy, interview with the authors, July 11, 2021; and Blakey, *Prisoner at War,* 154.

"His hands are cupped at his sides...and shuffles through a curtain and out of sight": Lee Lockwood, "U.S. prisoners and an eerie puppet show," *Life* magazine, April 7, 1967, 41–44.

Later that day, he confirmed the voice was Dick's: Alice and Dick Stratton interview with the authors, June 12 ,201; and Blakey, *Prisoner at War,* 153.

It is a deep-seated survival technique: Alice and Richard Stratton, "Seven years at war—A family story," community presentation, Jacksonville, Florida, January 26, 2012.

"I exposed, once again, the Foys": Blakey, *Prisoner at War,* 154.

***Time* magazine refers to the spectacle**: Stuart I. Rochester and Frederick Kiley, *Honor Bound: American Prisoners of War in Southeast Asia 1961–1973,* (Annapolis, MD: Naval Institute Press, 2007), 344; and Vernon E. Davis, *The Long Road Home: U.S. Prisoner of War Policy and Planning in Southeast Asia,* (Washington, DC: Historical Office, Office of the Secretary of Defense), 2000.

"it would appear that the North Vietnamese...professions of 'humane treatment' cannot be accepted": Alice and Dick Stratton, email and interview with the authors, June 12, 2017; and Lee Lockwood, "U.S. prisoners and an eerie puppet show," *Life* magazine, April 7, 1967, 41–44.

The Black Sedan (January 1967)

"It was as if everything suddenly stopped": Patrick Stratton, conversation with the authors, September 22, 2021.

"Is he dead?"...the men were not certain: Blakey, *Prisoner at War,* 85; and Patrick Stratton, conversation with the authors, April 22, 2021.

Alice wanted desperately..."Here, take this. It will help you sleep": Blakey, *Prisoner at War,* 84–88; Pat and Katie Foy, interview with the authors, July 11, 2021.

Alice thought growing up...Why God? Why me?: Patrick Stratton, conversation with the authors, April 22, 2021; Alice and Dick Stratton, email to the authors, June 12, 2017; and Blakey, *Prisoner at War,* 87.

Momentum (May 19, 1969)

"We wanted you to know that here in Washington": Stockdale and Stockdale, *In Love and War,* 308.

"When I sharpened the tone of my questions": Stockdale and Stockdale, *In Love and War,* 216; and Davis, *The Long Road Home,* 94–95.

Political kiss of death: Richard Capen, "Reflections on Mel Laird," July 10, 2015, personal collection of Richard Capen.

He pledged to serve four years and not one day longer: "Melvin Laird, Nixon defense secretary at the height of the Vietnam War, dies at 94," *The Washington Post,* November 16, 2016, *https://www.washingtonpost.com/politics/melvin-laird-nixon-defense-secretary-at-the-height-of-the-vietnam-war-dies-at-94/2016/11/16/7956cdca-ac44-11e6-8b45-f8e493f06fcd_story.html*; and Richard Capen, "Reflections on Mel Laird," *The San Diego Union-Tribune,* November 9, 2016.

Laird met with several POW and MIA wives: Smith, "The Reluctant Sorority," 222.

With more than 1,000 men missing or captive: "Laird asks freedom for GI prisoners," *Wisconsin State Journal,* May 20, 1969,

23, accessed on September 27, 2022, www.newspapers.com; and Davis, *The Long Road Home,* 180.

One wife smashes a painting: Alvin Townley, *Defiant: The POWs Who Endured Vietnam's Most Infamous Prison, The Women Who Fought for Them, and The One Who Never Returned,* (New York: St. Martin's Press, 2014), 380.

"Our government still had no reason...I marveled at his detached, casual attitude": Stockdale and Stockdale, *In Love and War,* 231.

In the process, it might shame Hanoi: Dale Van Atta, *With Honor: Melvin Laird in War, Peace, and Politics* (Madison, WI: The University of Wisconsin Press, 2008), 207; and Dale Van Atta, "Laird's Work for POWs may have saved McCain's life," *Marshfield News-Herald,* (Marshfield, WI), October 6, 2008, accessed February 13, 2021, www.newspapers.com.

Tucked away in file cabinets: Townley, *Defiant,* 381.

"By God, we're going to go public": Van Atta, *With Honor,* 207.

"Good morning, ladies and gentlemen...this is not the case" "Briefing on U.S. prisoners of war and missing in action personnel," News Release, Office of Assistant Secretary of Defense (Public Affairs), May 19, 1969, Box 176, Perot Family Archives, Dallas, Texas.

" Or we were going to mop up the floor with them": Stockdale and Stockdale, *In Love and War,* 314–5.

"As long as the United States does not cease its war": Davis, *The Long Road Home,* 204.

Cold Hard Truth (Summer 1969)

"All I'm interested in is for Hanoi": Press interview with Lieutenant Robert Frishman and Seaman Douglas Hegdahl, PPW Returnees Held by North Vietnam, Hearings Before the Subcommittee on National Security Policy and Scientific Developments of the

Committee on Foreign Affairs, U.S. House of Representatives, 91st Congress, First Session, November 13 and 14, 1969, 94.

Although he has never spoken to Stratton..."tied up in ropes to such a degree that he still has large scars on his arms from rope burns, which became infected": Blakey, *Prisoner at War,* 251; and Davis, *The Long Road Home,* 208.

Like an auctioneer: Jamie Howren and Taylor Kiland, *Open Doors: Vietnam POWs Thirty Years Later,* (Washington, DC: Potomac Books, Inc., 2005), 35–36.

Stratton further instructed Hegdahl: Blakey, *Prisoner at War,* 227.

"To acknowledge Vietnamese humanity and American Independence Day": Blakey, *Prisoner at War,* 245.

Pale and thin after losing 60 pounds in captivity: Samuel J. Cox, "Sojourn Through Hell"—Vietnamization and U.S. Navy Prisoners of War, 1969–70, H-043-2, March 20, 2020 Naval History and Heritage Command, *https://www.history.navy.mil/about-us/leadership/director/directors-corner/h-grams/h-gram-043/h-043-2.html*

First he sizes her up..."I remember walking out of that room and into an elevator in a total state of shock": Blakey, *Prisoner at War,* 245–247.

"We should apply...allowing the Red Cross Associations of some countries to visit the prisoners": "Politburo Resolution No. 194-NQ/TW, 20 November 1969," Nguyen Quy, Editor, Van Kien Dang Toan Tap, 30, 1969 [Collected Party Documents, Volume 30, 1969] (Hanoi: National Political Publishing House, 2004), pages 303–305. Translated for CWIHP by Merle L. Pribbenow, *https://www.wilsoncenter.org/publication/treatment-american-pows-north-vietnam.*

Chapter 4: Waist Deep

Ghosts in the Gulf (August 1964)

"Under attack by three PT boats...my main battery": Stockdale and Stockdale, *In Love and War*, 6.

President Johnson was unhappy with the results. He preferred a more aggressive approach: Robert Hanyok, "Skunks, bogies, silent hounds, and the flying fish: The Gulf of Tonkin mystery, 2–4 August 1964," *Cryptological Quarterly*, Winter 2000/Spring 2001, 6–9.

The attack was no surprise. Most likely the attack was retaliation for commando raids on Hon Me: Hanyok, 13.

"I had the best seat in the house": Stockdale and Stockdale, *In Love and War*, 19.

"Did you see any boats?": Stockdale and Stockdale, *In Love and War*, 23.

"We were about to launch a war": Stockdale and Stockdale, *In Love and War*, 25.

Johnson promised a quick passage: Lyndon Johnson Live Telecast to the Nation, August 4, 1964, *https://www.wnyc.org/story/president-johnson-announces-air-action-in-the-gulf-of-tonkin/*.

Only Detainees (September 1964)

"You were captured...no formal state of war between our countries": Everett Alvarez, Jr. and Anthony S. Pitch, *Chained Eagle*, (Washington, DC: Potomac Books, Inc., 2005), 91–92.

"This terminology is more appropriate...": Rochester and Kiley, *Honor Bound*, 99; and Alvarez and Pitch, *Chained Eagle*, 75.

Secretary of State Rusk appealed to Soviet Ambassador Anatoly Dobrynin: Memorandum of Conversation between Ambassador Anatoly F. Dobrynin, USSR, and Secretary of State Dean Rusk, March 19, 1964, Department of State, Central Files, POL

31–1 GER E–US. Confidential. Drafted by Valdes and approved in S on March 19. The meeting was held in Rusk's office. Foreign Relations of the United States, 1964–1968, Volume XV, Germany and Berlin – Office of the Historian, Document #21, https://history.state.gov/historicaldocuments/frus1964-68v15/d21

The men were released a few days later...In addition, they recommended punitive countermeasures in response to future captures": Davis, *The Long Road Home,* 33. Davis is citing: Memo (JCSM-158-64) JCS for McNamara, 26 Feb 64, ISA 383.6 (1964).

"...run the risk of being confused with military pressures... could impact overall U.S. policy in Vietnam: Davis, *The Long Road Home,* 35. Davis is citing Ltr Kitchen to Solbert, 22 May 64, ISA 383.6 (1964).

"We tried to treat this war as 'calmly' as possible": Dean Rusk, *As I Saw It,* (New York: W.W. Norton & Company, 1990), 500.

In Washington there appeared to be an unspoken resolution: Davis, *The Long Road Home,* 57.

The Bundy Factor (November 1964)

The Bundy Vietnam Working Group toils around the clock for two weeks: Kai Bird, *The Color of Truth*: *McGeorge Bundy and William Bundy*: *Brothers in Arms,* (New York: Touchstone, 1998), 293; and H. R. McMaster, *Dereliction of Duty*: *Lyndon Johnson, Robert McNamara, the Joint Chiefs of Staff, and the Lies that Led to Vietnam,* (New York: Harper Perennial, 1997), 181.

Johnson's famous insecurities: David Halberstam, *The Best and the Brightest,* (New York: Random House, 1969), 593, 656, 665.

Bill later writes: Bird, *The Color of Truth,* 295.

Option C opts for...this strategy was ineffective: Bird, *The Color of Truth,* 277; and McMaster, *Dereliction of Duty,* 158.

"Every time I get a military recommendation": Harold P. Ford, *CIA and the Vietnam Policymakers*: *Three Episodes, 1962–1968,*

(Washington, DC: History Staff, Center for the Study of Intelligence, Central Intelligence Agency, 1998), 71.

Hundreds of American aviators will be shot down and killed, captured, or lost: McMaster, *Dereliction of Duty*, 234.

Chapter 5: The Propaganda Wars

Propaganda Parade (July 1966)

The crowd jeers. They jab...The agitated throng breaks the Americans' nose, smashes teeth, spits, and punches: Maine Military Museum & Learning Center, "Hanoi March," April 10, 2016, video, *https://www.youtube.com/watch?v=JYWy0lbEerg*; and Gary Wayne Foster, *The Hanoi March: American POWs in North Vietnam's Crucible*, (Ashland, OR: Hellgate Press, 2022), 120–129.

"The girls loved watching Japanese cartoons...Tonight's footage has captured the attention of the family": Pat Mearns, conversation with the authors, August 22, 2021.

"First she sees Maj. Neal Jones...": Pat Mearns, interview with the authors, July 25, 2021, and September 2, 2022.

"The men were paraded like targets...": Pat Mearns, interview with the authors, July 25, 2021. Similar observation made in *Viet-Nam Information Notes,* Bureau of Public Affairs, August 1967, Department of State Publication 8275 USGPO 1967 0-272-209.

The previous year, the Viet Cong had executed: Davis, *Long Road Home,* 37, 59.

Casualties in Vietnam are mounting...": Townley, *Defiant,* 152; and McNamara, *In Retrospect: The Tragedy and Lessons of Vietnam,* (New York: Vintage Books, 1995), 244. McNamara cites George C. Herring, *America's Longest War: The United States and Vietnam, 1950–1975,* 2d ed., (New York: Knopf, 1986), 146.

"the United Nations secretary general denounces Hanoi's plan...": Davis, *The Long Road Home,* 81.

"Would incite a public demand for retaliation…": "Hanoi threatens U.S. prisoners," *The New York Times,* July 17, 1966, 141.

"Losing horse…the die for American commitment…defending the regime from communism": Rusk, *As I Saw It,* 432, 427.

"No trial is in view."…they admit they 'are by no means out of the woods,' Hanoi still refuses to accept: Townley, *Defiant,* 165; Confidential cable from Secretary of State Dean Rusk to American embassies in Seoul, Tokyo, Taipei, Djakarta, Vientiane, Colombo, Saigon, Kuala Lumpur, Manila, Singapore, Rangoon, Bangkok, and Hong Kong, July 29, 1966; and Davis, *Long Road Home,* 83–84.

"Nope, just on Wednesdays": Foster, *The Hanoi March,* 146.

Love in Code (October 1966)

The sources for this scene are the following:

Stockdale and Stockdale, *In Love and War,* 131–146, 193–195, 204–205.

James B. Stockdale, II, "My Father the Spy in the Hanoi Hilton," revised April 27, 2017, *The Daily Beast,* accessed on September 19, 2021, *https:www.thedailybeast.com/myfather-the-spy-in-the-hanoi-hilton*; and in conversation with the authors, August 18, 2021.

Pat Twinem, interview with the authors, March 12, 2019.

Capt. Gordon I. Peterson, USN (Ret.) and David C. Taylor, "Intelligence support to communications with US POWs in Vietnam," *Studies in Intelligence,* Vol 60, No. 1 (*Extracts,* March 2016), 6.

From Covert to Overt: The USS *Pueblo* Incident (January 1968)

"floating antenna" and he has a trip to Disneyland: Rose Bucher with Sandie North and David Hellyer, "Rose Bucher's Own Story: Agony, while U.S. talked," *Pittsburgh Press* (Pittsburgh, PA), May 25, 1969, 133, accessed on September 28, 2022, www.newspapers.com.

"We knew that if we wanted our men to return home alive...and we also might start a war": Rusk, *As I Saw It*, 392; and Lyndon Baines Johnson, *The Vantage Point: Perspectives of the Presidency (1963–1969)*, (London: Weidenfeld and Nicolson, 1971), 536.

"Through the months of its captivity...keep their mouths shut in public": Rusk, *As I Saw It*, 392.

"My purpose ... hope they eventually solve themselves": Rose Bucher with Sandie North and David Hellyer, "Rose Bucher's Own Story: Months of uncertainty drag on, but finally the awaited day comes," *Pittsburgh Press* (Pittsburgh, PA), May 28, 1969, 21, accessed on April 5, 202, www.newspapers.com.

Upset that Rose has become so overtly critical of the U.S. government: Stockdale and Stockdale, *In Love and War*, 228.

"If he knew I sat back in my rocking chair and did nothing": Beverly Beyette, "Pueblo skipper's wife fights to free ship," *Press Democrat* (Santa Rosa, CA), Copley News Service, August 25, 1968, 3, accessed on November 19, 2020, www.newspapers.com.

"I believe your husband is alive...What proof do you have that he isn't?": Rose Bucher with Sandie North and David Hellyer, "Rose Bucher's Own Story: Thousands write encouragement during Washington runaround," *Pittsburgh Press* (Pittsburgh, PA), May 27, 1969, 25, accessed on April 5, 2021, www.newspapers.com.

It takes eleven months: David Welna, "Remembering North Korea's audacious capture of the USS *Pueblo*," National Public Radio, January 23, 2018, accessed on April 7, 2021, *https://www.npr.org/2018/01/23/580076540/looking-at-the-saga-of-the-uss-pueblo-50-years-later*.

"This has been a frustrating episode...Christmas with their loved ones": Statement by Secretary Rusk, Department of State for the Press, No. 281, December 22, 1968, RG 59 Subject Files of Frank A. Sieverts, National Archives and Records Administration. A federal judge awarded the *Pueblo* survivors $2.3 billion in damages in February 2021. The Vietnam POWs have never been awarded any damages. *https://news.usni.org/2021/02/25/federal-judge-awards-uss-pueblo-survivors-and-families-2-3-billion-in-damages.*

Sidelines to Frontlines (October 1968)

The government has made a mistake: Nan Robertson, "POW Wives' Lament: 'Oh God—Just Get It Over With," New York Times News Service in *Honolulu Star Bulletin,* December 7, 1972, 83.

Boroughs feels the strength of an organization behind them: Stockdale and Stockdale, *In Love and War,* 225–226.

Where at least 200 men are believed to be held: "U.S. Rebuffed in Aid to Viet Prisoners," Associated Press in *Sacramento Bee,* September 8, 1967, accessed on August 24, 2021, www.newspapers.com.

"Experts in Torture...Hand and Leg Irons...16 hours a day": David Taylor, *"The Spy in the Hanoi Hilton,"* Smithsonian Channel, April 28, 2015, *https://www.smithsonianchannel.com/special/spy-in-the-hanoi-hilton-the*

"One high official...protect the authorities from criticism": Jack Anderson, "Is U.S. neglecting GI's held captive?," *Detroit Free-Press* (Detroit, Michigan), August 8, 1967, 9, accessed on September 13, 2021, newspapers.com.

"In reply to your telegram of yesterday...an early successful conclusion": Stockdale and Stockdale, *In Love and War,* 218–219.

"I'll just say one more thing...I think we could have forced them to release the POWs": John T. Mason, Jr., Interview with Adm. Thomas Moorer, chairman of the Joint Chiefs of Staff (1970–1974), U.S. Naval Institute Oral History Interview #15, February 25, 1976, 794–795, U.S. Navy Archives.

The summer of 1968..."What steps are being taken... uppermost in my mind": Stockdale and Stockdale, *In Love and War,* 298–300.

"Where is the evidence...The world does not know of their negligences and it should know!": Beverly Beyette, "Navy wife keeps vigil for captive husband," *The San Diego Union*, October 27, 1968, 1.

Chapter 6: Veering Off Course

Silent Night, Holy Night (December 1969)

But not tonight: Robert Timberg interview with Carol McCain, June 26, 1990, Robert Timberg Collection, U.S. Navy Archives.

"Okay, you're right....The car is cut almost in half": Robert Timberg, *John McCain: An American Odyssey*, (New York: Free Press, 1995), 104–105.

until she lands in a snowbank: Alex Leary, "A Florida foundation," *Tampa Bay Times*, July 20, 2008, 1, accessed on November 10, 2020, www.newspapers.com.

police find her mangled body in the snow: Robert Timberg, *The Nightingale's Song*, (New York: Simon & Schuster, 1995), 173.

"If you can hear us"...It will be several days before Carol can communicate: Timberg, *John McCain*, 105.

He inserts rods in her fractured legs: Amy S. Rosenberg, "McCain's Philadelphia Story," *Philadelphia Inquirer*, September 15, 2008, A04, accessed on November 10, 2020, www.newspapers.com.

"No! Don't do that."...but she may never walk again: Timberg, *John McCain*, 105.

She believes he has already suffered more than she: Amy S. Rosenberg, "McCain's Philadelphia Story," *Philadelphia Inquirer*, September 15, 2008, A04, accessed on November 10, 2020, www.newspapers.com.

"When he would ask me out...you think you're just the best": Carol McCain, from the documentary, *John McCain: For Whom the Bell Tolls*. Interviewed by Teddy Kunhardt. November 16, 2017, https://www.kunhardtfilmfoundation.org/interviewees/carol-mccain © HBO & Kunhardt Film Foundation.

Was Mary jealous of Carol? "I think so": Carol McCain, conversation with the authors, April 28, 2021.

"I was a brat"...Instead, she became a sought-after local model: Carol McCain, conversation with the authors, January 27, 2020.

"She did not think modeling required much talent."..."That's probably why I didn't": Carol McCain, conversation with the authors, April 28, 2021.

"My mother claimed that I was taken in by the Navy uniforms": Carol McCain, conversation with the authors, July 9, 2021.

Her father gave her away: "Events of social interest," *Philadelphia Inquirer,* December 28, 1958, 75, accessed on April 14, 2021, www.newspapers.com.

"His Academy yearbook calls him the Navy's answer to John Wayne...pretty decent description of him": Robert Timberg interview with Carol McCain, June 7, 1990, Robert Timberg Collection, U.S. Navy Archives.

She reconnected with John McCain: Timberg, *John McCain,* 72.

"He would tell you the crowd had thinned out by then, so when he asked me out, I went": Carol McCain, from the HBO documentary, *John McCain: For Whom the Bell Tolls.*

"The carefree life of a bachelor...as I was now": John McCain with Mark Salter, *Faith of My Fathers,* (New York: Perennial, 2000), 172.

"She was afraid I would get divorced again": Carol McCain, conversation with the authors, July 9, 2021.

"He was always kind of a legend...very good sense of humor": Carol McCain, from the HBO documentary, *John McCain: For Whom the Bell Tolls.*

Although the town was dry: Carol McCain, conversation with the authors, April 29, 2021.

"We all entertained a lot...it's sort of a great equalizer": Carol McCain, from the HBO documentary, *John McCain: For Whom the Bell Tolls.*

"Don't cry": Amy S. Rosenberg, "McCain's Philadelphia Story," *Philadelphia Inquirer,* September 15, 2008, A04, accessed on November 10, 2020, www.newspapers.com.

Reeling (January 1968)

He was in Hanoi on assignment...Chalais has offered to carry a message to his family: John McCain, with Mark Salter, *Faith of My Fathers,* (New York: Perennial, 2000), 194–197.

"John says he will be back...buy yourself a nice present": Robert Timberg interview with Carol McCain, June 20, 1990, Robert Timberg Collection, U.S. Navy Archives.

Parceling her three children out: Carol McCain, from the HBO documentary, *John McCain: For Whom the Bell Tolls.*

"He had no intention of giving it to me...but I asked him for it": Carol McCain, conversation with the authors, July 9, 2021.

"I plan to sell this...I have to make a living": Robert Timberg interview with Carol McCain, June 20, 1990, Robert Timberg Collection, U.S. Navy Archives.

"You have my word. I will not sell it": Carol McCain, from the HBO documentary, *John McCain: For Whom the Bell Tolls.*

Commander Boroughs...worried how it might affect John: Robert Timberg interview with Carol McCain, June 6, 1990, Robert Timberg Collection, U.S. Navy Archives.

"I could pretend I'm a French photographer...I've already used up my one chance I had to do it": Carol McCain, from the HBO documentary, *John McCain: For Whom the Bell Tolls.*

"I could just barely stand it...She was like a little muffin": Carol McCain, from the HBO documentary, *John McCain: For Whom the Bell Tolls.*

"Carol is that greatest thing...every happened to our family": Carol McCain, from the HBO documentary, *John McCain: For Whom the Bell Tolls.*

Carol was not the daughter-in-law Roberta envisioned: Robert Timberg interview with Carol McCain, June 20, 1990, Robert Timberg Collection, U.S. Navy Archives.

Roberta's favorite cookbook: Carol McCain, interview with the authors, April 29, 2021; and Carol McCain, from the HBO documentary, *John McCain: For Whom the Bell Tolls.*

"We don't think there are any survivors."..."I think Johnny's dead."..."I don't intend to."..."We have to believe he's alive": Robert Timberg interview with Carol McCain, June 20, 1990, Robert Timberg Collection, U.S. Navy Archives; and Timberg, *John McCain*, 85.

"What's the matter?": Doug McCain and Everett Alvarez interview transcript, Wondery's "Against the Odds," April 27, 2021.

"We don't know very much"..."This isn't good."..."When will he be home?"... "You can call me anytime . . . I'm in my office between eight and four": Carol McCain, from the HBO documentary, *John McCain: For Whom the Bell Tolls.*

"It was horrible...'This could be years'": Carol McCain, from the HBO documentary, *John McCain: For Whom the Bell Tolls.*

"I would just like to tell my wife...and just hope to see her soon": Frank Galey, "Captured airman says 'I love you' to wife on TV," *Delaware County Daily Times* (Chester, Pennsylvania), February 14, 1968, 1, accessed on April 26, 2021, www.newspapers.com.

Off-Kilter (December 1969)

"I was scared...just thinking about our meeting": Pat Mearns, interview with the authors, April 24, 2021 and August 21, 2022.

Col. Milt Kegley told her: Pat Mearns interview with the authors, October 27, 2020, April 12, 2021, and October 26 2021.

Duckles joined the WSP in 1943: Obituary of Madeline Duckles, *San Francisco Chronicle*, December 6, 2012, *https://www.legacy.com/us/obituaries/sfgate/name/madeline-duckles-obituary?id=18008032.*

"The North Vietnamese women are suffering....I have great admiration for their government and do not trust ours": Association of Wives and Families of Captured and Missing American Military Men newsletter, December 1969, from the personal collection of Pat Mearns.

When her roommate asked her to take a present: Betty Mearns Maxwell, interview with the authors, May 26, 2021.

"Electrifying": Pat Mearns, conversation with the authors, April 24, 2021.

"It wasn't fancy...to give it to me.": Pat Mearns, conversation with the authors, July 10, 2021.

"Whenever things were in a state of change...he always did the job the way I wanted": Jack Broughton, *Thud Ridge*, (Philadelphia, A: J. B. Lippincott & Company, 1969), 34.

She believes she is unsure of her convictions: Pat Mearns, interview with the authors, October 27, 2020, and April 12, 2021.

"That woman just does not care...Duckles wanted out... Here I am, sitting next to": Pat Mearns, interview with the authors, April 19, 2021, and April 27, 2021.

You Must Be Lonely (Summer 1969)

The sources for this scene are the following:

Pat Mearns, interview with the authors, March 3, 2017.

Letter to U.S. senators and U.S. representatives from Pat Mearns, Association of Wives and Families of Captured and Missing American Military Men, July 1969, from the personal collection of Pat Mearns.

Chapter 7: Taking It to The Enemy

Kushner to Cambodia (November 1969)

"Here. Please sit down."..."relax": "Valerie Kushner's Cambodia Trip More Successful Than Anticipated," *The Bee* (Danville, VA), December 1, 1969, 10, accessed on May 6, 2021, www.newspapers.com.

"He never was good with directions": Geraldine and Walter Sherman, interview with the authors, April 25, 2021. The two were neighbors and friends of Valerie Kushner in Danville, VA, during the Vietnam War.

"I decided that the only way...take them myself": Valerie Kushner testimony, "Hearing on Problems of Prisoners of War and Their Families," Committee on Armed Services, U.S. House of Representatives, 91st Congress, Second Session, March 6, 1970, U.S. Government Printing Office, 6017.

including a Cambodian doll: Valerie Kushner testimony, "Hearing on Problems of Prisoners of War and Their Families," 6017; and "Valerie Kushner's Cambodia trip more successful than anticipated," *The Bee* (Danville, VA), December 1, 1969, 10, accessed on May 6, 2021, newspapers.com.

Her father, a prominent Ph.D. chemist: "Anthony Moos, 75, developer of fuel cells," *The New York Times*, December 12, 1988, Section B, 14, *https://www.nytimes.com/1988/12/12/obituaries/anthony-moos-75-developer-of-fuel-cells.html.*

"Oh no, a Yankee": Toni Kushner Nee, interview with the authors, June 4, 2021.

She had three maxims: Toni Kushner Nee, interview with the authors, December 24, 2019.

"It was a hand-patting session...but the Viet Cong won't discuss it": "Virginia woman knows husband is prisoner alive; that's all," Associated Press wire story in *Progress-Index* (Petersburg, VA), August 15, 1969, 5, accessed on May 6, 2021, newspapers.com.

"She wasn't fearful of the world for herself or for us": Toni Kushner Nee, email to the authors, March 31, 2022; and Toni Kushner Nee, interview with the authors, June 4, 2021.

"The war has separated me from my family, too": "Valerie Kushner's Cambodia trip more successful than anticipated," *The Bee* (Danville, VA), December 1, 1969, 10, accessed on May 6, 2021, www.newspapers.com.

"But these can be used for other purposes, not just for the prisoners": "Viet Cong refuse to convey medical supplies to Kushner," Associated Press in *The Danville Register* (Danville, VA), November 3, 1969, 17, accessed on May 6, 2021, www.newspapers.com.

He also accepts letters from two other Army POW wives, including Andrea Rander: "VC official to deliver wife's letter to husband," UPI article in *Dayton Daily News* (Dayton, OH), November 30, 1969, 40, accessed on May 12, 2021, www.newspapers.com.

in hopes Kinh might change his mind: "Viet Cong refuse to convey medical supplies to Kushner," *Danville Register* (Danville, VA), November 30, 1969, 17, accessed on May 6, 2021, www.newspapers.com.

"Dear Mrs. Kushner...and you could meet again your husband shortly": Valerie Kushner testimony, "Hearing on Problems of Prisoners of War and Their Families," 6019.

Perot's Pocketbook (December 1969)

the Hanoi diplomats acquiesce: Thomas E. Meurer, *The Wild, Wild East: Adventures in Business from the Cold War to the War on Terrorism,* (Washington, DC, and London: Academica, 2022), (forthcoming); and Tom Meurer, interview with the authors, May 26, 2021.

"What in the hell do you think you are doing bringing a plane load of gifts and press into Laos?": Meurer, *The Wild, Wild East.*

"Haven't you been notified by Kissinger's office?": Meurer, *The Wild, Wild East.*

"the American people are being lied to...Because of all the widows and orphans in Hanoi, Perot cannot visit Hanoi": A Trip Report of "Operation Understanding," undated, Box 176, Perot Family Archives, Dallas, TX.

They wonder if his exploits will complicate diplomatic efforts in Paris: Richard Capen, email to the authors, September 3, 2021.

Perot lent executives to the campaign: Meurer, *The Wild, Wild East.*

Paid for by Perot and written by President Nixon's speechwriter William Safire: Michael J. Allen, *Until the Last Man Comes Home: POWs, MIAs, and the Unending Vietnam War,* (Chapel Hill, NC: The University of North Carolina Press, 2009), 34.

Perot's new group bought airtime on fifty-three television stations: Davis, *The Long Road Home,* 222.

Suspicious of his ties to Nixon: Although Perot initiated and underwrote this entire campaign, he worked in lock step with the Nixon administration. In a September 27, 1990, letter from Alexander Haig to Mr. Jeffrey Krames, executive editor of *Business One Irwin,* Haig assured the editor that Perot did not violate the Logan Act: "During the Vietnam War, I was directed by the President and Mr. Ross Perot to assist in improving the treatment of our prisoners of war. The resulting coordination with Mr. Perot's activities in this area was continuous and extensive and was warmly welcomed by the United States government. Mr. Perot's efforts were publicly presented as a private undertaking, thereby optimizing the impact of his activities on world opinion. To the best of my knowledge, from start to finish, Mr. Perot was working in complete coordination with the United States Government and, as such, his activities were in no way a violation of the Logan Act but rather a generous, patriotic and welcomed ancillary, private sector reinforcement of U.S. policies at the time." Box 187.1, Perot Family Archives, Dallas, TX.

They call Perot's global adventure a "provocation" and they call him the "dark scheme' of the Nixon Administration: Gifts for POWs reach Hong Kong," UPI article in *Anniston Star* (Anniston, AL), December 23, 1969, 13, accessed on May 24, 2021, newspapers.com.

"The North Vietnamese have shifted the monkey to the Russians' back": A Trip Report of "Operation Understanding," date unknown, Box 176, Perot Family Archives, Dallas, TX.

"Ross, you've done a great job of publicity. But you best now come home": Meurer, *The Wild, Wild East*; and Murphy Martin interview with Tom Marquez, March 27, 1976, 30, Box 176, Perot Family Archives, Dallas, TX.

They finish the task in ten hours: Davis, *The Long Road Home,* 223.

The answer is *also* no: "Paris Trip," undated, Box 176, Perot Family Archives, Dallas, TX.

A gold charm for her bracelet: Andrea Rander, interview with the authors, January 31, 2017.

"You might say it was a broken record": "Reds summon POW families sent by Perot, lecture them," The Times-Post Service in the *Longview Daily News* (Longview, WA), December 26, 1969, 5, accessed on May 24, 2021, newspapers.com.

Tell their children that their fathers are murderers . . . "They said gradually *all* the wives will hear": "Captives' names to be released 'gradually,'" Associated Press in *The La Crosse Times* (La Crosse, WI), December 26, 1969, 1, accessed on May 24, 2021, www.newspapers.com.

House Arrest in Moscow (January 1970)

The weather and the weak welcome have deflated her spirits: Pat Mearns, interview with the authors, March 12, 2022.

"We just had to do something significant."…"Nothing else was working": Pat Mearns, interview with the authors, September 5, 2021 and March 12, 2022.

"Life is empty…We're all missing so much.": Naomi Rock, Associated Press, "Wives or Widows? Agony of Uncertainty," in *Standard Speaker* (Hazelton, PA.), 21, March 17, 1970, accessed on October 26, 2022 newspapers.com.

"International Red Cross representatives told us…notified as to the status of each captured man": Pat Mearns interview with the authors, April 30, 2022, and in notes from her round the world trip, 1970, from her personal collection.

"I felt a really good feeling…I had no choice, but to crawl out for the stall…I didn't think I'd be wearing big boots to meet the Pope": Pat Mearns, telephone conversation with the authors, July 13, 2022, September 2 and 5, 2021, and August 22, 2021.

The Pope was struck by their narratives: Bob Dornan, interview with the authors, September 15, 2021.

They were waved onboard by a Russian guard: Pat Mearns, interview with the authors, September 2, 2021, and Bob Dornan in conversation with the authors, September 15, 2021.

"I was always convinced there had to be some leader…Our agony and terror are something…packed with meetings with anyone who might be able to help": Pat Mearns, interview with the authors, September 5, 2021.

"It was not comfortable, just furnished with a bed, a lamp and a desk": Bob Dornan, interview with the authors, September 14, 2021.

"We are Americans…What could possibly happen?": Pat Mearns, interview with the authors September 5 and 7, 2021.

An Associated Press photographer captures the group at the airport, looking careworn: Associated Press Wire Photo, "Still Waiting," *San Antonio Express* (San Antonio, TX), January 13, 1970, 31, accessed on September 4, 2021, www.newspapers.com.

"They were looking through our items": Pat Mearns, interview with the authors, May 5, 2021, and September 5, 2021.

he has compassion for all affected: their husbands, draft evaders, and deserters: Pat Mearns interview with the authors, July 13, 2021; "PW wives blister McCarthy," *Daily News* (New York), January 27, 1970, 217, accessed on May 5, 2021, www.newspapers.com.

So Close, Yet So Far Away (January 1970)

"And there we were, four Americans and a French girl, standing on the airstrip in Vientiane crying": "Hearing on Problems of Prisoners of War and Their Families Before the Committee on Armed Services," House of Representatives, 91st Congress, Second Session, March 6, 1970, 6007.

"I saw this handsome man sitting under a desk...He asked if he could call me": Carole Hanson Hickerson, interview with the authors, September 12, 2018.

"I never wore it again": Carole Hanson Hickerson, interview with the authors, August 10, 2022.

"They had fled the north some years ago...Someday, their sons will have the same opportunities our children have": Carole Hanson Hickerson, interview with the authors, April 6, 2019.

It was a white dove: "A symbol of the Holy Spirit, she really comforted me," Carole says. Author interview October 4, 2022.

His finger landed on Laos: Carole Hanson Hickerson, interview with the authors, April 6, 2019.

Chapter 8: Counterculture

No Man, No Mortgage (1970)

The sources for this scene are the following:

Candy Ellis, interview with the authors, January 20, 2014, and email message to authors, June 14, 2021.

Robert Fant, interview with the authors, April 7, 2014.

Candace Parish, "Is my husband dead or alive?" *Family Weekly*, February 1, 1970, 4–6.

Out in Front (May 1964)

The sources for this scene are the following:

Andrea Rander, interview with the authors November 17, 2017, December 2 and 18, 2021, and May 13, 2022.

Drifting Away (June 1967)

The sources for this scene are the following:

Emilee Reynolds, interview with the authors, June 19, 2019, August 8, 2019, March 11, 2020, November 9, 2020, and June 28, 2021.

Judy Holliday, interview with the authors, October 5, 2021.

Rebecca Grant, "The crucible of Vietnam," *Air Force Magazine*, February 1, 2013, *https://www.airforcemag.com/article/0213vietnam/.*

Robert S. McNamara with Brian VanDeMark, *In Retrospect: The Tragedy and Lessons of Vietnam*, (New York: Vintage Books, 1996), 212–213.

First Wives Club (Fall 1968)

The sources for this scene are the following:

Candy Ellis, interview with the authors, June 24, 2021.

Rotten Apples (Spring 1970)

This scene is drawn from the following sources:

Tape 6B Transcript of Video Interview with Carole Hanson, 29750123001. Vietnam Center and Sam Johnson Vietnam Archive. No Date, Box 01, Folder 23, Phillip Daniels Collection, Vietnam Center and Sam Johnson Vietnam Archive, Texas Tech University, accessed September 9, 2021, *https://www.vietnam.ttu.edu/virtualarchive/items.php?item=29750123001.*

Steve Murray, "Lady and the Flag," *Midweek.com*, July 7, 2010, *http://archives.midweek.com/content/story/midweek_coverstory/Carole_Hickerson/.*

Carole Hanson Hickerson, interview with the authors, September 12, 2021.

PART II: IN THE THICK OF THE FIGHT (1970-1973)

Chapter 9: In the Spotlight

Prime Time (December 1969)

"I felt he knew what was going on with us...we need traction": Pat Mearns, conversation with the authors, March 12, 2022.

"It would indicate concern at the highest levels of government for the welfare of these Americans": Memorandum for the President from Melvin Laird; "Meeting with Wives and Parents of Captured and Missing US Servicemen;" September 25, 1969; Ex ND 18-3/CO 165 Beginning–12/31/89 [2 of 2]; Folder 14; Box 1; Nixon Presidential Materials Staff, White House Central Files,

Subject Files, 1969–74, National Security–Defense; Richard Nixon Presidential Library, Yorba Linda, California.

"I would not disagree with this provided they are carefully screened for emotional stability and judgment": Memorandum for Steve Bull from Colonel James Hughes; September 27, 1969; Ex ND 18-3/CO 165 Beginning–12/31/89 [2 of 2]; Folder 14; Box 1; Nixon Presidential Materials Staff, White House Central Files, Subject Files, 1969–74, National Security–Defense; Richard Nixon Presidential Library, Yorba Linda, California.

Kissinger and Haig opposed a meeting: Memorandum for the President from Henry Kissinger; October 2, 1969; Ex ND 18-3/CO 165 Beginning–12/31/89 [2 of 2]; Folder 14; Box 1; Nixon Presidential Materials Staff, White House Central Files, Subject Files, 1969–74, National Security–Defense; Richard Nixon Presidential Library, Yorba Linda, California.

"I have serious doubts about the wisdom...she sounded almost bitter": Memorandum for Colonel Hughes from Alexander P. Butterfield; "POW Wives and Mothers Scheduled to Meet with the President and the First Lady on December 12th;" December 4, 1969; Ex ND 18-3/CO 165 Beginning–12/31/89 [1 of 2]; Folder 14; Box 1; Nixon Presidential Materials Staff, White House Central Files, Subject Files, 1969–74, National Security–Defense; Richard Nixon Presidential Library, Yorba Linda, CA.

"And then I got a phone call...By golly, it *was* the White House": Robert Timberg interview with Carol McCain, June 20, 1990, Robert Timberg Collection, U.S. Navy Archives.

"Mrs. Nixon greeted everyone personally": Andrea Rander, conversation with the authors, March 13, 2022.

"That didn't make any sense to me...separating them to the press?": Stockdale and Stockdale, *In Love and War*, 366.

"one of the most unconscionable in history": "Nixon meets with Wives of POWs, vows to seek better treatment of men,"

Associated Press, *Sacramento Bee* (Sacramento, CA), December 12, 1969, 30, accessed February 24, 2022, www.newspapers.com.

"There we were...flashbulbs flashing": Carole Hanson Hickerson, interview with the authors, August 10, 2022.

"It would be very damaging to us on the prisoner issue": "Nixon meets wives, vows Hanoi plea," Associated Press, *Modesto Bee* (Modesto, CA), December 12, 1969, 2, accessed October 27, 2022, newspapers.com.

She chimes in..."We send packages ... alive or dead": Pat Mearns, conversation with the authors, March 16, 2022; and Transcript of White House press conference of Sybil Stockdale, Pat Mearns, Andrea Rander, Carol Hansen [sic] and Louise Mulligan representing a delegation of wives and mothers of prisoners of war and of servicemen missing in action, December 12, 1969, from the personal collection of Pat Mearns.

"I just wished they had mentioned the MIAs on the broadcast I saw": Pat Mearns, conversation with the authors, March 16, 2022.

"Now has great interest, amazing what a little personal exposure will do. He now wants all sorts of actions": H. R. Haldeman, *The Haldeman Diaries: Inside the Nixon White House*, (New York: G. P. Putnam Sons, 1994), 114.

"I have changed my mind.–From now on until further direction from me–[American diplomat Philip] Habib is to talk only about prisoners": Memorandum for the President from Henry A. Kissinger; February 27, 1970; NSC Files, POW-MIA; Box 1; President's Daily Briefs February 20-28, 1970; Richard Nixon Presidential Library, Yorba Linda, CA.

"It should be composed of able and imaginative people... because there may be no specific end to the war through armistice or treaty.": Letter from Sybil Stockdale to Col. Hughes; December 12, 1969; Ex ND 18-3/CO 165 1/1/70-8/31/70; Box 1; Nixon Presidential Materials Staff, White House Central Files,

Subject Files, 1969-74, National Security–Defense; Richard Nixon Presidential Library, Yorba Linda, CA.

"I am sure you know of the existence...Therefore, we already have a 'task force' capability which should produce results if this type of approach is to be successful": Letter from Colonel James Hughes to Sybil Stockdale; January 2, 1970; Ex ND 18-3/ CO 165 1/1/70-8/31/70; Box 1; Nixon Presidential Materials Staff, White House Central Files, Subject Files, 1969–74, National Security–Defense; Richard Nixon Presidential Library, Yorba Linda, CA.

"I am going to be extremely frank...the Prisoner of War policy committee is a 'joke.'...I have seen nothing": Letter from Sybil Stockdale to Colonel Hughes; January 3, 1970; Ex ND 18-3/ CO 165 1/1/70-8/31/70; Box 1; Nixon Presidential Materials Staff, White House Central Files, Subject Files, 1969–74, National Security–Defense; Richard Nixon Presidential Library, Yorba Linda, California.

A Call to Action (May 1970)

bursting into resounding applause: Stockdale and Stockdale, *In Love and War,* 376.

"This administration has no more urgent goal...who have done so much for this country.": *Washington Post,* 2 May 1970: DPD. Commanders Digest, 23 May 70, 1-3; Program, Appeal for International Justice: DAR Constitution Hall—Washington, DC, May 1, 1970, from the personal collections of Candy Parish Ellis and Pat Mearns.

Six months ago, in October of 1969, more than 275 House members: Davis, *The Long Road Home,* 212.

"appeal for international justice for all the American prisoners of war and servicemen missing in action in Southeast Asia": Hearings Before the Subcommittee on National Security Policy and Scientific Developments of the Committee on Foreign

Affairs, U.S. House of Representatives, 91st Congress, Second Session, April 29, May 1, 6, 1970, 1.

"That every possible effort be made to secure their advance release from captivity": Appeal to International Justice event program, DAR Constitution Hall, May 1, 1970, from the personal collection of Candy Parish Ellis.

"That means cleaning out major North Vietnamese and Viet Cong-occupied territories...on both Cambodia and American and South Vietnamese forces in South Vietnam": "April 30, 1970: Address to the Nation on the Situation in Southeast Asia," Miller Center, University of Virginia, *https://millercenter.org/the-presidency/presidential-speeches/april-30-1970-address-nation-situation-southeast-asia.*

National Guardsmen have been summoned: "Guardsmen called at University of Maryland," UPI, *Redlands Daily Facts* (Redlands, California), May 1, 1970, accessed on March 11, 2022, www.newspapers.com.

"is fundamental to our negotiating stance in Paris": Margaret Scherf, "Families renew plea for pressure," *Salina Journal* (Salina, KS), May 3, 1970, 26, accessed on February 24, 2022, www.newspapers.com.

"Have we become...May Day, May Day!!! Please help!": Grubb and Jose, *You Are Not Forgotten*, 122; 28260000000, Louise Mulligan Collection, Vietnam Center and Sam Johnson Vietnam Archive, Texas Tech University; and "Jeremiah!," Echo Film Productions, Alabama Public Television, 2015, http://www.echofilmsproductions.com/documentary-films.html.

Crossed Wires (November 1970)

they write a message with the clothes: Benjamin F. Schemmer, *The Raid: The Son Tay Prison Rescue Mission*, (New York: Ballantine Books, 2002), 22–23.

new wall and a new guard tower: Schemmer, *The Raid*, 30.

Even more intriguing is...The letter begged for an evacuation: Schemmer, *The Raid,* 31–32; and George J. Veith, *Code-Name Bright Light: The Untold Story of U.S. POW Rescue Efforts During the Vietnam War,* (New York: Dell Publishing, 1998), 298.

"some focal point"...more than shaking his fist at the North Vietnamese: Schemmer, *The Raid,* 60–61.

The team rehearses under live fire at night 170 times with an inflatable mock-up: Mark Amidon, "Groupthink, politics, and the decision to attempt the Son Tay rescue," *Parameters: U.S. Army War College Quarterly,* Autumn 2005, 119; and Deposition of Thomas Hinman Moorer, April 22, 1992, Box 14, Senate Select Committee on Prisoner of War/Missing in Action Affairs, 1991–1993; Records of the U.S. Senate, Record Group 46, National Archives and Records Administration, Washington, DC.

Army Col. Arthur "Bull" Simons is in charge: Army Col. Arthur "Bull" Simons was notorious for leading the ill-fated Son Tay Raid in November 1970, but he became legendary in 1979 when he led a successful rescue of two of Ross Perot's EDS employees imprisoned in Tehran. The story was made into a bestselling book and movie, *On Wings of Eagles.*

The violence of the crash landing propels the door gunner from the aircraft.... "We're Americans...We'll be in your cells in a minute": Schemmer, *The Raid,* 213.

"I remember trying to inform DIA later that morning, only to discover the raid had just taken place": Veith, *Code-Name Bright Light,* 299.

In fact, officials also have significant photographic evidence..."95 to 97 percent assurance of success": Schemmer, *The Raid,* 139.

They approve the mission last minute: Van Atta, *With Honor,* 213.

"I do not like to say it was all a bad idea...There is no justification for it. Mr. Secretary, my time is up": "Bombing

Operations and the Prisoner-of-War Rescue Mission in North Vietnam," Hearing before the Committee on Foreign Relations, United States Senate, 91st Congress, Second Session with Hon. Melvin R. Laird, Secretary of Defense, November 24, 1970, 6–7.

Laird and Nixon believed the rescue attempt would demonstrate our love, caring, and affection for these POWs:" Schemmer, *The Raid,* 134.

Alan, in a Christmas letter to his wife: Veith, *Code-Name Bright Light,* 109.

"Alan was there, Bob": Bob Brudno, interview with the authors, March 4, 2022.

Chapter 10: Enduring Icons

Turning Point (fall 1970)

Carol is astonished as 30,000 envelopes and packages: Carol Bates Brown, interview with the authors, August 3, 2021.

"We were very skeptical about this idea...they would have to get permission [from the family].": Tape 12 Transcript of Video Interview with Sybil Stockdale, 29750112001. Vietnam Center and Sam Johnson Vietnam Archive. No Date, Box 01, Folder 12, Phillip Daniels Collection, Vietnam Center and Sam Johnson Vietnam Archive, Texas Tech University, accessed on August 5, 2021, https://www.vietnam.ttu.edu/virtualarchive/items.php?item=29750112001.

Where was the money going she wondered?: Pat Mearns, interview with the authors, July 27, 2021.

"VIVA was making so much money and the National League had so little": Carole Hanson Hickerson, interview with the authors, February 22, 2020.

She wrote an open letter to 250 newspaper editors all over the country: Marlene Meyer, "Service wife pushes drive for

U.S. prisoner release," *The Register* (Orange County, CA), August 20, 1969, C4.

only twenty responded: Toni Wood, "'Missing in Action' means loneliness for Marine wife," *Daily Sun-Post* (San Clemente, CA), September 16, 1969.

an opportunity to do more than bake cookies for soldiers: Mike Anton, "Vietnam War bracelets come full circle," *Los Angeles Times*, November 4, 2010, *https://www.latimes.com/archives/la-xpm-2010-nov-04-la-me-pow-bracelets-20101104-story.html.* VIVA was founded as Victory in Vietnam Association, but later changed its name to Voices in Vital America.

"Please, sir, do not stop wearing this bracelet...till my people are free": Bob Dornan, interview with the authors, September 6, 2021.

"When I work so hard and go without sleep...and it'll keep me going": Tape 7B Transcript of Video Interview with Carole Hanson, 29750124001. Vietnam Center and Sam Johnson Vietnam Archive. No Dates, Box 01, Folder 24, Phillip Daniels Collection, Vietnam Center and Sam Johnson Vietnam Archive, Texas Tech University, accessed on August 4, 2021, https://www.vietnam.ttu.edu/virtualarchive/items.php?item=29750124001.

"My parents were absolutely horrified": Carol Bates Brown, interview with the authors, March 3, 2022.

"These two girls called me with the obvious answer... Why can't we do this same type of thing for the prisoners of war?": Tape 7B Transcript of Video Interview with Carole Hanson, 29750124001. Vietnam Center and Sam Johnson Vietnam Archive. No Dates, Box 01, Folder 24, Phillip Daniels Collection, Vietnam Center and Sam Johnson Vietnam Archive, Texas Tech University, accessed August 4, 2021, *https://www.vietnam.ttu.edu/virtualarchive/items.php?item=29750124001.* This interview transcript also contains an interview transcript with Gloria Coppin.

At the taping of his Saturday night television show they shouted it from the audience: Letter to Bob Dornan from Carol Bates and Kay Hunter, February 9, 1970, personal collection of Carol Bates Brown.

"What did you just say? That's a fantastic idea": Bob Dornan, interview with the authors, September 6, 2021.

Ross Perot rebuffed them, as did Howard Hughes: Carole Bates Brown, History of the POW/MIA Bracelet, *http://thewall-usa.com/bracelet.asp.*

Gloria's husband, the owner of an aircraft parts manufacturer, donated enough metal for the first 1,200 bracelets: Dick Kaukas, "POW bracelet distributors face criticism, legal problems," *Courier-Journal* (Louisville, KY), August 28, 1973, 3, accessed on September 29, 2020, newspapers.com.

work around the clock creating bracelets: Mike Anton, "Vietnam War bracelets come full circle," *Los Angeles Times,* November 4, 2010, *https://www.latimes.com/archives/la-xpm-2010-nov-04-la-me-pow-bracelets-20101104-story.html.*

Vowing to keep the bands on their wrists until all the men return home: Janet L. Koenigsamen, "Mobilization of a Conscience Constituency: VIVA and the POW/MIA Movement," A dissertation submitted to the Kent State University Graduate College in partial fulfillment of the requirements for the degree of doctor of philosophy, August 1987, 50.

"The bracelet campaign is an insidious campaign...All of that's a lot of nonsense": Transcript of Cora Weiss speech to NARMIC Philadelphia, August 1972, in the

Committee of Liaison with Families of Servicemen Detained in North Vietnam Records (DG 227), Box 2, Swarthmore College Peace Collection.

You Are Not Forgotten (1972)

"I used to fly within range of the Japanese...I thought how easy it would be to forget these guys.": The Story of the POW-MIA Flag, Annin Flagmakers web site, *https://web.archive.org/web/20140101223329/http://www.annin.com/about_powmia.asp.*

"We were playing on victimhood, trying to win hearts and minds": Bob Brudno, interview with the authors, November 30, 2021.

A banner emblazoned with the design is first presented to Secretary Laird: "History of the POW/MIA Flag," National League of Families, revised July 2022, *https://www.pow-miafamilies.org/history-of-powmia-flag.html.*

"I recall no discussion about getting it trademarked since all we wanted was to see the war end": Bob Brudno, email to the authors, February 17, 2021.

"We didn't even think about trademarking it. We were novices": Carole Hanson Hickerson, interview with the authors, August 10, 2022.

Chapter 11: Breaking Down

Lambs to Lions (January 15, 1970)

in front of a fireplace: Diary, 1965–1970, Sybil Bailey Stockdale papers, Box 11, Hoover Institution Archives; and Margaret Cifrino, Deputy Chief of Staff to Secretary of State Colin Powell, interview with the authors, March 8, 2022.

"she loudly and firmly makes her case... "I just can't believe a country as big as ours can't win this war if they want to!": Stockdale and Stockdale, *In Love and War,* 370.

"Any sign of good faith by the other side in this matter would provide encouragement for our negotiations in Paris": Davis, *Long Road Home,* 205.

"When I started here"...he was never seen as an influential secretary of state: Michael Viorst, "William Rogers thinks like Richard Nixon," *The New York Times,* February 27, 1972, *https://www.nytimes.com/1972/02/27/archives/william-rogers-thinks-like-richard-nixon-rogers-thinks-like-nixon.html*

"Nixon considered Rogers's unfamiliarity...would remain in the White House": Henry Kissinger, *White House Years,* (Boston: Little, Brown, and Company, 1979), 26.

"I felt pleased...from botching up the peace efforts the president and Dr. Kissinger are working on": Stockdale and Stockdale, *In Love and* War, 370.

Lions to Lambs (Fall 1970)

The sources for this scene are the following:

"Captain's wife quits 'Free POWs' cause," *Hartford Courant* (Hartford, CT), September 11, 1970, 2, accessed on February 2, 2021, www.newspapers.com.

Note handwritten by Sybil Stockdale on State Department note pad, from the collection of Dr. James B. Stockdale II, and Diary, 1965–1970, Sybil Bailey Stockdale papers, Box 11, Hoover Institution Archives.

Sybil Stockdale First Person Recollections of Psychotherapy, Sybil Bailey Stockdale papers, Box 4, Hoover Institution Archives, and Stockdale and Stockdale, *In Love and War*: 380–382.

Chapter 12: Breaking Out

Moving On vs. Moving In (January 1972)

The sources for this scene are the following:

Candy Parish Ellis, interview with the authors, January 20, 2014, and January 14, 2022.

Letter from Capt. F. C. Turner, USN, commanding officer, USS *America* (CVA-66), to Mrs. Charles Parish, August 9, 1968, from the personal collection of Candy Parish Ellis.

Letter from Capt. Dean E. Webster, USN, director, Personal Affairs Division of the Bureau of Naval Personnel, to Mrs. Charles Carroll Parish, January 8, 1970, from the personal collection of Candy Parish Ellis.

Letter from Col. T. H. Curtis, USAF, to Mrs. Charles C. Parish, December 29, 1969, from the personal collection of Candy Parish Ellis.

Don McLeod, "The families whose men are missing," Associated Press in *Santa Cruz Sentinel* (Santa Cruz, CA), February 23, 1971, 19, accessed on November 15, 2021, www.newspapers.com.

Diverging Paths (April–May 1971)

"We've got to be doubly sure we are keeping the POW wives in line": Memo for Gen. Hughes from H. R. Haldeman, April 26, 1971, Box 176, The Perot Family Collection, Dallas, Texas.

"tender-box [sic] that is about to explode": Memorandum for The President's File from H. R. Haldeman, Meeting with Senator Dole, Wednesday, April 14, 1971, Box 176, The Perot Family Collection, Dallas, Texas.

"There is a strong possibility...efforts...will be devoted to keeping the families on the reservation in order to buy us time": Memorandum for Bob Haldeman from Brigadier General James D. Hughes, POW/MIA Families, April 27 1971, Box 176, The Perot Family Collection, Dallas Texas; and Memorandum for H. R. Haldeman from Brig. Gen. James D. Hughes, POW/MIA Wives, April 29, 1971, Box 176, The Perot Family Collection, Dallas, TX.

Almost 200,000 remain on the ground...and several hundred men die every month: National Archives, "DCAS Vietnam Conflict Extract File record counts by CASUALTY CATEGORY (as of April 29, 2008)," https://www.archives.gov/research/military/vietnam-war/casualty-statistics#toc-dcas-vietnam-conflict-extract-file-record-counts-by-casualty-category-as-of-april-29-2008-.

"If our goal is a total withdrawal of all our forces...we would have thrown away our principal bargaining counter to win the release of American prisoners of war": "President Nixon Address on Vietnam War," April 7, 1971, C-SPAN.org, *https://www.c-span.org/video/?67889-1/president-nixon-address-vietnam-war#*!

"let them rot in comfort": John Gehrke, "Kin rip 25M ads on PW policy," *Daily News* (New York, NY), August 13, 1971, 6.

"When we incorporated, it was believed that *broad* appeal was more important to us than partisanship": National League of Families of American Prisoners and Missing in Southeast Asia newsletter, April 13, 1971.

"The POWs have become political hostages...should take precedence over its obligation to the Government of South Vietnam": "POW politics," *New York Times*, October 3, 1971, Section SM, 56, *https://www.nytimes.com/1971/10/03/archives/pow-politics.html.*

"We must not let them go off on a tangent here".... "That's why we've got to keep that residual force thing alive": "Richard Nixon and Henry Kissinger on 14 April 1971," Conversation 001-091, Presidential Recordings Digital Edition [Nixon Telephone Tapes 1971, ed. Ken Hughes] (Charlottesville: University of Virginia Press, 2014) URL: *http://prde.upress.virginia.edu/conversations/4001707.*

As long as there are POWs still in Southeast Asia, some troops will remain in Vietnam: Davis, *The Long Road Home*, 460.

"Bargaining counter": Henry Kissinger, *Ending the Vietnam War: A History of America's Involvement in and Extraction from the Vietnam War*, (New York: Simon & Schuster, 2003), 209.

"...they've got to not fight on one of these withdrawal programs...Remember everybody is working on them.": Conversation 001-091, The President/Mr. Kissinger, April 14, 1971, White House Tapes: Sound Recordings of Meetings and Telephone

Conversations of the Nixon Administration, 1971–1973, Richard M. Nixon Presidential Library and Museum, *https://www.nixonlibrary.gov/white-house-tapes/001/conversation-001-091.*

The POWs, a tiny fraction of the total American casualties, are upstaging the men fighting and dying on the front lines: "Reflections: The time of illusion," *New Yorker*, June 23, 1975, 60.

Chapter 13: Out of Line

Crying Foul (1971)

"Most importantly…It was no mere coincidence that the position of the Nixon Administration and the league were identical": "Secret link proven," Rep. Les Aspin (D-Wis.), as quoted in the Extension of Remarks, *Congressional Record,* January 31, 1972, U.S. House of Representatives, 92nd Congress, 1863.

Free office space…$25 million campaign sponsored by the Ad Council: Captain Douglas L. Clarke, USN, The National War College, *The Missing Man: Politics and the MIA,* (Washington, DC: National Defense University Press, 1979), 34.

"Of course, we all want the war to end…and its allies for answering this plea": Letter from National League National Coordinator Joan M. Vinson to membership, September 1, 1971.

"If I were a prisoner of war in North Vietnam…and the advertising business couldn't lend a hand": "Global POW campaign," *The Bee* (Danville, VA), June 17, 1971, 6, accessed on October 27, 2021, www.newspapers.com.

"We're all in favor of free inspections…and all our energies should be devoted to that end": "Families of American POWs To Challenge Advertising Council–White House Campaign," Press Release issued by the Families for Immediate Release, August 12, 1971.

"We are surprised and shocked...even one day's delay in emptying the prisons in Southeast Asia": Letter from National League of Families National Coordinator Joan Vinson to the League membership, September 1, 1971.

"sabotaged": Evelyn Grubb and Carol Jose, *You Are Not Forgotten: A Family's Quest for Truth and the Founding of The National League of Families,* (St. Petersburg, FL, Vandemere Press, 2008), 216.

Wives Compete with Nixon (January 1972)

The sources for this scene are the following:

"POW Wives–Bombing," *60 Minutes,* Season IV, January 2, 1972.

"President Nixon Informs Henry Kissinger of Television Appearance by Skeptical Wives of Prisoners of War," Transcript Prepared for the Digital National Security Archive by C. Lewis; DNSA Collection: The Kissinger Telephone Conversations: A verbatim record of U.S. diplomacy, 1969–1977, Time Stamp: 1835 Local Time; National Archives; Richard Nixon Presidential Library and Museum, White House Tapes; WHT 17-150, January 2, 1972.

"Henry Kissinger and President Nixon Discuss Skepticism of Wives of Prisoners of War and Effect of Bombing on Vietnam Peace Prospects," Transcript Prepared for the Digital National Security Archive by C. Lewis; DNSA Collection: The Kissinger Telephone Conversations: A verbatim record of U.S. diplomacy, 1969–1977, Time Stamp: 1909 Local Time; National Archives; Richard Nixon Presidential Library and Museum, White House Tapes; WHT 17-151, January 2, 1972.

"A Conversation with the President–Richard M. Nixon," (1-2-1972), *CBS News,* January 2, 1972, *https://www.youtube.com/watch?v=6P6HfUHqExk.*

Jumpin' Joe (May 1972)

"That resolution is aiding and abetting the enemy!": Taylor Branch, "Prisoners of war, prisoners of peace," *Washington Monthly*, August 1972, 42.

Sometimes over his family's objections: "When a powerful admiral feels powerless…," *The Town Talk* (Alexandria, LA), March 13, 1971, 17, accessed on November 1, 2021, *www.newspapers.com*.

"Fuck, no": Joe McCain, interview with the authors, June 13, 2019.

"Well, you have Joe": Carol McCain, conversation with the authors, July 7, 2021.

And he rolls out 26 million signatures: "POW's kin eats Thanksgiving meal for prisoners: rice, fat," *Chicago Tribune*, November 27, 1970, 3, accessed November 1, 2021, www.newspapers.com; "Half-mile of POW petitions offered," *Arizona Republic*, February 1, 1971, 3, accessed November 1, 2021, www.newspapers.com; and Fred Esplin, "Pony express rides Again—for POWs," *Deseret News* (Salt Lake City, UT), January 17, 1972, 15, accessed on December 6, 2021, *www.newspapers.com*.

Political Pawns (July 1972)

The sources for this scene are the following:

Valerie Kushner's speech to the Democratic National Convention seconding the nomination of Sen. George McGovern for president, Miami, FL, July 12, 1972.

"Transcript of President Nixon's News Conference Emphasizing Foreign Affairs," *New York Times*, June 30, 1972, *https://www.nytimes.com/1972/06/30/archives/transcript-of-president-nixons-news-conference-emphasizing-foreign.html*

"'Fantastic!' 'Wow!' 'Just Great!' Shout Members of Virginia Delegation After McGovern Victory," *The Bee* (Danville, VA), July 13, 1972, 15, accessed on October 1, 1972, *www.newspapers.com*.

Ann Compton, interview with the authors, August 16, 2022.

Clark's Charade (August 1972)

"I wasn't particularly close to him growing up...I knew enough to fear that many of the POWs might not survive until the end of the war": Bob Brudno, email to the authors, August 16, 2021.

"Whole villages had been wiped off the earth...There are only people": "Talk of the town," *The New Yorker*, September 2, 1972.

But he was allowed to visit ten captives in one wing of a prison: "Special Report: Meetings with Ramsey Clark," National League of Families newsletter, undated; and Grubb and Jose, *You Are Not Forgotten*, 249–52.

"bull session": "Clark denies claim," United Press International in *The Times Standard* (Eureka, CA), August 15, 1972, 1, accessed on August 8, 2021, *www.newspapers.com.*

Their devotion to freedom and their just cause..."There can be no question that the prisoners would be returned immediately": Rowland Evans and Robert Novak, "Clark's POW Charade," *Cincinnati Enquirer*, September 11, 1972, 5, accessed on August 8, 2021, *www.newspapers.com.*

"If you are worried about their health...and I'm a healthy man": "U.S. POWs are 'healthy,' Clark reports," United Press International in *Miami Herald*, August 13, 1972, 2, accessed on August 8, 2021, www.newspapers.com.

Statements like these threaten the lives of the POWs: Bob and Sheila Brudno, interview with the authors, June 13, 2019.

wood-paneled office: Bonnie Metzger, interview with the authors, September 23, 2021.

"No, you can't...Clark insists that the ten men he met were not "showcase" prisoners: Grubb and Jose, *You Are Not Forgotten*, 250–251.

"While you're all fighting over how to end the war...but these are still *our* boys": Bob Brudno, interview with the authors, October 22, 2020.

Through a mutual friend: Mike Harrigan, interview with the authors, August 23, 2021. Harrigan introduced Brudno to Novak's secretary.

"If I can get my hands on the entire recording...will you listen to it?": Bob Brudno, interview with the authors, October 22, 2020.

"Simply put, the August 10 meeting was a charade, giving the dubious impression of American POWs splendidly treated by their captors and infuriated by U.S. war policies": Rowland Evans and Robert Novak, "Clark's POW Charade."

Taking Sides (October 1972)

"Do you think, if the president appears tomorrow night... and I think I can assure you that he will be received the way he should be": Tape 6B Transcript of Video Interview with Carole Hanson, 29750123001. Vietnam Center and Sam Johnson Vietnam Archive. No Date, Box 01, Folder 23, Phillip Daniels Collection, Vietnam Center and Sam Johnson Vietnam Archive, Texas Tech University, accessed October 15, 2021, https://www.vietnam.ttu.edu/virtualarchive/items.php?item=29750123001.

More than 700 fired up family members are attending: National League of Families of American Prisoners and Missing in Southeast Asia, October 1972 newsletter.

"...where does there exist...Most prisoner-of-war families find it impossible to muster that kind of faith": Carole Hanson, "Leverage for Return of the Prisoners," *Los Angeles Times,* July 3, 1972, 21, accessed on October 20, 2021, www.newspapers.com.

He is their commander-in-chief, and he has the power to end the war and bring the men home: Tape 5B: Carole Hanson Hickerson, 2975VI3675. Vietnam Center and Sam Johnson Vietnam Archive. ca. 1997–2000, Phillip Daniels Collection, Vietnam Center and Sam Johnson Vietnam Archive, Texas Tech University, accessed October 18, 2021, https://www.vietnam.ttu.edu/virtualarchive/items.php?item=2975VI3675.

"[The president] did the POW wives thing at the last minute...He had a great reception, gave one of the best talks he's given": H. R. Haldeman, *The Haldeman Diaries*, 521.

"This is the thing you've got to keep in mind...will be a continuing, nagging problem.": "Richard Nixon and Henry A. Kissinger on 14 December 1972," Conversation 823-001 (*PRDE* Excerpt A), *Presidential Recordings Digital Edition* [*Fatal Politics*, ed. Ken Hughes] (Charlottesville: University of Virginia Press, 2014–), *http://prde.upress.virginia.edu/conversations/4006751.*

publicly endorses the president for re-election: "I waited until I was no longer chairman of the board...I did not want to disengage with the people in power. They were the ones who could close the door on you." Carole Hanson Hickerson, interview with the authors, March 3, 2022.

"Mr. McGovern's proposals would dishonor this country...I don't want my husband's sacrifice to have been in vain": "POW league leader stands up for Nixon," *Honolulu Advertiser* (Honolulu, HI), October 19, 1972, 4, accessed on October 20, 1972, www.newspapers.com.

Betrayal (October 1972)

inside that little foil container: "Cora Weiss, News Conference, October 3, 1972/Philadelphia," Folder 207C, Box 3, RG-46 Records of the U.S. Senate Subcommittee on POW/MIA Affairs, 102nd Congress, National Archives and Records Administration, Washington, DC.

in suits, high heels, and gloves: "Cora Weiss Oral History Project: The Reminiscences of Cora Weiss," Columbia Center for Oral History, Columbia University, 2014, Session 2, 33–34.

But she has a housekeeper who can stay the night: "Cora Weiss Oral History Project: The Reminiscences of Cora Weiss," Session 2, 74.

"None of the last three presidents...I think they are mostly concerned with creating propaganda": Tom Tiede, "Nixon using POWs, antiwar leader insists," *La Crosse Tribune* (La Crosse, WI), December 27, 1970, 12, accessed on June 16, 2022, www.newspapers.com.

"The women are going around as if their men had been kidnapped...The Geneva Convention doesn't say they have to be comfortable": Christopher S. Wren, "What is Christmas to the P.O.W. wives?," *Look*, December 15, 1970, 40.

"The only way to secure the eventual release of prisoners is through the decision by the United States to end the war": Committee of Liaison, 2150804004. Vietnam Center and Sam Johnson Vietnam Archive. 27 January 1970, Box 08, Folder 04, Douglas Pike Collection: Unit 03–Antiwar Activities, Vietnam Center and Sam Johnson Vietnam Archive, Texas Tech University, accessed June 16, 2022, https://www.vietnam.ttu.edu/virtualarchive/items.php?item=2150804004.

"It looks to us an unmistakably professional job": Peter Arnett, "Electronic device in toothpaste," *San Francisco Chronicle*, September 27, 1972.

"The charges are too ridiculous...to negotiate meaningfully for all our prisoners of war.:" Peter Arnett, "Spy devices in POW mail?" *Washington Star*, September 26, 1972.

"My family would never take part...Conclude from that what you want.": "No. Viets say spy devices mailed to Quincy POW," *Quincy Patriot-Ledger*, September 27, 1972.

Bob never asked questions: Bob Brudno, interview with the authors, April 11, 2022.

"...we were doing...embarrassment is a good form of diplomacy": "Cora Weiss Oral History Project: The Reminiscences of Cora Weiss," Session 4, 4.

"From home a few came seeking truth (?)...And to press them for better conditions": Bob Brudno, email to the authors,

December 11, 2021. The complete poem written by Capt. Alan Brudno is in the personal collection of Bob Brudno.

Chapter 14: Reunions

The List (January 1973)

"For us, we were close to the end. For them, it was just the beginning": Bob and Sheila Brudno, interviews with the authors on December 9 and December 16, 2021.

Freewheeling (February 1973)

The sources for this scene are the following:

Emilee Reynolds, interview with the authors, November 9, 2020, and November 19, 2021.

"POW on Captivity: 'Catching a rat was a big event,'" *Pacific Daily News* (Agana Heights, Guam), February 24, 1973, accessed on November 16, 2021, www.newspapers.com.

Homecomings (February–April 1973)

A military color guard standing at attention forms a gauntlet at the base of the ramp…He rushes down the ramp to salute the receiving line of American military officers: Scott Blakey, *Prisoner of War*, 320–321.

She is apprehensive, told by military briefers that the longest-held group of POWs in American history might be hostile to those they loved: Stockdale and Stockdale, *In Love and War*, 440.

Sybil breaks free and embraces Jim with so much intensity that they nearly topple over: Stockdale and Stockdale, *In Love and War*, 441.

That evening, fourth son Sidney joins the family for a steak dinner in Jim's suite at Balboa Naval Hospital: Sidney played in a championship hockey game that same day and flew home in time for dinner.

"Syb, I just can't do it. I'm so happy": Stockdale and Stockdale, *In Love and War,* 442.

where they passionately rekindle their relationship: Stockdale and Stockdale, *In Love and War,* 443.

"he would not have anything to do with them because that was the past and it should have no reflection on our marriage": "After The Call Came," unpublished memories written by Andrea Rander, undated, from the personal collection of Andrea Rander.

She is first in line to greet him, while everyone else waits: Andrea Rander, interview with the authors, March 19, 2018.

"with love, lust, and happiness": "After The Call Came," unpublished memories written by Andrea Rander, undated, from the personal collection of Andrea Rander.

"He needs to know the war was wrong." Bob is stunned. "No, he doesn't, and certainly not from you": Bob Brudno, interview with the authors, August 15 and September 1, 2022.

Several returning POWs, aware of Alan's periods of deep depression while in captivity, try warning the Air Force about his mental state, urging medical intervention: Col. Carlyle "Smitty" Harris (Ret.) and Sara W. Berry, *Tap Code: The Epic Survival of a Vietnam POW and The Secret Code That Changed Everything,* (Grand Rapids, MI: Zondervan, 2019), 202 and 215.

"I don't think Richard Nixon will end this war and I don't think he wants to end it on any terms except a good old military victory"..."When it's time for it to happen, I will permit it to happen rather than prevent it from happening": Al Eisele, "POW 'widow" to give up vigil, reassess wife role," *Press-Telegram* (Long Beach, CA), November 12, 1972, 1, accessed on March 9, 2022, www.newspapers.com.

"...I said to her that her devotion, her loyalty, and her love were my sustenance and surcease": Kushner press conference,

Valley Forge, Pennsylvania, April 3, 1973, from the personal collection of Toni Kushner Nee.

"Must have an end to this war: I see no end…That death takes away all that was taught by Christ's birth": Valerie M. Kushner, "I Cannot Rejoice," *New York Times*, December 24, 1971, *https://www.nytimes.com/1971/12/24/archives/i-cannot-rejoice.html.*

"Your daddy is coming home. He is out. They cannot get him anymore": Robert Timberg, *John McCain*, 113–114.

"Where will he sleep? And what will we feed him?": Robert Timberg, *The Nightingale's Song*, 198; and Mark Salter, *Faith of My Fathers: A Family Memoir*, (New York: Random House, 1999), 302.

One of her legs no longer bends: Robert Timberg interview with Carol McCain, June 26, 1990, Robert Timberg Collection, U.S. Navy Archives.

"I already know," he says. "I know you had an accident."… "Well, you know, I don't look so good myself. It's fine": Timberg, *John McCain*, 115; and Timberg, *The Nightingale's Song*, 230.

"Now the other thing is, the boys have long hair": Robert Timberg interview with Carol McCain, June 26, 1990, Robert Timberg Collection, U.S. Navy Archives.

Carole had received definitive news that Steve was not among the 591 men who survived the war: TELEGRAMS TO NEXT OF KIN: NAME OF SUBJECT NOT ON LIST OF US PRISONERS HELD IN LAOS. 1973. Manuscript/Mixed Material. *https://www.loc.gov/item/powmia/pwmaster_74804/*.

Cius doubted he survived the ensuing barrage of gunfire: John L. Plaster, *SOG: The Secret Wars of America's Commandos in Vietnam*, (New York: Onyx, 1998), 97; and UPDATED BIOGRAPHIC/SITE REPORT FOR REFNO. 1996. Manuscript/Mixed Material. *https://www.loc.gov/item/powmia/pwmaster_147786/*; and Carole Hanson Hickerson, interview with the authors, April 6, 2019.

"I deeply regret to confirm that the status of your husband, Major Stephen P. Hanson, has been changed from missing in

action to deceased": TELEGRAMS TO NEXT OF KIN: STATUS CHANGED FROM MISSING IN ACTION TO DECEASED. 1974. Manuscript/Mixed Material. *https://www.loc.gov/item/powmia/pwmaster_74807/*.

"This noon Nancy dedicated a display case in the corridor of the Capitol...I, too, shall miss him": Letter from Gov. Ronald Reagan to Carole Hanson, June 20, 1973, from the personal collection of Carole Hanson Hickerson.

guests are treated to an Air Force flyover and a concert with Bob Hope as MC: Martha Hand, "Vietnam vets honored at Dallas celebration," *Fort Worth Star-Telegram* (Fort Worth, TX), June 3, 1973, 1, accessed on June 8, 2022, www.newspapers.com.

"Jim leaned over and gave me a little kiss on the cheek": Jim and Carole married on December 14, 1974. Carole took both of Todd's hands in hers and asked him, "Do you think we are doing the right thing? Because it was something *we* were doing." Jim adopted Todd and the family adopted two more children. Jim Bell also remarried an MIA wife, Dora Griffin.

"I found myself getting angry"..."I was so happy for them and for the men who got home. But I cried a lot": Pat Mearns, interview with the authors, March 3, 2022.

"I found myself wondering why they had Art fly the same exact route each day. The enemy was just waiting for his plane so they could shoot it down": Pat and Missy Mearns, conversation with the authors, February 26, 2022.

"As all of you know, this is the largest dinner ...": Richard Nixon Remarks at the White House Honoring Returning Vietnam POWs, May 24, 1973, courtesy of the Maine Military Museum, *https://mainemilitarymuseum.org/photos-and-videos/the-white-house-salutes-our-prisoners-of-war/*.

PART III: THE LONG AND WINDING ROAD (1973-PRESENT)

Chapter 15: Mythmaking

Into the Jungle (July 1973)

"It hurt like hell": Pat Mearns, interview with the authors, September 2, 2021.

She believes he might still be alive, here: Leah Larkin, "A futile search brings new awareness," *Courier-Journal* (Louisville, KY), August 27, 1973, 1, accessed on September 29, 2020, www.newspapers.com.

The goal is to meet with as many Communist party heads as possible: Steve Franks, interview with the authors, September 23, 2020. Steve Franks worked closely with Carole Bates Brown and Kay Hunter on VIVA campaigns, including the creation of the POW/MIA bracelets.

Known for her naiveté, she questioned little: Carol Bates Brown and Ann Mills Griffiths, interview with the authors, December 9, 2020.

it was best not to ask too many questions until Marian's father sobered up: John Shelton, interview with the authors, April 28, 2022.

She was seventeen and pregnant when she married Charles: Lea Ann Shelton, interview with the authors, March 14, 2022.

marrying Charles helped her get over the loss: Susan Katz Keating, *Prisoners of Hope: Exploiting the POW/MIA Myth in America*, (New York: Random House, 1994), xvii.

Johnny Shelton and eight-year-old Michael were transfixed by an extensive and colorful vinyl album collection...Johnny caught a glimpse of his mother, surrounded by guests, crying

and shaking in a flowery mu-mu: John Shelton, interview with the authors, February 4, 2022; and Michael Shelton, interview with the authors, March 23, 2022.

spied Shelton on a steep, sloping hill about 30-40 yards from his parachute, which was caught in a tree: RECORD OF TELEPHONE CONVERSATION CONCERNING MIA STATUS OF CHARLES SHELTON. 1974. Manuscript/Mixed Material. *https://www.loc.gov/item/powmia/pwmaster_64728/*.

"I told him to *git out*! And then he came back in and was telling me some more...She was covered up with people, handing her drinks. And pills": Lea Ann Shelton, Charles Shelton, John Shelton, and Joan Shelton May, interview with the authors, December 11, 2021.

"Landlocked, lousy little place": Deposition of William Sullivan, July 20, 1992, 23, Box 25, Senate Select Committee on POW/MIA Affairs–Unclassified and Declassified Depositions, RG-46 Records of the U.S. Senate Select Committee on POW/MIA Affairs, 102nd Congress, National Archives and Records Administration.

"...I am consciously jeopardizing entire Air America [CIA] operation in this country and am risking severe embarrassment to both U.S. and Lao governments": Veith, *Code-Name Bright Light,* 71.

"This has been the best thing on the whole trip...I can see why they can't get him out": Leah Larkin, "A futile search brings new awareness," *Courier-Journal* (Louisville, KY), August 27, 1973, 12, accessed on September 29, 2020, www.newspapers.com.

The Trouble with Laos (1973–1975)

Nixon's chief of staff H. R. Haldeman has spent the week managing the barrage of meetings about the grand jury investigation into the growing scandal: H. R. Haldeman, *The Haldeman Diaries,* 618–619.

today's news stories are full of words like "sabotage," "espionage," "obstruction of justice," and "cover up": Joseph Kraft, "Watergate: A time bomb," *Sacramento Bee*, March 29, 1973, 31, and Jack Anderson, "Washington merry-go-round: Capitol buzzing about White House role," *Bangor Daily News* (Bangor, Maine), March 29, 1973, 14, accessed on March 13, 2022, www.newspapers.com.

"For the first time in twelve years, no American military forces are in Vietnam. All of our American POWs are on their way home": "President Richard Nixon's 14 Addresses to the Nation on Vietnam," Richard Nixon Foundation, *https://www.nixonfoundation.org/2017/09/president-richard-nixons-14-addresses-nation-vietnam/*; and "President Richard Nixon Address to the Nation on Vietnam and Domestic Problems," March 29, 1973, https://www.youtube.com/watch?v=0BYwpNy7vd4.

350 who were lost or captured in Laos have never been heard from again: Memorandum for the Secretary of Defense from Lawrence S. Eagleburger, Acting Assistant Secretary of Defense for International Security Affairs, and Memorandum for the Assistant to the President for National Security Affairs, March 28, 1973, "U.S. POW/IA Personnel in Laos," Box 220, Perot Family Archives, Dallas, TX.

"There was no other single objective as important to us as the POWs": Deposition of Henry Alfred Kissinger, September 14, 1992, page 28, Box 10, Senate Select Committee on POW/MIA Affairs–Unclassified and Declassified Depositions, RG-46 Records of the U.S. Senate Select Committee on POW/MIA Affairs, 102nd Congress, National Archives and Records Administration, Washington, D.C.

U.S. troops in Vietnam were instructed not to withdraw until the last C-141 Starlifter carrying the last group of American POWs have left Hanoi air space: Minutes of the Washington Special Action Group Meeting, March 6, 1973, folder

"POW-MIA Data (1970–1980) (1 of 8)," RAC Box 24, Box 32, Robert Kimmitt Files, Ronald Reagan Presidential Library and Museum, Simi Valley, California.

"the [Lao Patriotic Front] may hold a number of unidentified U.S. POWs although we cannot accurately judge how many. The American embassy, Vientiane, agrees with this judgment": Memorandum for the Secretary of Defense from Lawrence S. Eagleburger, Acting Assistant Secretary of Defense for International Security Affairs, and Memorandum for the Assistant to the President for National Security Affairs, March 28, 1973, Box 220, Perot Family Archives, Dallas, Texas.

Kissinger delivered a letter from Nixon detailing the economic aid the United States was prepared to give North Vietnam under Article 21 of the Paris Peace Accords: Kissinger, *Ending the Vietnam War,* 448–449; and Deposition of Henry Alfred Kissinger, Select Committee on POW/MIA Affairs, September 14, 1992, 120–121, RG 46 Records of the U.S. Senate Select Committee on POW/MIA Affairs, 102nd Congress, Transcripts of Depositions, Box 10, National Archives and Records Administration.

Article 21: "Agreement on ending the war and restoring peace in Viet-Nam. Signed at Paris on 27 January 1973," *https://treaties.un.org/doc/Publication/UNTS/Volume%20935/volume-935-I-13295-English.pdf.*

Although Kissinger had said publicly that Congress would be consulted: "Kissinger vows a Congress role in aid in Hanoi," *New York Times,* January 27, 1973, 61, *https://www.nytimes.com/1973/01/27/archives/kissinger-vows-a-congress-role-in-aid-for-hanoi-promises.html.*

"My major concern was not to have people go around saying we owed them reparations and to avoid any possibility of their linking this thing together....It was something to reassure the ladies that I have been meeting with for several years, to tell them that the release of their husbands could not be

held up on the basis of any of these positions": Deposition of Henry Alfred Kissinger, Select Committee on POW/MIA Affairs, September 14, 1992, 133–134, RG 46 Records of the U.S. Senate Select Committee on POW/MIA Affairs, 102nd Congress, Transcripts of Depositions, Box 10, National Archives and Records Administration.

"Where Are Our MIAs?"..."We know with modern ejection methods there is a great chance of pilot and crew survival when a plane goes down. This figure ... is ludicrous": "Ads ask: 'Where are our MIAs?'," *The Bee* (Danville, VA), February 21, 1973, accessed on February 9, 2022, *www.newspapers.com.*

"...our members have become increasingly alarmed...We cannot allow this to happen, and our organization does not intend to keep silent indefinitely": Letter from the National League of Families to Brig. Gen. Brent Scowcroft; February 20, 1973; folder Vietnam (POW) Vol. VI Jan 1973 [1 of 2]; Box 2; Vietnam Subject Files; Richard Nixon Presidential Library and Archives, Yorba Linda, California.

Kissinger advocated for air strikes in Laos, along the Ho Chi Minh Trail: Memorandum for the Secretary of Defense from Lawrence S. Eagleburger, Acting Assistant Secretary of Defense for International Security Affairs, and Memorandum for the Assistant to the President for National Security Affairs, March 28, 1973, Box 220, Perot Family Archives, Dallas, Texas; and Deposition of Henry Alfred Kissinger, Select Committee on POW/MIA Affairs, September 14, 1992, 156, RG 46 Records of the U.S. Senate Select Committee on POW/MIA Affairs, 102nd Congress, Transcripts of Depositions, Box 10, National Archives and Records Administration.

"We have no indications at this time that there are any Americans alive in Indochina," he asserts...Since many of the crash sites are near the DMZ or in Hanoi-controlled territory, it was reasonable to assume that Hanoi could provide answers: Memorandum for the Chairman, Joint Chiefs of Staff from Lt. Gen. John R. Deane, Jr., Acting Director of the Defense Intelligence Agency, prepared in response to a request from Dr. R.E. Shields, Assistant to the Assistant Secretary of Defense/International Security Affairs, 21 MAR 1973, POLICY FOR PROCESSING OF RETURNED U.S. POW AND OTHER DETAINED MILITARY PERSONNEL/INFORMATION PERTAINING TO PW/MIA SITUATION IN LAOS, RADIO PATHET LAO BROADCAST, FILE RECORD SUMMARIES. 1973. Manuscript/Mixed Material. *https://www.loc.gov/item/powmia/pwmaster_86650/*.

"No Americans are still being held alive as prisoners in Indochina, or elsewhere, as a result of the war in Indochina": "Americans Missing in Southeast Asia," Final Report Together with Additional and Separate Views of the Select Committee on Missing Persons in Southeast Asia, United States House of Representatives, December 13, 1976, vii.

Other refugees talk of bedraggled Americans begging for cigarettes: Jack Anderson, "Fate of MIAs in Vietnam haunts Pentagon," *The Central New Jersey Home News* (New Brunswick, NJ), United Press Syndicate, Inc., July 16, 1978, 52, accessed on March 17, 2022, www.newspapers.com.

a small group of Americans in chain gangs building roads or being moved around the jungles of Laos and Cambodia: Marianne Lester, "Twisting slowly, slowly in the breeze," *Family* magazine, June 19, 1974, 6.

Some 64,000 Vietnamese flee their homeland in the month of May alone: Harry F. Young, "Refugees—An International Obligation: Department of State Bulletin." *December Monthly Labor Review* 103:10, 41.

Marian's Megaphone (February 1974)

The trio sits in the jostling camper, driving around the White House for a week: Mike Huber, "The last POW," *Courier-Journal* (Louisville, KY), August 2, 1981, 91, accessed March 14,

2022, www.newspapers.com; and author interviews with Lea Ann Shelton and Joan Shelton May, December 12, 2021.

"There are some 'dissident' members on the board who advocate actions such as the 'vigil' at the White House January 27... may divert our energy from other important aspects of the Indochina situation": Memorandum to the Secretary [of State] from Frank A. Sieverts; Your Meeting With MIA Families 11:30 a.m., February 9 [1974]; folder Vietnam (POW) Vol. VI Jan. 1973 [1 of 2]; Box 2; WH NSC Files: POW/MIA; Richard Nixon Presidential Library, Yorba Linda, California.

"World conditions could change, and the League should be prepared to take advantage of any such changes": Excerpt from the newsletter published by the National League of Families, February 26, 1974; folder POW/MIA Policy (1976-1985) (2 of 3); RAC Box 15 – Box 14; Richard T. Childress Files; Ronald Reagan Presidential Library and Museum, Yorba Linda, CA.

Chapter 16: Desperately Seeking Answers

In Pursuit (December 1980–May 1981)

Squinting through a magnifying glass: former Director of Naval Intelligence, interview with the authors, February 9, 2022.

They show what resembles a large detention camp: SYMBOL READOUT/ANALYSIS. 1980. Manuscript/Mixed Material. *https://www.loc.gov/item/powmia/pwmaster_128559/*.

The figures milling about the camp do not appear Asian... seem too long for use by Asians: Keating, *Prisoners of Hope*, 131; George C. Wilson and Art Harris, "Mercenaries sent to Laos seeking MIAs," *Washington Post*, May 21, 1981, *https://www.washingtonpost.com/archive/politics/1981/05/21/mercenaries-sent-to-laos-seeking-mias/4b7be40b-037e-41c6-b987-c24b924746cb/*; and Thomas W. Lippman, "U.S. Team To Inspect Possible POW Prison in Laos," *The Washington*

Post, January 16, 1994, *https://www.washingtonpost.com/archive/politics/1994/01/16/us-team-to-inspect-possible-pow-prison-in-laos/c9f4690e-1c2d-4eb9-a417-8052f7f67a48/*.

Nearby is what looks like the letter "K": Jack Murphy, "Op Pocket Change: The Delta Force operation to rescue U.S. POWs allegedly left behind after the Vietnam War," June 21, 2021, *https://www.audacy.com/connectingvets/news/delta-force-top-secret-mission-to-rescue-vietnam-era-pows.*

and only visible from above: Michael Ross, "Senate panel hears of covert POW hunt," *Los Angeles Times*, October 17, 1992, 41, accessed on January 30, 2022, *www.newspapers.com*.

Over a two-month period, they appear four times: SYMBOL READOUT/ANALYSIS. 1978. Manuscript/Mixed Material. *https://www.loc.gov/item/powmia/pwmaster_128541/*.

Defense Intelligence Agency (DIA) has received more than 1,000 reports...three hundred are alleged first-hand, eyewitness sightings of live American POWs: Memorandum for the Chairman, Joint Chiefs of Staff from Lt. Gen. Eugene F. Tighe, Jr., USAF, Director, Defense Intelligence Agency, 28 January 1981, CURRENT POW INTELLIGENCE/CURRENT US PRISONER OF WAR STATUS. 1981. Manuscript/Mixed Material. *https://www.loc.gov/item/powmia/pwmaster_86683/*.

"They might have seen Americans...it's really got the families stirred up": Dan Lohwasser, "Refugees' Stories Rekindle Hopes of POW-MIA Families," *Los Angeles Times*, April 5, 1981, 3, accessed on February 16, 2021, *www.newspapers.com*.

"I am an American. Are you interested?": Wendell Rawls, Jr., "A Marine court finds Garwood helped foe as a Vietnam P.O.W.," *The New York Times*, February 6, 1981, *https://www.nytimes.com/1981/02/06/us/a-marine-court-finds-garwood-helped-foe-as-a-vietnam-pow.html#:~:text=Pfc.&text=Garwood%20of%20the%20Marine%20Corps,days%20before%20returning%20the%20conviction.*

Collaborated with their captors: Ginny Carroll, "Former POW says Garwood remained after 'liberation,'" *Washington Post*, January 10, 1980, *https://www.washingtonpost.com/archive/politics/1980/01/10/former-pow-says-garwood-remained-after-liberation/4764cc8f-d729-4eb2-bcde-fa3c53bfdaa8/*.

In addition, in intercepted radio chatter, a top Laotian military leader is heard ordering American POWs be moved to central Laos: Douglas Waller, "The Americans left behind," *Time* Magazine, October 17, 1994, 50.

"Let's get it going": A handwritten comment by Richard V. Allen in the margins of a Memorandum from Robert M. Kimmitt to Richard V. Allen, National Security Advisor; March 20, 1981; Legal: POW-MIA 1980-7/1981 (11) folder; RAC Box 7, Box 5; Robert Kimmitt Files; Ronald Reagan Presidential Library.

Authorizing a reconnaissance mission only: Michael Ross, "Senate Panel Hears of Covert POW Hunt," *Los Angeles Times*, October 17, 1992, 41, accessed on January 30, 2022, *www.newspapers.com*.

They slip into Laos...close enough for first-hand observation: Waller, "The Americans left behind;" and Murphy, "Op Pocket Change."

The degree of planning was not very deep: Lt. Col. Lewis H. Burruss, Jr., interview with the authors, January 28, 2022.

"The Post has learned... concluded that there are no Americans in the camp in Laos, defense officials said": Wilson and Harris, "Mercenaries Sent to Laos Seeking MIAs"; and Thomas W. Lippman, "U.S. Team To Inspect Possible POW Prison in Laos," *Washington Post*, January 16, 1994, *https://www.washingtonpost.com/archive/politics/1994/01/16/us-team-to-inspect-possible-pow-prison-in-laos/c9f4690e-1c2d-4eb9-a417-8052f7f67a48/*.

"Highest national priority": Remarks at a Meeting of the National League of Families of American Prisoners and Missing in Southeast Asia, January 28, 1983, *https://www.reaganlibrary.*

gov/archives/speech/remarks-meeting-national-league-families-american-prisoners-and-missing-southeast.

"Governor Reagan, will you bring my daddy home?": Derek Pogson, "'Bring my daddy home': Reagan vows to seek return of California fliers held by reds," *Sacramento Bee* (Sacramento, CA), June 24, 1970, 4, accessed on April 11, 2022, www.newspapers.com; and Carole Hanson Hickerson, interview with the authors, March 23, 2022.

The Over-the-Hill Gang (March 1981)

to keep tabs on the group's leader: TRANSCRIPT OF HEARINGS BEFORE THE SENATE SELECT COMMITTEE ON POW-MIA AFFAIRS: DEPOSITION OF ANN MILLS GRIFFITHS. 1992. Manuscript/Mixed Material. *https://www.loc.gov/item/powmia/pwmaster_91847/* Note: At the time, Mills-Griffiths said, "Gritz is quite a talker and I was awfully dumb in those days. I certainly talked to General Tighe about it and told him what was going on, in fact at his request flew down. He sort of wanted me to sort of keep track of what was going on, and I did and I would become appalled and come back. At the time, however, as Gritz would put it, he was sort of running this parallel thing and if the U.S. government got serious he would cease and desist. And I can't remember what the date was, but at one point General Tighe asked me to fly down and ask [Gritz] to cease and desist, which I did."

She spies Gritz leading his men in a calisthenics routine: Carol Bates Brown, interview with the authors, March 2, 2021.

"It is too bad we have to proceed this way...absolute need to know": Jack Anderson, "Search for POWs got some official support," *Marion Star* (Marion, OH), October 15, 1984, 4, accessed on February 3, 2022, www.newspapers.com; AFFIDAVIT FROM LT. COL. RET. JAMES "BO" GRITZ. 1986. Manuscript/Mixed Material. https://www.loc.gov/item/powmia/pwmaster_36801/

Note: Many DoD officials who saw the original of this memo doubt its authenticity. General Aaron died in 1980.

"This thing is so sensitive it could result in a real inquisition if word leaked out that we were proceeding unofficially": James "Bo" Gritz, *A Nation Betrayed,* (Boulder City, NV: Lazarus Publishing Company, 1989), 161.

Ross Perot has encouraged him on these missions: Carter Harrison and Bill Bond, "Vets planned Viet raid to free POWs," *Chicago Tribune,* March 26, 1981, 1, and "Ex-Green Berets trained for POW rescues," *News-Press* (Fort Myers, FL), March 27, 1981, 32, accessed on March 24, 2022, www.newspapers.com.

"I have been handpicked...and you are my disciples": Alex McColl, "Operation Velvet Hammer: Gritz's first trip through the looking glass," *Soldier of Fortune's POW/MIA Special, Bo Gritz: Hero or Huckster?*, Spring 1983, 29.

Gritz has seen the DIA overhead images...digging up bamboo: Keating, *Prisoners of Hope,* 133.

It can supposedly cut a car in half...and sustain seven bullet holes before losing air: Charles J. Patterson and G. Lee Tippen, *The Heroes Who Fell from Grace,* (Canton, OH: Daring Books, 1985), 27; Gritz, *A Nation Betrayed,* 186; and Keating, *Prisoners of Hope,* 133.

The helicopters will hoist...celebratory parade on Fifth Avenue: McColl, "Operation Velvet Hammer," 26-31; Keating, *Prisoners of Hope,* 134; and Harrison and Bond, "Vets planned Viet raid to free POWs."

The entire team is expected to commit suicide: Keating, *Prisoners of Hope,* 134; and Patterson and Tippen, *The Heroes Who Fell from Grace,* 32.

"To the vulnerable people we were at the time, and to the uninformed populace, Gritz can be very persuasive": Gerald Posner, *Citizen Perot: His Life and Times,* (New York: Random House, 1996), 195.

Gritz estimates the mission could cost...MIA families also contribute $30,000: Harrison and Bond, "Vets planned Viet raid to free POWs"; TRANSCRIPT OF HEARINGS BEFORE THE SENATE SELECT COMMITTEE ON POW-MIA AFFAIRS: DEPOSITION OF ANN MILLS GRIFFITHS. 1992. Manuscript/Mixed Material. https://www.loc.gov/item/powmia/pwmaster_91847/; and Alex McColl, Operation Velvet Hammer: Gritz's first trip through the looking glass," *Soldier of Fortune*'s POW/MIA Special, Bo Gritz: Hero or Huckster?, Spring 1983, 28.

"Even if one came out alive, it would be worth it": Harrison and Bond, "Vets planned Viet raid to free POWs."

The "Mystery Box" (October 1981)

"We had come up on a knoll...a detainee camp": Deposition of Scott Tracy Barnes, U.S. Senate Select Committee on POW/MIA Affairs, Friday, March 6, 1992, 180, RG 46 Records of the U.S. Senate Select Committee on PW/MIA Affairs, 102nd Congress, Transcripts of Depositions, Box 2, National Archives and Records Administration.

...to make it difficult to discern the truth: Bob Cohn, "The strange tale of Mr. Barnes," *Newsweek,* November 8, 1992, *https://www.newsweek.com/strange-tales-mr-barnes-196798.*

"the worst condition... 'I can't believe we would leave them behind'": Deposition of Scott Tracy Barnes, U.S. Senate Select Committee on POW/MIA Affairs, Friday, March 6, 1992, 183–191, RG 46 Records of the U.S. Senate Select Committee on PW/MIA Affairs, 102nd Congress, Transcripts of Depositions, Box 2, National Archives and Records Administration.

As instructed by Mike Baldwin: Scott Barnes also claimed that his companion on the adventure into Laos, Mike Baldwin, was really a CIA operative named Jerry Daniels. Also, according to Barnes, Baldwin (a.k.a. Daniels), the only man who could verify the claims of sighting live American POWs, died from carbon monoxide poisoning a few weeks later. Source: Lee Davidson, "Agencies deny man's charges of POWs, chemical arms, murder in Southeast Asia," *Deseret News*, July 17, 1988, *https://www.deseret.com/1988/7/17/18772168/agencies-deny-man-s-charges-of-pows-chemical-arms-murder-in-southeast-asia.*

"If merchandise confirmed, then liquidate...I'll have no part in this": "DIA cover up/testimony of Mark A. Smith and Scott T. Barnes before the U.S. Senate Committee, Veterans Affairs," January 27, 1986, DIA COVER UP/TESTIMONY OF MARK A. SMITH AND SCOTT T. BARNES BEFORE THE U.S. SENATE COMMITTEE, VETERANS' AFFAIRS. 1986. Manuscript/Mixed Material. https://www.loc.gov/item/powmia/pwmaster_85697/.

A scuffle ensues: Donna DuVall and Jim Graves, "Scott Barnes: Many of Mystery," *Soldier of Fortune*'s POW/MIA Special, Spring 1983, 35. This article says the fight broke out over a piece of camera equipment.

Barnes did not trek into Laos, and he did not photograph POWs: "Agent exposes secret mission," *CovertAction Quarterly*, Summer 1982, 40; Gritz, *A Nation Betrayed*, 198–9; and Patterson and Tippen, *The Heroes Who Fell From Grace*, 53; and Deposition of James Gordon "Bo" Gritz, U.S. Senate Select Committee on POW/MIA Affairs, November 23, 1992, 12, RG 46 Records of the U.S. Senate Select Committee on PW/MIA Affairs, 102nd Congress, Transcripts of Depositions, Box 8, National Archives and Records Administration.

who brings a new dimension to the term Walter Mitty: Gritz, *A Nation Betrayed*, iii.

She mortgages her home to help pay his bills: B. G. Burkett and Glenna Whitley, *Stolen Valor: How the Vietnam Generation Was Robbed of its Heroes and its History*, (Dallas, TX: Verity Press, Inc., 1998), 423; and Susan Katz Keating notes from phone call with Marian Shelton, December 1988, from the private collection of Susan Katz Keating.

Chapter 17: Turning a Cause into A Profession

The Rise of Ann Mills-Griffiths (September 1982)

Shelton is the only missing man officially listed as a POW: Scott Harris, "POW's children surrender the legend," *Los Angeles Times,* September 25, 1994, *https://www.latimes.com/archives/la-xpm-1994-09-25-me-42914-story.html.*

She and the National League initiated it: Richard Childress, interview with the authors, August 19, 2022.

"That sounds like it": David E. Hendrix, "U.S., Laos to discuss last official POW," *Riverside Press-Enterprise* (Riverside, CA), July 7, 1985.

American bombs destroyed the men's graves: Garnett "Bill" Bell with George J. Veith, *Leave No Man Behind: Bill Bell and the Search for American POW/MIAs from the Vietnam War,* (Madison, WI: Goblin Fern Press, 2004) 189; NATIONAL LEAGUE OF FAMILIES NEWSLETTER – LEAGUE DELEGATION TRIP TO SOUTHEAST ASIA. 1982. Manuscript/Mixed Material; *https://www.loc.gov/item/powmia/pwmaster_64778/*; and LEAGUE OF FAMILIES PRESS CONFERENCE – EXCERPTS. 1982. Manuscript/Mixed Material *https://www.loc.gov/item/powmia/pwmaster_64814/*; and DIA Memo to Department of State 02 MAR 89, David Hrdlicka Case File, Folder C-13 06, Box 7, RG 46 Records of the U.S. Senate Select Committee on POW/MIA Affairs, 102nd Congress, National Archives and Records Administration, Washington, D.C.

"major breakthrough": National League of Families of American Prisoners and Missing in Southeast Asia newsletter October 13, 1982, Folder A01.01.0004.20b, Box HRP008, Perot Family Archives, Dallas, TX.

It is the first time representatives from the Lao People's Democratic Republic and the United States have discussed the fate: Anne Keegan, "Searching a jungle crash site to solve a 10-year mystery," *San Francisco Examiner*, October 10, 1982, 20, accessed on April 6, 2022, *www.newspapers.com*.

The Real Rambo (October-November 1982)

"I told Gritz I would bring this up with President Reagan... and he assured me he wouldn't": "Agent exposes secret mission," CAIB's *Covert Action*, Summer 1982, 39.

Gritz also has financial backing: Patterson and Tippin, *The Heroes Who Fell from Grace*, 50.

"It's a good night to die": Patterson and Tippin, *The Heroes Who Fell from Grace*, 110.

U.S. officials assure him that the U.S. government has not sent Green Berets and has neither supported nor condoned this activity: This is not technically true. Gritz was given an "advance of funds and equipment totaling $16,000 by the Intelligence Support Activity, a subordinate element of the Army's Intelligence and Security Command (INSCOM) after the command had belatedly submitted a [redacted] to Headquarters Department of the Army for further coordination with the Defense Intelligence [redacted]. ... In October 81, USAISA submitted a [redacted] for Army, DIA and [redacted] approval. The [redacted], known as GREAT EAGLE, envisioned using Gritz in a collection capacity to confirm/deny and efinitively [sic] locating live PWs in Southeast Asia. DIA declined to approve the [redacted] due to Gritz's notoriety." Source: Memorandum Thru Director of the Army Staff for Mr. Robert Winchester from Robert F. Gaudet, LTC, GS, Special Projects Officer; "GAO Inquiry – LTC (Ret) Bo Gritz"; 11 July 1988; DOD/OSD; Box 6; RG Records of the U.S. Senate 102nd Select Committee on POW/MIA Affairs, National Archives and Records Administration.

"Why can't the U.S. government do something about this fellow?": Cable from AMEMBASSY Vientiane to SECSTATE, 092136ZFEB83, POW-MIA Technical Meetings – Laos Feb. 1983–May 1985 folder, RAC Box 16 – Box 18, Richard T. Childress

Files, National Security Council Staff & Offices, Ronald Reagan Presidential Library & Museum

"Both Teddy Roosevelt and John Wayne are dead": Patterson and Tippin, *The Heroes Who Fell from Grace,* 183.

Mindset to Debunk (Summer 1985)

The office team basically "runs itself": Rear Adm. Tom Brooks, interview with the authors, June 2, 2022.

"Rabbit warren": Carol Bates Brown, interview with the authors, March 2, 2022.

disingenuous at best and an outright lie at worst: Rear Adm. Tom Brooks, interview with the authors, April 30, 2019.

"Mindset to debunk" and "we will not withstand scrutiny very well": Memorandum for BGEN Shufelt from Thomas A. Brooks, Commodore, USN, Assistant Deputy Director for Collection Management, Defense Intelligence Agency, September 25, 1985, from the personal collection of Rear Adm. Thomas A. Brooks.

Loose Cannon (May 1987)

"Have covered up…And that's what caused the people to be left in Hanoi.": Barbara Crossette, "Perot criticizes U.S. Hanoi policy," *The New York Times,* August 12, 1992, A9, *https://www.nytimes.com/1992/08/12/world/perot-criticizes-us-hanoi-policy.html.*

They came up empty-handed, reporting to Perot that no live POWs were left: Tom Meurer, interview with the authors, May 26, 2021; and Posner, *Citizen Perot,* 193.

"I do know the Communist mind": Tom Meurer, interview with the authors, May 26, 2021.

"People kept calling Ross…found their way to him.": Posner, *Citizen Perot,* 194. Perot told Ann Mills-Griffiths, "I'll handle the POWs. You handle the bones." Source: Ann Mills-Griffiths, interview with the authors, December 14, 2021.

"Do I have your promise...you will follow up?": Posner, *Citizen Perot,* 199.

"...go all the way to the bottom of it and figure out what the situation was": "Reagan asks Perot to go to bottom of POW issue," *El Paso Times,* November 14, 1986, 6-B.

Bush rebutted that he had never asked Perot for money..."I told [Vice President Bush] I did not want to...and proved it again": Posner, *Citizen Perot,* 199–201; and Deposition of H. Ross Perot, July 1, 1992, 28–29, U.S. Senate Select Committee on POW/MIA Affairs, RG 46 Records of the U.S. Senate Select Committee on POW/MIA Affairs, 102nd Congress, Transcripts of Depositions, National Archives and Records Administration, Washington, DC.

"Spasmodic, temporary, no organized, sustained effort to get it done": Deposition of H. Ross Perot, July 1, 1992, 281, U.S. Senate Select Committee on POW/MIA Affairs, RG 46 Records of the U.S. Senate Select Committee on POW/MIA Affairs, 102nd Congress, Transcripts of Depositions, National Archives and Records Administration, Washington, DC.

"Getting out of it": Letter from Vice President Bush to Ross Perot, March 23, 1987, NLGB Control #9437, Staff and Office Files, The George H. W. Bush Presidential Library, Houston, TX.

"He feels he has been badly treated by all": Posner, *Citizen Perot,* 211; and Memorandum for the Files from the Vice President, Office of the Vice President, March 21, 1987, "phone call from Ross Perot – 2:00 P.M.," Box 176, The Perot Family Archives, Dallas TX.

"Why did your government declare...looking for live Americans?": Memo from Ross Perot to The Honorable Ronald Reagan, April 8, 1987, Box 176, The Perot Family Archives, Dallas, TX.

"Once I saw those national security guys": Posner, *Citizen Perot,* 213–214.

Perot takes a seat next to the president . . . "probably time for me to get out of this and go back to my business.": Posner,

Citizen Perot, 213–214; Memorandum for the Vice President from Gregg Mattke, Subject: May 6, 1987 Ross Perot Meeting with President, NLGB Control #9399, Staff and Office Files, The George H.W. Bush Presidential Library, Houston, Texas; Deposition of General Colin L. Powell, Chairman, Joint Chiefs of Staff, July 16, 1992, 93–98, U.S. Senate Select Committee on POW/MIA Affairs, RG 46 Records of the U.S. Senate Select Committee on POW/MIA Affairs, 102nd Congress, Transcripts of Depositions, National Archives and Records Administration, Washington, DC.

Lost Causes (October 1990)

Marian called her son Michael to bring her vodka...He could tell she was depressed.": County of San Diego Investigative Report, Office of the Medical Examiner, Case #90-2078, December 14, 1990, from the personal collection of Susan Katz Keating; Michael Shelton, interview with the author, March 23, 2022.

She has done the best she could to find their father: Keating, *Prisoners of Hope,* xx.

And she pens an apology: Michael Clark, interview with the authors, February 4, 2022.

Her blood alcohol content was .30: County of San Diego Toxicology Report, Case #90-2078, Approved October 19, 1990, by Richard F. Shaw, Chief, Toxicology Laboratory, from the personal collection of Susan Katz Keating.

Strangely, the sliding glass door: Lea Ann Shelton, Charles Shelton, John Shelton, and Joan Shelton May, interview with the authors on December 11, 2021.

she died instantly: Michael Shelton, interview with the authors, March 23, 2022.

She tried her best: Michael Clark, email to the authors, December 20, 2020.

Chapter 18: POW Politics

"Shut Up and Sit Down!" (July 1992)

"We live in a marvelous time...America's values have indeed changed the world.": President George H.W. Bush, "Remarks to the National League of Families of American Prisoners and Missing in Southeast Asia in Arlington, Virginia," July 24, 1992, *https://bush-41library.tamu.edu/archives/public-papers/4605.*

After so many dashed hopes, could this be real photographic evidence?: "Hoping against hope," *Newsweek,* July 29, 1991, 20-26, and H. D. S. Greenway, "Rage, questions continue for families," *The Boston Globe,* July 21, 1991, 1, accessed on February 9, 2021, www.newspapers.com.

70 percent of the country believed the North Vietnamese were holding Americans prisoner: Keating, *Prisoners of Hope,* 224.

A man jumps up and approaches the podium...some turn their back on the president in protest with their hands clasped behind them: *The Phil Donohue Show,* October 26, 1992. Donohue hosted some MIA family members on his show and then showed a clip from the National League's July annual meeting, where a small group families stand in protest.

"Would you please shut up and sit down?": "Remarks to the National League of Families of American Prisoners and Missing in Southeast Asia in Arlington, Virginia," July 24, 1992, *https://bush-41library.tamu.edu/archives/public-papers/4605.* Ann Mills-Griffiths, who was on stage, and Richard Childress, who was sitting in the front row, claim that President Bush was shouting at a reporter, not the dissident families. Mills-Griffiths said a reporter in the back of the room was asking President Bush a question about homeless veterans in Washington, DC. Source: Richard Childress, interview with the authors August 19, 2022; and Ann Mills-Griffiths, interview with the authors, October 10, 2022.

"To suggest that a commander-in-chief...Now, what kind of an allegation is that to make against a patriot?": "Remarks to the National League of Families of American Prisoners and Missing in Southeast Asia in Arlington, Virginia," July 24, 1992, *https://bush-41library.tamu.edu/archives/public-papers/4605*; and "POW-MIA families shout down Bush," *Post-Crescent* (Appleton, WI), July 25, 1992, 10, accessed on March 15, 2022, newspapers.com.

"If the United States should announce that we will quit... thrown away our principal bargaining counter to win the release of American prisoners of war": "Address to the Nation on the Situation in Southeast Asia," April 7, 1971, *https://millercenter.org/the-presidency/presidential-speeches/april-7-1971-address-nation-situation-southeast-asia.*

"The McGovern-Hatfield "end the war" amendment: John W. Finney, "Senate, 55 to 42, defeats McGovern-Hatfield plan," *The New York Times,* June 17, 1971, 1, *https://www.nytimes.com/1971/06/17/archives/senate-55-to-42-defeats-mcgovernhatfield-plan-administration-backed.html.*

"That's right": Ken Hughes, *Fatal Politics: The Nixon Tapes, The Vietnam War, and The Casualties of Reelection,* (Charlottesville, VA, and London: University of Virginia Press, 2015), 8. Hughes's cite is "Conversation 471–472, 19 March 1971, 7:03-7:27 p.m., Oval Office.

"any bad results would be too late to affect the election": H. R. Haldeman, *The Haldeman Diaries,* 221.

"Darn that Ross Perot...to find them": Barbara Bush, *Barbara Bush: A Memoir,* (New York: Lisa Drew Books, 1994), 476. On page 126 of President George H. W. Bush's memoir *All the Best, George Bush: My Life in Letters and Other Writings* (New York: Scribner, 2013), he reveals: "Perot's number one cause for years was the release of American prisoners in Vietnam. I was sympathetic to this cause and even suggested to Jerry Ford that Congress hold a special session to address the POW problem. However, years down the road, I believe it is this same issue that drove a wedge between Perot and me."

"sparked up": Richard Childress, interview with the authors, August 16, 2022.

published an apology: Thomas Ferraro, "Divided MIA families apologize to Bush," United Press International, July 30, 1992, *https://www.upi.com/Archives/1992/07/30/Divided-MIA-families-apologize-to-Bush/8712712468800/.*

"So, all I'm asking...I don't care how long it takes": President George H. W. Bush, "Remarks to the National League of Families of American Prisoners and Missing in Southeast Asia in Arlington, Virginia," July 24, 1992, *https://bush41library.tamu.edu/archives/public-papers/4605.*

The Outsider (*October 13, 1992*)

The sources for this scene are the following:

"James Stockdale Interview," Jim Lehrer Hosts Debating Our Destiny, PBS, September 4, 1999, *https://www.pbs.org/newshour/spc/debatingourdestiny/interviews/stockdale.html.*

"Gore, Quayle, Stockdale: The 1992 vice presidential debate," PBS Newshour, October 13, 1992, *https://www.youtube.com/watch?v=BIq_mW-nSnQ.*

Compromising Positions (*October 25, 1992*)

He is the most serious independent challenger to the two-party system in modern American history: George J. Church, "The Other Side of Perot," *Time,* June 29, 1992, 39; and Posner, *Citizen Perot,* 322.

"I have a daughter": Transcript of Lesley Stahl interview with Ross Perot on *60 Minutes,* October 25, 1992, Box 181, Perot Family Archives, Dallas, TX.

"Compromising lesbian-related situations": Posner, *Citizen Perot,* 311.

Marian Shelton's suicide brought them closer: Jim Coyne, "Scott Barnes: The flake that changed America's future," *Soldier of Fortune*, March 1993, 76.

"My hope is that a bunch of zealots were doing stupid things": Transcript of Lesley Stahl interview with Ross Perot on *60 Minutes*, October 25, 1992.

He has lost faith in his president: Kenneth T. Walsh, "The world according to Ross," *U.S. News & World Report*, June 1, 1992, 25.

He always thought President Bush was "weak." Now, he believes Bush is corrupt...narcotics trafficking in the region: Posner, *Citizen Perot*, 215; and Kenneth T. Walsh, "The world according to Ross," 24–28.

Perot's anger over this failure is at the heart of his bid to unseat President Bush.: Richard S. Dunham and Douglas Harbrecht, with Wendy Zellner, "Is Perot after the presidency—Or just the president?", *Business Week*, April 16, 1992, 41; John Mintz, "MIA issue shaped Perot's view of Bush," *Washington Post*, April 18, 1992, *https://www.washingtonpost.com/archive/politics/1992/04/18/mia-issue-shaped-perots-view-of-bush/2a0c0ff8-dada-4fe5-8329-829bbd5b408d/*; Richard Armitage, interview with the authors, March 22, 2022; and Tom Meurer, interview with the authors, May 26, 2021.

"It was a big lie": From Tribune News Services, "Ex-Perot aide reveals 'a lie' that backfired," *Chicago Tribune*, March 29, 1997, https://www.chicagotribune.com/news/ct-xpm-1997-03-29-9703290088-story.html.

Sparring (August 11, 1992)

"The Vietnamese could be cruel, but": Mark Salter, *The Luckiest Man–Life with John McCain*, (New York: Simon & Schuster, 2020), 185–186.

McCain is having a tough time...call him "nuttier than a fruitcake": During the 1992 Senate Select Committee hearing where Ross Perot testified, Senator McCain ran into Ross Perot's former aide Tom Meurer in the bathroom. Meurer had also been called to testify before the committee. McCain stopped Meurer, looked him in the eye, and asked, "Tom, why does Perot hate me so much?" Meurer chuckled nervously and dismissed the notion: "Oh, senator, he doesn't hate you." But that was not exactly true. Meurer knew that while Perot respected McCain's service and resilience as a POW, he had lost respect for McCain for two reasons: (1) Perot believed McCain "hushed up" evidence of live POWs long after the war ended, and (2) Perot was angry at how McCain treated Carol after the war. Indeed, when McCain took his first run for president in 2000, his good friends and fellow former POWs Everett Alvarez and Orson Swindle convinced him he must make amends. They did not want Perot to be another presidential spoiler. Alvarez told McCain, "You don't need him to support you, but you don't want him working against you." The two told McCain he must apologize to Perot for his "nuttier than a fruitcake" comment and *he must thank Perot for taking care of Carol during the war.* Alvarez dragged McCain to Dallas for a private meeting with Perot, where McCain took Alvarez's advice. According to Alvarez, Perot was gracious. Sources: Tom Meurer, interview with the authors, May 26, 2021; Jonathan Alter, "The Bushed and the Bored," *Newsweek*, March 13, 2000; "When Ross Perot calls...," *Newsweek*, January 16, 2008; and Everett Alvarez, interview with the authors, July 18, 2022.

He is giving McCain a "101 lesson on negotiations" with the Vietnamese: "The Vietnamese, if you would spend time listening to them...We'd have to really sit down and come up with a good plan on to get Laos's attention": Ross Perot testimony to the U.S. Senate Select Committee on POW/MIA Affairs, C-SPAN, August 11, 1992, *https://www.c-span.org/video/?30918-1/powmia-affairs.*

Who want to keep Hanoi diplomatically and economically isolated: In 1995, Senator McCain would be one of the highest profile Republicans to back President Clinton's move to normalize relations with Vietnam. In an editorial published in the *Washington Post* on May 21, 1995, he argued that the Vietnamese were already cooperating with the United States to account for the missing. Moreover, "The Vietnamese are already developing complex relations with the rest of the free world. So instead of vainly trying to isolate Vietnam, let us test the proposition that greater exposure to Americans will render Vietnam more susceptible to the influence of our values." Vehemently opposed to normalization were the National League of Families and Rep. Bob Dornan. When Senator McCain ran for president in 2008, he was vilified by Dornan and many MIA families for abandoning their men.

"Nuttier than a fruitcake": Richard A. Oppel, Jr., "The 2000 Campaign: The Perot Connection; McCain and Perot Stealing Glances, Some Say," *New York Times*, February 26, 2000, A1, *https://www.nytimes.com/2000/02/26/us/2000-campaign-perot-connection-mccain-perot-stealing-glances-some-say.html.*

"No compelling evidence that proves any Americans remain alive in captivity in Southeast Asia": Executive Summary of the "Report of the U.S. Senate Select Committee on POW/MIA Affairs," January 13, 1993, 13.

It is Time (October 4, 1994)

"It's hung over us for so long": Sally Streff Buzbee, "Still agonizing, children ask to have POW dad declared dead," *Star Tribune* (Minneapolis, MN), September 29, 1994, 22, accessed on February 16, 2021, www.newspapers.com.

Other sources for this scene are media coverage of the funeral, including *The Today Show*, October 5, 1994.

The Shelton/Sheldon family crest, on display at the home of youngest daughter Joan Shelton May, contains the Latin words "Optimium [est] pati," or "The best is to suffer." Oldest son Charlie Shelton says, "Oh yes, we are really good at suffering."

Chapter 19: The Trailblazer

The sources for this scene are the following:

USS *Yellowstone* statistics: *Dictionary of American Naval Fighting Ships*, U.S. Navy Archives, https://*www.history.navy.mil/yellowstone.*

Christine Cugini, interview with the authors, July 14, 2022.

Ambassador Charles Untermeyer, interview with the authors, June 10, 2022; email to the authors, June 20, 2022.

10 work diaries, Alice M. Stratton, DASN, (1985–1989), Richard A. Stratton papers, Box 13, Hoover Institution Library and Archives.

"Dreams are Real, Dare to Dream—Make a Difference," speech written by Alice Marie Robertson Stratton for the Beaches Women's Partnership, undated, from the personal collection of Richard and Alice Stratton.

"The Beginning of the Family Service Center at the United States Naval Academy," undated, from the personal collection of Richard and Alice Stratton.

Chapter 20: Resolution

Back to Son Tay (1995)

"a reminder of a better life, far from the prison wall and Vietnam": William A. Guenon, Jr., *Secret and Dangerous: Night of the Son Tay P.O.W. Raid,* (Ashland, MA: Wagon Wings Press, 2002), 4.

"I was able to separate myself...I wanted to see him. You know?": Emilee Reynolds, interview with the author, November 9, 2020.

Almost exuberant: Elizabeth Reynolds Peltz, interview with the authors, May 31, 2022.

Was it emotional going back to Son Tay? "No, it wasn't": Jon Reynolds, interview with the authors, March 16, 2022.

"I think the most fortunate thing in my life...If you haven't experienced it, maybe you don't miss it": Emilee Reynolds, interview with the author, June 28, 2021.

Remains of the Day (1977 and 2000)

The sources for this scene are the following:

Pat Mearns, interview with the authors, July 13, 2022, August 21, 2017, and September 2, 2022.

"21 more Vietnam war dead identified," *Corpus Christi Times* (Corpus Christi, TX), October 26, 1977, 66, accessed on July 13, 2022, www.newspapers.com.

Carole Hanson Hickerson, interview with the authors, July 12, 2022.

JANUARY UPDATED BIOGRAPHIC/SITE REPORT: REFNO 0720. 1996. Manuscript/Mixed Material. *https://www.loc.gov/item/powmia/pwmaster_143747/*.

To the West Wing (1981)

"Carol, can you believe we are here?...Four years ago, if you told me what I'd be doing now, I would have told them they are dreaming.": Students and leaders with Carol McCain, Director of the White House Visitors Office," *C-SPAN*, May 13, 1982, Ronald Reagan Presidential Library, Simi Valley, CA.

He married a much younger woman six weeks later: Paul Farhi, "The separate peace of John and Carol," *South Coast Today*, October 12, 2008, *https://www.southcoasttoday.com/story/lifestyle/2008/10/12/the-separate-peace-john-carol/52233029007/*.

"I owe a lot to people like Mr. Reagan who helped me get through that period....I didn't know whether to take the job... Listen, bring Sidney to California...And John, while I was gone, move out": Robert Timberg interview with Carol McCain, July 12 and 17, 1990, Robert Timberg Collection, U.S. Navy Archives.

"held my life together...was really a blessing": Marguerite Sullivan, "Building a creative Christmas," *Odessa American* (Odessa, TX), December 20, 1981, 22, accessed on April 26, 2021, www.newspapers.com.

"Wedding Bells Are Breaking Up That Old Gang of Mine"... "What exactly does that do?": Robert Timberg interview with Carol McCain, July 17, 1990, Robert Timberg Collection, U.S. Navy Archives.

brainchild behind the White House Christmas ornament campaign: Carol McCain, conversation with the authors, July 9, 2021.

"I didn't know where to go"...She waves to Doug, and limps into the West Wing: Robert Timberg interview with Carol McCain, July 17, 1990, Robert Timberg Collection, U.S. Navy Archives.

Discordant (1993)

This scene is drawn from the following sources:

Andrea Rander, interview with the authors, December 18, 2017, January 29, 2018, and August 24, 2022.

Andrea Rander, "After the call came," undated, from the personal collection of Andrea Rander.

Donald Baker, "The POW," *Washington Post*, October 20, 1974.

Michael Pousner, "The PWs: It can be from here to eternity," *Daily News* (New York, NY) March 25, 1975, from the personal collection of Andrea Rander.

Getting Answers (2017)

Sources for this scene:

Jeff and Nui Clark, interview with the authors, December 20, 2021.

Bradley Taylor, Stony Beach Program Manager, Defense Intelligence Agency, interview with the authors, August 8, 2022.

INTERIM SEARCH AND RECOVERY REPORT CIL-065-R, AN ALLEGED BURIAL SITE LA-00630 ASSOCIATED WITH

REFNO 0079, VIENGXAI DISTRICT, HOUAPHAN PROVINCE, LAO PEOPLE'S DEMOCRATIC REPUBLIC, 29 JANUARY THROUGH 24 FEBRUARY 2019. Manuscript/Mixed Material. *https://www.loc.gov/item/powmia/s147-078/.*

A Long Time Coming (2017)

Hunter Ellis, interview with the authors, May 13, 2022.

Chapter #21: One Last Dive (2018)

The sources for this scene are the following:

"The Fullest Accountability: A Conversation With Ann Mills-Griffiths About the POW/MIA Issue," West Point Center for Oral History, June 4, 2019, *https://www.westpointcoh.org/interviews/the-fullest-accountability-a-conversation-with-ann-mills-griffiths-about-the-pow-mia-issue.*

Ann Mills-Griffiths, interview with the authors, June 13, 2022 and October 10, 2022, and email to the authors, August 29, 2022.

Paul Mather, interview with the authors, August 29, 2022.

Charles H. Briscoe, Ph.D., "Vietnam Casualty Resolution: Top U.S. Peace Priority," *Veritas*, Vol. 12, No. 1, 2016, *https://arsof-history.org/articles/v12n1_casualty_resolution_page_1.html.*

INDEX

Page numbers in **bold** indicate photos.

E

F

M

N

O

Q

R

T

U

V

W

Y

Z